Endorsements

"In a confusing world, with high stresses, Christians know that our model for doing life right is Jesus Christ. However, learning the *how* of living like Jesus can often be confusing in and of itself, and we wonder where to start. The authors of this book have provided a clear biblical path for the reader, in showing how Jesus was the perfect example of emotional intelligence, and then following up with specific assessments, behaviors, skills and tools to get us on our way. You'll find your own situation in the many scriptural case studies, and answers for your own *how*."

—John Townsend, Ph.D., Author of the New York Times bestselling Boundaries series, *Psychologist Founder*, Townsend Institute for Leadership and Counseling, and the Townsend Leadership Group

"It's been said, 'it's not what you know, but who you know.' More importantly, 'it's not who you know but who you are!' That cannot happen apart from 'Emotional Intelligence'. Being certified in two EQ assessments I am convinced this will not happen at a deep and ongoing level without an encounter with Jesus—the model, source and sustainer of deep dispositional growth. The clarity of this book is highly beneficial and encouraging!"

—Mick Ukleja, Ph.D., Founder, LeadershiptraQ, Professor, Author, Speaker, Generational Strategist

"*Emotional Intelligence in Christ* will change lives from the inside out! It will open your minds and hearts to a new understanding of Jesus,

His leadership, and how we can more powerfully follow His example in our own lives. Combining *Emotional Intelligence* and the *Biblical DISC* provides a clear understanding of the application to our lives and our interactions with others. Using both Biblical and real-life examples and case studies gives a much-needed practical depth to Jesus' teachings—I will never read the Bible the same way again! Even after many years of being a Christian and studying the Bible, this book has given me a completely new and practical application of how I can be a much better messenger of the Lord. Thank you for the clarity you have given me both in my self-understanding as well as a better understanding of the needs and behaviors of others from a Biblical and EIC perspective. I know it will make a difference in my life and ministry."

—Barbara A. Glanz, Hall of Fame Speaker and the author of *CARE Packages for the Workplace, Priceless Gifts: Using What God's Given You to Bless Others,"* and co-author with Ken Blanchard of *The Simple Truths of Service Inspired by Johnny the Bagger*

"Revelation and life-change are certain outcomes when Jesus takes the main stage. That is exactly what is waiting for you in the pages of *Emotional Intelligence in Christ*. Through the collaboration of gifted authors and experts, you gain compelling new perspectives on the life of Christ plus access to assessments that will guide your quest to lead more like Jesus. Today is your day to discover how you can more closely follow the Leader!"

—Tami. Heim - President and CEO, Christian Leadership. Alliance

"The book, *Emotional Intelligence in Christ* skillfully uses Jesus Christ as an example to explain the elements of emotional intelligence. The book focuses on the notion that there is no better role model than Christ when it comes to controlling one's emotions, displaying empathy, and developing relationships. The authors expertly use Scripture and

Christ's teachings to provide guideposts that will help anyone become a better leader and person."

—Major General John L. Gronski (USA Retired) and author of the books, *Iron-Sharpened Leadership* and *The Ride of Our Lives*

"In a world where uncertainty has gone viral and taking offense has become a salutation, Emotional Intelligence in Christ is a beacon of light which provides refuge as well as strength to pilgrims seeking the Way, Truth and Life. Apart from Christ we can do nothing. With Christ as our emotional intelligence mentor, self-control and purposeful communication become our way. This book pulls back the curtain of Jesus in action, offering you the opportunity to do what Jesus did . . . and continues to do as He connects and positively impacts the lives of people who encounter Him. The how to becomes a reality in these pages . . . how to be like Jesus in your relationships with others. You will learn what makes you tick and how to use that knowledge in a strategic way to manage yourself and relationships in a way that witnesses Christ's example of loving your neighbor as yourself. This is an interactive read that will change your life in, with and through Christ."

—Johnny Hunt, Pastor Emeritus FBC Woodstock, Former SBC President, Senior VP of NAMB in Evangelism and Leadership

"In 1536 John Calvin said, 'There is no deep knowing of God without a deep knowing of self, and no deep knowing of self without a deep knowing of God.' In the Gospels, Jesus offers us a clear invitation to self-knowledge when He said, 'Why do you see the speck in your neighbor's eye but do not notice the log in your own eye, … First take the log out of your own eye and then you will see clearly to take the speck out of your neighbor's eye.' David in Psalm 51:6 also recognized that God wants us to be honest with ourselves: 'Surely you desire truth in the inward being; therefore, teach me wisdom in my secret heart.' A lack of self-awareness keeps us from knowing God intimately because we can only give the parts of ourselves to God that we know. In *Emotional Intelligence in Christ* you will discover practical tools that will help you know you and others in the deeper ways by looking intensely at the only model who will change you and all those around you—Jesus.

—Phyllis Hendry Halverson, President Emeritus, Lead Like Jesus, Co-Author *Lead Like Jesus Revisited*

"We live in a world of seemingly unparalleled offense. The enemy of our soul has trapped us in cycles of anger, fear, and isolation. *Emotional Intelligence in Christ* will equip you with a Spirit-empowered set of tools so that you can live, love and relate like Jesus."

—Dr John Jackson, President of William Jessup University; Author & Speaker on Leadership & Transformation

"Why do you respond to people and situations the way you do? How can you be better prepared for the unexpected? Understanding and mastering your God-given emotions is one of the best tools you can develop as a leader. Too many people operate at one extreme or the other—they either completely hand off the steering wheel to their emotions or they seek to box them up completely, never letting them out. This book shows us a better way. Starting with knowing ourselves better through Christ and the identity He gives; you will learn healthy ways to manage yourself and your responses. Ultimately that gives us a much better way of relating to and responding to others."

—Kevin Ezell, President, North American Mission Board, SBC

As an Executive Coach and Leadership Development Facilitator, it is my goal to support managers and teams as they attempt to become more aware of their own behaviors. How their very actions impact the business positively or negatively. This is very difficult. If we knew how to adjust our behaviors, we would likely have done it. They must be given a method in which to think. An environment to learn about themselves. As believers in Christ, we recognize the Divinity of Jesus. We also know that he was able to walk circumspectly in the world as a human. He is our model. Through the stories of the Bible and the actions of Jesus we learn that we possess the capacity to be aware of, control and express our emotions with empathy, compassion, mercy and justice. This is the very definition of 'Emotional Intelligence'. Many things have been written on knowing God and his character yet how in a very practical sense remains a mystery. This book brilliantly uses the structure of 'Emotional Intelligence' to frame the mentorship of Jesus Christ. The How. I can't wait to use it.

—Judith Colemon Kinebrew, Coach, Educator and Facilitator, Sherpa Coaching LLC

"The timing of this book is brilliant. Our culture is in desperate need of emotionally intelligent leaders, whether that be parent to child or manager to direct report. Any time we are in position to influence another person, we are leading. Jesus is our ultimate model to follow. The authors of *Emotional Intelligence in Christ* have done a magnificent job offering the reader an interactive road-map that reveals how to become an emotionally intelligent leader in Christ, ultimately resulting in the resurrection of the spirit that God gave us."

—Father Nathan Cromly, CSJ, Founder & President of St. John Leadership Institute

"Emotional intelligence is an underappreciated and underrated leadership skill. Understanding your EQ is critical to leading well in a diverse and globalized world. As a Christ follower, this book provides a framework based on the life and principles of the King of Kings. Every believing leader, at any level, needs to read this book. It will heighten their awareness and improve their effectiveness as a Christ-like leader."

—Debbie Bresina, President Dare 2 Share

"From its opening salvo exploring offenses to its thoughtful treatment of behaviors that influence all of our lives, *Emotional Intelligence in Christ* presents a thoughtful and Biblical approach to emotional Intelligence. I found the combination of Biblical case studies, emotional intelligence self-assessments, teaching and questions most helpful. What makes this different to so many books is that it is not a self-help book, while it encourages deep self-reflection, it is a press into Jesus, help me lead, help me change, help me serve well kind of book. It's worthy of a slow, purposeful read."

—Ivan L. Filby, Founding Executive Director, Gordon Global Adult Education, Gordon College, Wenham, MA

"Manners matter! There is nothing more irritating than engaging with a leader who does not possess emotional intelligence. Those who lack emotional intelligence, often try to bolster their own image through loud and aggressive behaviour. They always want to be seen, heard, and acknowledged. There is a pervasive toxic corporate culture that is becoming mainstream in certain sectors of the marketplace on the watches of these type of leaders. This phenomenon has adverse consequences and its implications for value destruction is not fully appreciated. Very bright and promising professionals' careers are prematurely aborted, and energy is diverted into undue contestation instead of being applied to productive and beneficial output.

"To be credible as a leader, you have got to be centered in your soul. *Emotional Intelligence in Christ*, is a timeous contribution to equip leaders to excel in this regard. I want to commend the authors for the outstanding work done in broadening our understanding of this important aspect that every leader has to master. What is however of significance, is that they anchored their work on the best possible example i.e., our Lord Jesus Christ. This book gives us a fresh perspective, to mastermind what the Master had in mind. The power game leaders play with their exaggerated sense of self–importance, is increasingly running out of options and cannot be sustained indefinitely. There is a better way. Are you ready to make that change?"

—Martin Kuscus, Chairperson, Lead Like Jesus South Africa

Emotional Intelligence in Christ

Estella Chavous, EdD
Richard Cummins, MAOL
Lauren E Miller, M.Ed

With Ken Voges

DocUmeant *Publishing*
244 5th Avenue
Suite G-200
NY, NY 10001
646-233-4366
www.DocUmeantPublishing.com

Copyright © 2022 Dr. Estella Chavous, Rich Cummins, Lauren E Miller, and Ken Voges.

Published by

DocUmeant Publishing
244 5th Avenue, Suite G-200
NY, NY 10001
646-233-4366

Limit of Liability and Disclaimer of Warranty: The publisher has used its best efforts in preparing this book and the information provided herein is provided "as is."

No part of this book may be reproduced or transmitted in any form or by any means, electronic or mechanical, including photocopying, recording or by any information storage or retrieval system, except as may be expressly permitted by law or in writing from the publisher, or except by a reviewer who may quote brief passages in review to be printed in a magazine, newspaper, or online website.

Permission should be addressed in writing to: publisher@DocUmeantPublishing.com

All Scripture quotations, unless otherwise indicated, are taken from the Holy Bible, New International Version®, NIV®. Copyright ©1973, 1978, 1984, 2011 by Biblica, Inc.™ Used by permission of Zondervan. All rights reserved worldwide. www.zondervan.com The "NIV" and "New International Version" are trademarks registered in the United States Patent and Trademark Office by Biblica, Inc.™

All Scripture quotations marked "KJV" are taken from the Holy Bible, King James Version, Cambridge, 1769.

Cover Design and Layout by DocUmeant Designs, www.DocUmeantDesigns.com

Library of Congress Cataloging-in-Publication Data

Names: Chavous, Estella, 1957- author.
Title: Emotional intelligence in Christ / Estella Chavous, EdD, Richard Cummins, MAOL, Lauren E Miller, M.Ed with Ken Voges.
Description: NY, NY : DocUmeant Publishing, [2021] | Summary: "Jesus Christ of Nazareth modeled the highest form of emotional intelligence, connecting the hearts of humanity: love in action. Using His acute awareness, words, intonation, body language, and self-control, Jesus won the hearts of the people who encountered Him from the youngest to the oldest; He positively impacted people's lives. What if you could do the same? As you read through this book, you will have the opportunity to: Encounter the living Christ so much so that your ability to love and be loved is expanded. See how Jesus, the ultimate leader in EIC, impacted so many lives with varied personalities, backgrounds, and stories. Learn how to influence behavior with the EIC methodology through its connection with Biblical DISC™. Are you ready to up your game and discover what makes you tick? Emotional Intelligence in Christ (EIC) gives you the opportunity to learn how to master yourself in order to positively impact people around you. It provides tools, case studies, and real world applications using the EIC formula teaching you how to become emotionally intelligent in Christ. Step out of your old ways into Christ's way today"-- Provided by publisher.
Identifiers: LCCN 2021048196 (print) | LCCN 2021048197 (ebook) | ISBN 9781950075683 (pbk) | ISBN 9781950075690 (epub)
Subjects: LCSH: Emotions--Religious aspects--Christianity. | Emotional intelligence--Religious aspects--Christianity. | Jesus Christ--Example.
Classification: LCC BV4597.3 .C43 2021 (print) | LCC BV4597.3 (ebook) | DDC 152.4--dc23/eng/20211008
LC record available at https://lccn.loc.gov/2021048196
LC ebook record available at https://lccn.loc.gov/2021048197

CONTENTS

Foreword xvii
Preface xxi

CHAPTER 1: Overview of Emotional Intelligence in Christ 1
   Identity Crisis - 2
   Finding Christ - 3
   Freedom - 4
   A New Life - 5
   What is Emotional Intelligence? - - - - - - - - - - - - - - - - 6
   Prayer - 14

CHAPTER 2: Biblical EIQ Assessment for EIC Application 15
   Self-Awareness - 18
   Self-Management - 20
   Social-Awareness - 23
   Relational Management - 28

CHAPTER 3: Behavior 1 Personal Identity in Christ (Self-Awareness) 43
   Define the Trait - 44
   Biblical Examples - 52
   Focused Case Study - 61

Tools for Application ---------------------------- 70

The Six Phase Ripple Impact for Emotional Intelligence in Christ -- 71

Coaching Questions ------------------------------ 80

Prayer -- 81

CHAPTER 4: Behavior 2 Self-Control (Self-Management). 82

Define the Trait--------------------------------- 82

Biblical Examples ------------------------------- 87

Focused Case Study ------------------------------ 89

Tools for Application ---------------------------- 92

The Being Habits -------------------------------- 93

Coaching Questions ------------------------------121

Prayer --123

CHAPTER 5: Behavior 3 Altruistic Attitude (Social-Awareness). 124

A Biblical Example ------------------------------ 130

Focused Case Study ------------------------------ 134

Tools for Application ---------------------------- 137

Coaching Questions ------------------------------ 142

Prayer -- 143

CHAPTER 6: Behavior 4: Christ Connections (Relational Management) 144

EIC Trait Defined: Christ Connections ------------ 144

Biblical Example in Jesus's Life----------------- 153

Focused Case Study ------------------------------ 159

Tools for Application ----------------------------161

Coaching Questions	170
Prayer	172

CHAPTER 7: DISC Meets EIC Bible Case Studies 173

The Connection Between DISC and EIC	173
3 R's of DISC Relationships: Respond | Relate | Reinforce	174
Jesus Adapts to Different DISC Profiles	176
Biblical DISC® Assessment	176
How Fear Impacts Your DISC	186
Case Studies	188
How to Respond, Relate and Reinforce a High D DISC	196
Jesus is our EIC Mentor	197

CHAPTER 8: Applying the Chavous/Cummins/Miller/Voges EIC Method 199

The Application of the EIC Method	203
Scripture Study Reference 1: Moses and the Burning Bush	205
EIC Case Study 1: Moses (burning bush)	208
EIC Case Study 2: God EIC toward Aaron (burning bush)	212
Scripture Study Reference 2: The Golden Calf (Exodus 32)	215
EIC Case Study 3: Aaron (golden calf)	218
EIC Case Study 4: EIC of God towards Aaron—God empowerment of Moses (golden calf)	222
Scripture Study Reference 3: Death and Resurrection of Lazarus—Jesus's response to our behaviors (Martha and Mary)	226
EIC Case Study 5: Martha (death of Lazarus)	229
EIC Case Study 6: Mary (death of Lazarus)	231
EIC Case Study 7: Jesus to Martha and Mary Summary	233

Scripture Study Reference 4: At the Home of Martha
and Mary - 235

Scripture Study Reference 5: Jesus and the Miraculous Catch
of Fish (John 21) - 238

   EIC Case Study 8: Jesus Reinstates Peter   239

Scripture Study Reference 6: Sanhedrin Story
(Acts 4: 1–13) - 243

   EIC Case Study 9: Peter (Sanhedrin Story)   244

Next Steps 251

Author's Personal Testimonies to the Power of Emotional Intelligence in Christ 257

Estella Chavous's EIC Story - - - - - - - - - - - - - - - - - - - 257

Rich Cummins's EIC Story - 258

Lauren E. Miller's EIC Story - - - - - - - - - - - - - - - - - - - 260

Ken Voges's Story - 262

Author Bios 265

Estella Chavous, MBA, EdD - - - - - - - - - - - - - - - - - - - 265

Rich Cummins, MAOL, CFRE - - - - - - - - - - - - - - - - - 266

Lauren E Miller, M.Ed, MSC, ICF-PCC - - - - - - - - - - - - 267

Ken Voges Bio - 268

Acknowledgements 269

Emotional Intelligence in Christ Journal 271

Your EIC Learnings and Reflections - - - - - - - - - - - - - - - 273

This book is dedicated to Jesus Christ of Nazareth, the ultimate Mentor when it comes to emotional intelligence. He was and is brilliant in His ability to tune into the greatest need of a person along with His ability to meet that need in a way that transforms lives forever. We love because *He first loved us* (1 John 4:9). Lead us on Lord . . . lead us on. Show us *The Way* to connect with each other as You connect with us.

FOREWORD

FOLLOWING JESUS IS an inside-out job. Why? Because you can't give away what you haven't mastered within. Are you ready to up your game and discover what makes you tick? This book, *Emotional Intelligence in Christ*, gives you an opportunity to learn how to understand yourself so that you may make a positive difference in the lives of others.

"Jesus is after you" to do mighty work through our lives, say authors Estella Chavous, Rich Cummins, and Lauren Miller—and it all starts with a simple choice for us to hear and act upon: *Come and follow me and I will make you fishers of men (Matthew 4:9). Come and learn from me, for I am gentle and humble in heart and you will find rest for your souls (Matthew 11:29). All things are possible for those who believe (Mark 9:23).* Step out of the old ways of thinking and behaving that often leave you overwhelmed and stressed out. Increase your emotional intelligence in Christ and reclaim the power to connect and relate to others as Jesus guides your way. God adores you right where you are today—and loves you enough to not leave you there.

When things are going well for you in life, it's easier to be aware of and manage your own emotions as well as those of other people. However, when life doesn't show up the way you want it to, those abilities quickly fade. Rather than you being the boss of your emotions, your emotions quickly become the boss of you. Your ability to relate and connect to people in a positive way can become compromised when things don't go your way.

Emotional Intelligence in Christ is a story of love. It helps teach the behavior of Jesus using emotional intelligence. The stories in this book share how God works in your life, in His time. He strategically places people to help you gain more insight into His Word through emotionally intelligent behaviors.

You have a unique opportunity to discover what you and the people around you desire most in life. Jesus is our role model in every arena. He is masterful when it comes to connecting to people in life-changing ways, regardless of where they are physically or emotionally.

Jesus always leads with love. He knows love unlocks the human heart and each person's God-given purpose and potential. As you read this book, you will learn how Jesus does this and how you can follow His lead as you increase your ability to empower the people around you. You will read about Jesus' encounters with different personalities and how He continually calls people to action: *"get up," "pick up your mat," "go and sin no more," "come follow me."* You will also read how Jesus maintains an inner calm, confidence, and peaceful purpose in the midst of raging emotions all around.

Life doesn't always show up the way you want it to. This can compromise your ability to make a positive difference in your world. Emotions are messy, yet they are a part of who we are. They serve a beautiful purpose when it comes to our ability to experience the gift of life. Emotion is our body's response to our thoughts. Jesus wants to be a guide for our minds, which connect to our wills and emotions.

It's the authors' intention in writing this book to make the complex simple, applicable, transferable, and sustainable. They invite you to linger in the chapters that speak to you personally. But before you continue on, take a moment to invite God to join you on this journey. Simply ask: *Holy Spirit, as I read, show me what's for me. What do you want me to lean into, learn from, and apply in my daily life? I want to experience closer intimacy with Jesus.*

There is no doubt that this is a God project. When you prayerfully and thoughtfully travel through the following pages, we want you to:

1. Have a personal encounter with Jesus in a new and refreshing way.

2. Learn how and why Jesus is the ultimate model and mentor for emotional intelligence.
3. Become aware of your own emotions and those around you and learn how to manage those emotions.
4. Notice where the Holy Spirit moves you to transfer your learnings into behavior. Take notes and listen closely.
5. Practice what you learn so that you can make a positive difference in the lives of people around you.

A leader who follows Jesus is a constant student who is curious to discover new and innovative ways to guide others back to themselves and unlock their potential to outshine the darkness. Wherever you are in your journey of life—parent, student, pastor, executive, entrepreneur—you are called by God to lead well the people entrusted to your care. This book offers a method- to make that happen.

Emotional Intelligence in Christ is designed to be an interactive educational experience. As such, the authors include coaching questions in each chapter. Each question gives you, the reader, the opportunity to reflect and respond to the information you are learning. So grab a highlighter and a pen and read on!

Lauren Miller's involvement in the Lead Like Jesus ministry (LeadLikeJesus.com) connected her to Rich Cummins, president and CEO of Lead Like Jesus, whose passion for emotional intelligence was the element God needed to carry this project forward. Estella Chavous and Lauren Miller discussed the benefits of having Christ-like Emotional Intelligence and their Edge God In Podcast on emotional intelligence in Christ was a significant factor. Rich further moved the mission ahead, introducing Lauren and Estella Chavous to Ken Voges who develped the Biblical DISC™ Assessment and which is a registered trademark of Lead Like Jesus and In His Grace, INC. Ken's published materials focus on Jesus' words "love your neighbor as yourself." His biblical case studies are used throughout this book.

You can learn more about the authors' individual spiritual journeys at the back of the book.

May God's wisdom, insight and power be yours as you journey into the *Emotional Intelligence in Christ* experience.

God bless,

Ken Blanchard
Co-founder of Lead Like Jesus
Co-founder and chief spiritual officer of The Ken Blanchard Companies
Co-author of *The One Minute Manager*® and *Lead Like Jesus Revisited.*

PREFACE

JESUS IS AFTER you. He sees and loves you right where you are and loves you enough not to leave you there. We live in a world that is full of fragmented relationships, broken hearts and emotional outbursts fueled by offense and fear. We are told in the end times that offense will increase.

Stress is the power you give to outside circumstances to define your worth, value, and capability. You will learn as you enter into your own emotional intelligence in Christ experience, how to take back the power you give away. You will learn that you have the God-given ability to link to the power of Christ within you in such a profound way that you, through Him, become the master of your emotions rather than giving them the power to master you. This is emotional intelligence in Christ.

Have you have noticed, in the past couple of years particularly, an increase in this one behavior: taking offense?

It's one of the devil's tactics to divide and conquer the people of God. Can you relate? The word offense has its history in the Greek word "*skandalon*" which is actually the part of a trap (to catch animals) that holds the bait. It's been noted as the trigger point on the trap that closes down on an unsuspecting victim. The victim in this case is you.

Effective fly fishing involves a skill called reading the hatch. Simply put, the hatch are the flies that the fish are feeding on at the particular time you are fishing. If you do a good job figuring out which "fake" fly looks most like the real fly, then SHAZAM the fish will take the fake bait. Satan is using offense to cause us to bite. Once he has us on the line, our emotions go from dormant to live, and chaos and division too often take center stage; killing, stealing, and destroying our inner peace, confidence, and ability to scale walls and climb the mountains of challenging times and moments. Not to mention disconnecting our awareness of God's mighty power within us that gives us the ability to love those who persecute us as well as those who have different personalities than we have.

To be offended is at an all-time high these days which is one of the main reasons we are responding with a solution: Emotional Intelligence in Christ. To be offended simply means to take something someone said or did personally. When you are offended you give power to something outside of you to determine your ability to handle it successfully.

Offense flows directly from self-focus. In the King James version of Matthew 24:10–12, Jesus says this about the end times: *"and then shall many be offended and shall betray one another and shall hate one another."* The mental serpent of offense slithers in between your two ears and produces resentment, accusation and frustration which is often founded on smoke and mirrors used to distract you from God's love for you and those around you.

Offense also walks hand in hand with another reptile that Satan uses to keep you stuck: victimization. If he can render you mentally tuned out to the strength of God within you to overcome and tune into possible solutions to life's roadblocks then he's got you. Victimization fuels offense and vice versa and Jesus died to set you free from both:

> ***"It is for freedom that Christ has set us free.** Stand firm, then, and do not let yourselves be burdened again by a yoke of slavery"* (Galatians 5:1).

What offends you these days? Taking offense has gone viral in our society, blocking our ability to see through the lens of emotional intelligence in Christ. Are you rising and falling these days emotionally depending upon exterior circumstances and how the world judges you?

It's time to wake up and resist the urge to be offended and feel like a victim, incapable of positive forward momentum. This is only possible through Christ's power within you. Jesus was not confined by status or the opinions of other people. Can you imagine waking up tomorrow morning and you had no mental space given to concern over your status and the opinions of other people? What would you do with that freed up mind space? Good news: Jesus has come to free you from that mental bondage and emotional muck.

Come and follow Jesus's lead and you will learn how to fill up what is lacking in your emotional bandwidth. Restore what has been hijacked by the world around you. It's time. Time to begin again with the Lover of your soul.

The "how" question is what Jesus believed to be important. The answer is in a question asked by a Pharisee on which one law was the greatest. Jesus gave him two that are connected.

> "'Teacher, which is the greatest commandment in the law?' 'Jesus replied, love the Lord your God with all your heart and with all your soul and with all your mind.' This is the first and greatest commandment and the second is like it: 'Love your neighbor as yourself'" (Matthew 22:36-39).

The first was to embrace the love guided emotional intelligence of God the Father. The second is to understand the unique emotional "Want" of any individual one meets and a personalized love strategy for that individual. This involves connecting two separate behavioral models in meeting individual "Needs": Biblical DISC™ meets Emotional Intelligence in Christ, which we will explore together.

The journey of this book is a testimony to God's plan, which started several years ago, when friends, colleagues, and co-hosts of Edge God In Podcast (EdgeGodIn.com) Estella and Lauren facilitated a four-part series on emotional intelligence from a Biblical perspective. Their interest in following Jesus's example of Emotional Intelligence continued to grow, as did the need for it in this chaotic world. As God often does, He had a master plan on how He wanted to roll this out.

You will notice that Chapter 3 is the longest chapter in the book. Why? Because the first phase of *Emotional Intelligence in Christ* is the anchor that makes the other 3 phases possible. It is the foundation that allows phase 2, 3 and 4 to come alive in our behavior. The next longest chapter is Chapter 4. Chapter 6 explores the final phase of *Emotional Intelligence in Christ* and is possible for us to experience because of our encounter with Christ in the third chapter and played out in phase 2 and 3 (Chapters 4 and 5) of *Emotional Intelligence in Christ*.

Emotional Intelligence in Christ is a journey that must be accompanied by prayer, self-reflection, and the willingness to embrace behavioral shifts as guided by the Holy Spirit. Take time to thoughtfully reflect and respond within each chapter. As you come across pieces of information that stand out to you. Invite the Holy Spirit to help you transfer those ah-ha moments into behavior that glorifies God and represents the power of Christ within you. Allow the emotional intelligence that is linked to your encounter with Christ spill out into your relationships. *Stand firm, then, and do not let yourselves be burdened again by a yoke of slavery*, to your emotions or the emotions of those around you. Jesus invites you to learn from him (Matthew 11:29) as He guides you into His ultimate model of emotional intelligence that will anchor the second greatest commandment in your life: love your neighbor as yourself.

Emotional Intelligence in Christ Course
coming in 2022

For More Information Visit:
EmotionalIntelligenceinChrist.com

CHAPTER 1

OVERVIEW OF EMOTIONAL INTELLIGENCE IN CHRIST

"A gentle answer turns away wrath, but a harsh word stirs up anger.

"The tongue of the wise adorns knowledge, but the mouth of the fool gushes folly.

"The eyes of the Lord are everywhere, keeping watch on the wicked and the good.

"The soothing tongue is a tree of life, but a perverse tongue crushes the spirit" (Proverbs 15:1–4).

HAVE YOU EVER caught yourself-in a situation where your mouth spills out words that negatively trigger the people around you? Perhaps you have cut others down when they disagree with your point of view? Or you find yourself-wide-eyed staring at the ceiling at night, wondering: "Why did I say that?" or ruminating about a strong negative emotion that has a firm grip on your mind and is stealing your inner peace?

Questioning yourself-in situations like this is normal. Being a human being can be emotionally messy. Good news, God knows this and meets us right where we are, inviting us to explore a higher mental ground called: *Emotional Intelligence in Christ* (EIC).

Emotional Intelligence in Christ is the activation of the Holy Spirit within you to discern and manage personal emotions and behavior in a way that honors God by loving others well as Jesus did.

Let's start with a "boots on the ground" example of Emotional Intelligence in Christ in action. This is the story of Christian Music Artist/Speaker Billy Ballenger. Perhaps you can relate to Billy's "BC", *before Christ* encounter, and the *after Christ* encounter as you read through his story. *The following testimony is used with the permission of Billy Ballenger.*

You will notice that an identity crisis is often the fuel that Satan uses to confuse the mind enough to forget whose you are and who you are. We will discuss this more in Chapter 3. Emotional Intelligence in Christ is made possible when we see with our eyes, hear with our ears, understand with our hearts, and turn as we allow the love of Jesus to heal and override the pain and false beliefs (Matthew 13:15) we've encountered.

IDENTITY CRISIS

As a young boy, Billy faced many challenges. Before coming to know Jesus at the age of 10, he discovered that he was adopted and that his parents were his maternal aunt and uncle. Billy's biological mother had her own struggles and decided to give him up for adoption at age 3. Before age 11, the sense of security that Billy once had started to fray as his adoptive parents divorced, eventually marrying other people. As a result, he moved in with his dad, but he never felt a strong sense of stability or connection. According to Billy, "*It was a very difficult time emotionally. I struggled to find common ground with my stepparents. I was mocked, ridiculed, and bullied by other students well into high school. Friends were hard to find and this consumed my thinking and affected my learning throughout school. I hated life, I had no self-esteem; I was very unhappy as a child and began to run away from my problems.*"

By the time Billy reached age 16, he was ordered by the court to attend a residential juvenile facility called Josiah White's New Possibilities in Wabash, IN. Josiah White's was a pivotal experience for Billy. For the first time in a long time, he felt the possibility of a new start in a place where no one knew of his past struggles. He learned to serve others and began to work on character development. At the facility, he also met his future wife, Jodie.

After completing the program at Josiah White's, Billy was placed on probation and sent back to his former surroundings. By age 17, Billy ran away to where Jodie lived, who was 16 at the time. Billy moved in with Jodie and her mother in Muncie, IN and Jodie soon became pregnant. Shortly after, the couple married and delivered a healthy baby girl named Mindy.

Billy and Jodie were living a chaotic life while raising Mindy. Fueled by excessive drinking and drug use, the couple engaged in a dangerous lifestyle, including illegal drug dealing, receiving stolen property, and engaging in violent behavior. This conduct came to a boiling point with a dramatic SWAT team raid on their house leading to losing their freedom and their daughter in the same day. Recounting those moments, Billy laments "All my hope was gone."

Billy's *identity* had been hijacked by exterior circumstances along with the ability to experience *self-control, care for others* and *connections with people around him that were grounded in Christ*. Little did he know, Jesus was after him.

FINDING CHRIST

Billy and Jodie were released from jail on bond and awaiting and upcoming trial when they had an encounter of a lifetime. Billy met a man at a gas station who hired him on the spot for a construction job. The man invited the couple to church, where they both re-dedicated their lives to Christ. While both had salvation experiences through altar calls as children, this was different. According to Billy, "*My life was a mess. I was broken and afraid. However, I somehow knew God was my only hope."*

As life moved on, both were eventually given 6-year prison sentences after being found guilty on charges of possession of stolen goods. Life had never been so low for Billy. *"It was a bad day. I thought my life was over. However, I was determined to not spend the next few years in prison. To fight off depression and loneliness I began reading my Bible and then my faith began to grow. As I studied the Scriptures, I realized God was changing my heart and desires and had made me a new man. I didn't run to God to worship Him. I hardly knew anything about worship. I wanted my wife and my daughter back. I wanted to be free. It was my number one desire. As I read the Scriptures my faith got stronger, and I realized that God loved me and that He was on my side. Not only did He want me free and restored to my little family, but He also wanted me to follow His plan for my life. I began to thank God for setting me free from prison."*

As the Holy Spirit began the mighty work of identity recovery for Billy, his emotional intelligence in Jesus began to take over his perceptions. Love replaced fear, which ignited the courage to declare behind prison bars that freedom was and is God's plan for his life. *"It is for freedom that Christ has set us free. Stand firm, then, and do not let yourselves be burdened again by a yoke of slavery"* (Galatians 5:1).

FREEDOM

God can turn all things around. Billy and Jodie understood that, knew that their freedom would someday be restored and that they would eventually be reunited as a family. While the couple was eternally freed from the bondage of sin, a miracle was about to happen that would radically change their lives, release them from incarceration, and escort them right out of the prison one year early. The judge had originally stated that she would not grant an early release for the couple. But God had another plan. Due to a technical error with sentencing, the couple received a special hearing intended to correct the mistake of the court.

While at the hearing, the original judge and prosecutor agreed to set aside the remainder of the couple's sentences, and they walked out of the courtroom free that day. The best part was being reunited right away with Mindy, who had been in the custody of Billy's mom. Just as being incarcerated was one of his worst days, the day they got their freedom back was monumental for Billy. "*I just felt indescribable elation. God's word was alive, and it really works. It was miraculous.*"

A NEW LIFE

Freedom from prison was just the beginning for Billy and Jodie. God had big plans for their lives, and everything was about to change. Soon Jodie became pregnant and gave birth to their son, Jared. Billy and Jodie and their children started faithfully attending a local church and eventually Billy accepted a pastorate at an urban ministry. The couple was drawn to minister to the hopeless and joined Chuck Colson as instructors for his Prison Fellowship Ministry. Billy started leading worship at church and in 2002 began recording music and traveling in full-time ministry. It didn't take long for Billy to land music opportunities in prisons, churches, and schools in North America. Through their nonprofit ministry, Break the Grey, Inc., Billy and Jodie have impacted over half of a million people in search of hope with the same gospel message that brought them freedom years ago. Additionally, Billy has performed as a national touring Christian music artist along with some of the industry's most prolific names.

Billy's message is simple, "*Don't quit. If you can just get a glimpse of what your future could be and that God has a plan for your life – look out!*

Billy is now filled with Emotional Intelligence in Christ which has made all the difference in transforming one life, hijacked by a lost identity, now recovered for the purpose of God's glory. He experienced a personal encounter with Jesus which resulted in transformative behavior and a course correction, you will learn more about this process in Chapter 8.

WHAT IS EMOTIONAL INTELLIGENCE?

Peter Salovey and John D. Mayer coined the term 'Emotional Intelligence' in 1990, describing it as "a form of social intelligence that involves the ability to monitor one's own and others feelings and emotions, to discriminate among them, and to use this information to guide one's thinking and action." Although the term first appeared in 1964, it gained popularity in the 1995 best-selling book Emotional Intelligence (EI), written by science journalist Daniel Goleman. Goleman defined EI as the array of skills and characteristics that drive leadership performance. Various models have been developed to measure EI, and they use four emotional intelligence skills that fall under two competencies of personal and emotional competence.

God is the ultimate example of emotional intelligence.

> *"For the message of the cross is foolishness to those who are perishing, but to us who are being saved it is the power of God"* (1 Corinthians 1:18).

Jesus Christ of Nazareth modeled the highest form of emotional intelligence, connecting the hearts of humanity: love in action. Using His words, intonation, body language and self-control, Jesus won the hearts of the people who encountered Him from the youngest to the oldest; He positively impacted people's lives.

Emotional Intelligence in Christ is the activation of the Holy Spirit within you to discern and manage personal emotions and behavior in a way that honors God by loving others well as Jesus did.

> Jesus Christ is where the true transformation happens. Modeling His behavior and those of His anointed is how you become emotionally intelligent in Christ.

God is the ultimate example of emotional intelligence. The focus of this book is emotional intelligence as showcased by Jesus Christ of Nazareth when He walked this earth as a man. We believe Jesus Christ is the ultimate model of emotional intelligence, as fully man and fully God, He offers us the bridge between man and God. Our mission on earth is to make God recognizable by loving our neighbor as ourselves, just as Jesus did.

Jesus Christ is where the true transformation happens. Modeling His behavior and those of His anointed is how you become emotionally intelligent in Christ.

We refer to Emotional Intelligence in Christ in terms of behaviors. The definition of behavior is how a person acts or responds to a particular situation. As you identify and anchor specific behaviors that connect with Christ's emotional intelligence, you are then in a position to gain clarity of focus around the specific action steps you want to integrate into your daily life to form habits. This chapter will give you an overview of Emotional Intelligence and define each of the four behavior traits associated with becoming Emotionally Intelligent in Christ (EIC).

> Love is the basis of emotional intelligence, and it is through Jesus Christ, you can live and develop the behaviors that make you emotionally intelligent in Christ.

The Scripture in John 1:1 refers to Jesus Christ: *In the beginning was the Word, and the Word was with God, and the Word was God.* The Bible, God's Word, answers the following questions: Who am I? Why am I here? What does it matter? What is the truth? These questions are answered by reading the Bible and understanding Jesus and His nature. The definition of nature is referred to as understanding the particular characteristic of a person. What is the nature of Jesus, and how does emotional intelligence play into this?

Jesus is the Son of God. 1 John 4:8 tells us that God is Love and that he that does not love doesn't know God because God is Love. God's nature, which is love, includes all that He is in Spirit and person. Because it is so hard for us to comprehend this love, He gave us the ultimate teacher, Jesus, to explain and model it for us.

Love is the basis of emotional intelligence, and it is through Jesus Christ, you can live and develop the behaviors that make you emotionally intelligent in Christ.

The Apostles witnessed the emotional intelligent nature of Jesus Christ. How? They personally encountered His presence in their lives and therefore, their nature was transformed into His nature which spilled over into their behavior. The Apostles were the A-team that Jesus brought together to tell the world about our inherent divine nature. The Book of Acts helps us understand how we are directed by the Holy Spirit to know the role of Jesus's lessons in our lives. The story in Acts 15 demonstrates the modeling of Jesus's emotional intelligence through the Apostles, which is seen in their investment in others, the release of responsibility, servant leadership, treatment of others with love and grace, people over rules and regulations, and focus on a Godly vision.

So, what specific behaviors are essential to become emotionally intelligent in Christ? We identify four phases as behaviors that reflect how Jesus showed up with emotional intelligence: *Personal Identity, Self-Control, Altruistic Attitude, and Christ Connections.*

Behavior 1: Personal Identity (Self-Awareness in Christ)

> *I have been crucified with Christ, and I no longer live, but Christ lives in me. The life I now live in the body, I live by faith in the Son of God, who loved me and gave himself-for me"* (Galatians 2:20).

Whose am I? How does my relationship with Christ shape my understanding of myself? Your personal identity, when grounded in Christ, leads with a humble acknowledgment that its identity, worth and value flows directly from knowing itself-to be loved and adored by God who has a good plan that overrides any emotional life "pop-ups."

Behavior 2: Self-Control: (Self-Management)

The last fruit of the Spirit that resurrects the other fruits to the frontline of our behaviors: *"But the fruit of the Spirit is love, joy, peace, forbearance, kindness, goodness, faithfulness, gentleness, and self-control"* (Galatians 5:22–23).

Self-control is the ramification of surrender to the presence and authority of Jesus Christ of Nazareth in your life. The resulting relationship is a face-to-face encounter with the One who died to win you over to eternal love and security. Your awareness of the presence of Christ within you gives you the ability, through Him, to be the boss of your emotions rather than allowing them to be the boss of you.

Behavior 3: Altruistic Attitude (Social-Awareness)

Philippians 2:5 tells us, *"You must have the same attitude as Christ."*

The result of our encounter with Christ and the gift of the Holy Spirit reminds us of the attitude we are to have. This attitude enables us to think less of our own ambitions and selfish focus and more about other people's needs and wants.

Altruism is the unselfish concern for other people—doing things simply out of love, not because you feel obligated to out of guilt, shame, duty, loyalty, or religious reasons. It refers to behavior that benefits another individual at a cost to oneself.

Behavior 4: Christ Connections: (Relational Management)

Jesus himself-invited us into the freedom of this final phase of EIC when He said in John 13:34–35: *"A new command I give you: Love one another. As I have loved you, so you must love one another. By this, everyone will know that you are my disciples if you love one another."*

As a direct result of your deeper relationship awareness in Christ you are able to make Christ connections. Through Christ, you have the authority to cast down the emotional drama, which flows from the I, me, my mindset, to make way for the awareness of other people's perspectives and emotions to connect with others in a meaningful way.

Throughout this book, we will focus on someone who is the ultimate model for Emotional Intelligence: Jesus Christ of Nazareth. You will also notice case studies of people who encountered Christ woven into each chapter. As you read through each case study, reflect on where you recognize yourself-and what you want to model in your own behavior based on what you learn. Jesus had an extraordinary ability to meet people where they were and adapt His response to them based on how they processed life.

A powerful Scripture taken from John 8:1–11 showcases Jesus's ability to transition into each of the four Emotional Intelligent strategies:

- Self-Awareness (Personal Identity)
- Self-Management (Self-Control)
- Social-Awareness (Altruistic Attitude)
- Relational Management (Christ Connections)

We will use the following Scriptures as a case study. Take a moment to read through John 8:1–11 before we break it down for you:

> *"... but Jesus went to the Mount of Olives.*
>
> *"At dawn he appeared again in the temple courts, where all the people gathered around him, and he sat down to teach them. The teachers of the law and the Pharisees brought in a woman caught in adultery. They made her stand before the group and said to Jesus, 'Teacher, this woman was caught in the act of adultery. In the Law Moses commanded us to stone such women. Now what do you say?' They were using this question as a trap, in order to have a basis for accusing him.*
>
> *"But Jesus bent down and started to write on the ground with his finger. When they kept on questioning him, he*

straightened up and said to them, 'Let any one of you who is without sin be the first to throw a stone at her.' Again he stooped down and wrote on the ground.

"At this, those who heard began to go away one at a time, the older ones first, until only Jesus was left, with the woman still standing there. Jesus straightened up and asked her, 'Woman, where are they? Has no one condemned you?'

"'No one, sir,' she said.

"'Then neither do I condemn you,' Jesus declared. 'Go now and leave your life of sin.'"

Let's unpack and take a closer look at this story. In order to connect to the people around Him, Jesus changed his responses and strategic direction, five different times:

1. SITUATION: Jesus was in the temple area telling stories which are referred to as parables. He was divinely aware of what people needed and what He needed to give to them. The Pharisees decide they are going to catch Jesus, so they bring to Him a woman caught in adultery. They choose to have a trial smack in the middle of Jesus's teaching the people about the things of God. We have a mob event that raises the emotions really high that uses half-truths of a law to get Jesus's attention and attempt to discredit Him: the law says that a woman caught in adultery is to be stoned. They conveniently leave out the other part of the law: in the presence of two witnesses, they do not point out which man was caught in

> As you continue your journey into Emotional Intelligence in Christ, you will experience a change in your ability to direct your thoughts to be more Christ-like, link your will to God's will, and adjust your emotional responses to yourself-and others around you.

the act. In spite of the high-pitched emotions, the first thing Jesus does is ignore them. Emotionally Intelligent behavior: Social-Awareness/Altruistic Attitude.

2. **CHALLENGE(S):** *He was dealing with all the EIC behaviors.* He takes the emotions and settles them down. How? By not reacting. Knowing His personal identity, Jesus does not allow the behavior of other people to shift Him off course. The guys who are playing the blame-game try to raise it up another notch by asking Jesus: *What do you say about this?* As General Patton says: *If you're going to give an order, stand up even if you are talking on the phone.* Jesus stands up and declares a Scripture in response to their inquiry: *He who is without sin, cast the first stone.* Drop the mic. At the Biblical time of this particular situation this was the protocol: If you are accusing someone of adultery, you need at least two witnesses. One of the witnesses is the man who committed the act. Where is the guilty man? Have these men visited the woman too? These men are now obligated to come up with names and have them stand up . . . and if anyone is lying, they will be stoned too. Emotionally Intelligent behavior: Personal Identity/Self-Awareness.

3. **BEHAVIORAL GOAL:** Jesus flips the scene by using Self-Awareness (staying on mission), self-control (not stepping onto the stage of drama), Social-Awareness (being alert and attentive to the people's emotions around Him), and social management (flipping the lesson back on the people for their ultimate good). The greatest teachers are those who guide others back to themselves as connected to God. Jesus, being God's Son, nailed it. Rather than the woman, now the crowd of judgmental onlookers are on trial. The oldest leaves

first. Why? According to the law, the oldest guilty of lying would be stoned first. You could feel the thickness in the air as each man came face-to-face with their own transgressions. Everything settles down as one-by-one they drop their stones and walk away.

4. **RESULT:** Jesus now speaks using a term of respect: *Woman, where are they? Has no one condemned you?* To which she replies: *No one, sir.* Then with much compassion and expression of altruism (Social-Awareness), Jesus makes a Christ connection that will change her entire life as He says: *"Then neither do I condemn you, go and leave your life of sin."* The only person there worthy of bringing her to trial is Jesus and He says go and change your life. That woman was sure she was going to die and instead she received grace.

The case study[1] above , reveals Jesus's ability to adapt His DISC behaviors to the emotional intelligence needs of the crowd around him without compromising God's mission of salvation through Him.

As you continue your journey into *Emotional Intelligence in Christ*, you will experience a change in your ability to direct your thoughts to be more Christ-like, link your will to God's will, and adjust your emotional responses to yourself-and others around you.

---

1 *DISCovering the Leadership of Jesus*, Ken Voges & Mike Kempainen, ©2001, Ken R. Voges, pages 160–167)

Prayer

Holy Spirit I invite You into this experience of resurrecting emotional intelligence in Christ within my spirit, mind, emotions, and body. Strengthen my ability to tune into people's needs and respond to them in an emotionally intelligent way that makes You recognizable to them and brings glory to Your name. Lead me onward and upward, Lord. I invite You into the words of my mouth and meditations of my heart now and moving forward. In Jesus name, Amen

CHAPTER 2

BIBLICAL EIQ ASSESSMENT FOR EIC APPLICATION

"A pure, simple and steady spirit is not distracted by flitting about from one thing to another, for he does all things to the honor of God and tries in his heart to be free from all selfishness. What gets in your way and troubles you more than the undisciplined passions (emotions) of your own heart? A good, devout person first arranges inwardly the things to be done outwardly. He does not let his passions (emotions) get the best of him, but he subjects them to the ruling of sound judgment. Who has a more fierce struggle than the person who strives to master himself? And this must be our occupation: to strive to master ourselves and daily to grow stronger and to advance from good to better. (In, with, and through Christ)."[2]

"WE LOVE BECAUSE God first loved us" (1 John 4:19). We cannot give out to the world around us what we have not first experienced within. When you personally encounter the love of God, you can't help but share that love in meaningful and impactful ways to the people around you.

---

2 Thomas A Kempis, *The Imitation of Christ, A Timeless Classic for Contemporary Readers*, William C. Creasy, (Notre Dame, IN: Ave Maria Press, 1989), 33.

The Biblical EIQ and Biblical DISC Assessments will offer you powerful insights into Christ-like ways to manage the behaviors of yourself-and others. Jesus is our ultimate mentor and guide into the experience of emotional intelligence as God designed it to be fulfilling the greatest commandment and ultimate guidepost to effective leadership and healthy relationships:

> *"Love the Lord your God with all your heart and with all your soul and with all your mind and with all your strength.' The second is this: 'Love your neighbor as yourself.' There is no commandment greater than these"* (Mark 12:30–31).

We have included two Bonus Assessments as a part of your learning experience in this book: Biblical EIQ and Biblical DISC. You can access these assessments here:

Biblical EIQ Link: https://bit.ly/39e3f0M

Biblical DISC Link: https://bit.ly/3EomOBW

For link issues call: 1-800-383-6890.

These are easy and quick assessments that will take approximately 15 minutes each. You will receive a summary of your results for each assessment. Keep them nearby as you read through this book as they will offer you clarity of focus around the human operating system, how God wired you for His glory. It will also help you apply the EIC Method, enabling you to explore how to best use your findings for His glory and the edification of the people around you, whether that be strangers, children, family members, friends, co-workers, etc. colleagues or direct reports.

Congratulations if you have taken both the Emotional Intelligence In Christ Assessment known as *Biblical EIQ* and the *Biblical DISC® (Developed by Ken Voges)*. You received a summarized version of the Biblical EIQ and Biblical DISC assessment. This is valuable feedback that offers you a framework to build on in order to model Christ-like behavior. In this chapter, you will focus on the use of Biblical case studies and how they relate to each of the EIC subcategories. This begins the process of reflecting on what you are learning about yourself, your EIQ and DISC strengths and opportunities.

The Biblical Emotional Intelligence Assessment contains four traits of focus and five subcategories, detailed below. As you will notice, we include after each EIC trait the behavior that we will use in this book. For example, Self-Awareness will be referred to as Personal Identity:

- **SELF-AWARENESS/PERSONAL IDENTITY:** Self-Awareness/Self-Understanding | Connection of cause and effect | Self-appreciation, acceptance, and confidence | Consciousness and Assertiveness | Emotional Identification.
- **SELF-MANAGEMENT/SELF-CONTROL:** Self-Control/Discipline | Goal-Directed Performance, Targeted Actions | Integrity and Trustworthiness | Motivation and Positive Psychology | Creativity, Agility, Flexibility, Adaptability
- **SOCIAL-AWARENESS/ALTRUISM:** Empathy | Sensitivity | Appreciation| Understanding| Compassion | Benevolence: | Aiding | Helping | Coaching | Giving | Holistic Communication | Situational Perceptual | Awareness.
- **RELATIONAL MANAGEMENT/CHRIST CONNECTIONS:** Developing Relationships, Getting Along with Others | Leadership and Influence | Change Catalyst and Response | Negotiation and Conflict Management | Teamwork and Collaboration

Within each of the subcategories you will notice details associated with the subcategory and a Biblical case study. Take a moment to explore where you recognize yourself-now and where you want to be. Journal a few of your thoughts as you consider your personal EIC.

SELF-AWARENESS

Take a moment to self-reflect on your EIQ Self-Awareness results and the subcategories. If you have also taken the Biblical DISC Assessment, you will know your personality style and how your style intertwines with the subcategories.

Sub-Category #1 Self-Awareness/Understanding: a conscious, deliberate reflection on personal identity, image, feelings, motives, desires and how these are associated with perceptions of self-in the context of various situations.

Biblical case study: Matthew 16:15–21 *"Who do you say I am?"* (Matthew 16:15). Regarding His personal identity, Jesus used the term **"I AM"** 153 times in the New Testament.

In what ways do you relate to Christ when it comes to your sense of identity and purpose?

_____

_____

_____

_____

Sub-Category #2 Connections of Cause and Effect: recognition of the impact and consequence of behaviors on feeling and moods; separating external and internal factors affecting emotions; knowing how feelings relate to performance.

Biblical case study: Luke 22:39–44 Jesus in the Garden of Gethsemane. *"Take this cup . . . sweating drops of blood"* (Luke 22:42–44), Jesus was asking the Father to let the cup pass from Him yet surrendered to God's will.

Ultimate surrender and self-assurance which leads to acceptance of God's will.

When was a time in your life emotionally, you wanted to let the cup pass yet you chose to surrender to the will of God and experienced the divine power to overcome your emotional moods?

Sub-Category #3 Self-Appreciation, Acceptance and Confidence: development of self-esteem; personal worth and value; and coming to grips with personal attributes. Operating with realistic, self-assurance.

Biblical case study: Matthew 26:37–42 Jesus in the Garden of Gethsemane: *"My Father, if it is not possible for this cup to be taken away unless I drink it, may your will be done"* (Matthew 26:39).

Ultimate surrender and self-assurance which leads to acceptance of God's will.

Describe your level of self-confidence and personal worth.

Sub-Category #4 Consciousness & Assertiveness: intentional establishment of personal boundaries and appropriate limits; choosing a path that expresses self- worth through personal care and outward presentation (presence).

Biblical case study: Mark 3:1–6 Jesus Heals on the Sabbath: *"He looked around at them with anger, being grieved by the hardness of their hearts . . . he stretched out the withered hand of the man and it was restored"* (Mark 3:5). Jesus was not confined by status or the opinions of other people. He was driven by the will of God to do good in spite of the emotional outbursts of people around Him.

What do you need to remember to give yourself-permission to speak the truth in love in the face of adverse reactions? To be conscious and assertive about your identity in Christ and yet remaining humble and kind?

....
....
....
....

Sub-Category #5 Emotional Identification: ability to identify and name personal feelings; vocabulary and definition of emotions allowing choices, responses, and performance; effective reflection on intra-personal information.

Biblical case study: John 11:1–35 *"Jesus wept"* (John 11:35).

When was the last time you allowed yourself to identify with your emotions and personal feelings in a way that helped you move through them? Describe your experience.

....
....
....
....

SELF-MANAGEMENT

Take a moment to self-reflect on your EIC Self-Management results and the subcategories. If you have also taken the Biblical DISC Assessment, you will know your personality style and how your style intertwines with the subcategories.

Sub-Category #1—Self-Control, Discipline: effectively handling impulses; maintaining composure while experiencing stressful, trying emotions . . . the ability to emotionally persist to achieve strategic objectives.

Biblical case study: Matthew 4:1–4: Jesus's Temptation: Following a 40-day fast, Jesus was tempted by Satan to change a stone to bread.

Jesus's answer — *"It is written, "MAN SHALL NOT LIVE ON BREAD ALONE, BUT ON EVERY WORD THAT PROCEEDS OUT OF THE MOUTH OF GOD"* (Matthew 4:4).

When have you felt God's strength within you to resist temptation? Perhaps in the area of a potential emotional outburst? Explain.

....

....

....

....

Sub-Category #2 Goal-Directed Performance, Targeted Actions: focus to achieve long-term desired goals; emotional tenacity and persistence; drive to choose challenging objectives and assume acceptable risk.

Biblical case study: Matthew 4:5–7: Jesus's Temptation: Satan suggested Jesus prove He was God by jumping off the pinnacle of the Temple.

Jesus's answer— *"On the other hand, it is written, YOU SHALL NOT TEMPT THE LORD YOUR GOD"* (Matthew 4:7).

What Scripture have you recently used to talk back to the devil as Jesus did in the desert? Describe the ways you acted on that Scripture.

....

....

....

....

Sub-Category #3 Integrity, Trustworthiness: the ability to work with conscience, ethics and integrity; operating with personal standards, principles, and values; being dependable, reliable, and authentic.

Biblical case study: Matthew 4:8–10: Jesus's Temptation in the desert. Satan offered Him the world's kingdoms if Jesus would fall down and worship him.

Jesus's answer— *"Away from me, Satan! For it is written, YOU SHALL WORSHIP THE LORD YOUR GOD, AND SERVE HIM ONLY"* (Matthew 4:10).

Based on Jesus's response above, what triggers does Satan use to spin you emotionally in daily life? Use Jesus's words to help you resist worldly temptations that trigger emotions: *"Away from me Satan! I will worship the Lord my God and serve Him only!"*

....
....
....
....

Sub-Category #4 Motivation, Positive Psychology, Initiative: self-energizing; the ability to be mentally and emotionally engaged; limiting negative emotions, patterns, and spirals.

Biblical case study: Matthew 4:11: Jesus Alone *"Then Satan left Jesus alone until a more opportune time . . ."*

Jesus's action plan *". . . and behold, angels came and began to minister to Him."* When was a time when you resisted temptation and felt the strength of God ministering to your emotions? What did you identify and adjust, with the strength of God, to limit negative emotions and spirals?

....
....
....
....

Sub-Category #5 Creativity, Agility, Flexibility, Adaptability: coping with change, transition and developments; adjusting to situations, relationships and feelings; the ability to problem solve and 'think outside the box.'

Biblical case study: John 4:1–26: Jesus and the Samaritan Woman: While alone, Jesus engaged in a conversation with a Samaritan woman who had been married five times and was currently living with yet another man.

Jesus's out-of-the-box dialogue with the woman resulted in her saying *"I know that Messiah is coming (He who is called Christ); when that One comes, He will declare all things to us"* (John 4:25).

Jesus said to her, *"I who speak to you am He"* (John 4:26).

This is the first of 153 times in which Jesus used the words I AM to declare his true identity. I believe this case study qualifies as an "out-of-the-box" encounter.

When have you experienced the ability to adjust to a situation, relationship, or feelings with the assistance of the Holy Spirit in your life?

....
....
....
....

SOCIAL-AWARENESS

Take a moment to self-reflect on your EIC Social-Awareness results and the subcategories. If you have also taken the Biblical DISC®Assessment, you will know your personality style and how your style intertwines with the subcategories.

Sub-Category #1 Empathy, Sensitivity, Appreciation: understanding others; accurately picking up emotional cues from communication (including words, tone, and nonverbal signals).

Biblical case study: Luke 1:26–56 Mary and Gabriel: The initial dialogue between Gabriel and Mary concerning her giving birth to Jesus, the Messiah.

Mary said to the angel, *"How can this be since I am a virgin?"* (Luke 1:34)

And Gabriel answered and said to her, *"The Holy Spirit will come upon you, and the power of the Most High will overshadow you; and for that reason, the holy offspring shall be called the Son of God. And behold, even your relative Elizabeth has also conceived a son in her old age; and she who was called barren is now in her sixth month. For nothing will be impossible with God"* (Luke 1:35–37).

Notice the sensitivity of Gabriel, the Lord's messenger, when speaking with Mary, this is emotional intelligence in action.

In what ways do you use your words, tone, and nonverbal signals to make God recognizable in your communication with people He entrusted to your care?

_____

_____

_____

_____

Fun fact about effective communication: 8% are the words you use, 38% comes from your intonation and 54% from your body language.

What area do you want the Holy Spirit to influence for stronger connections? The words you use? Your intonation? Body language? Invite feedback from people who know you well. Ask: Describe the ways I allow Christ's love to come through me in my voice. Words I use? Body language? Jesus used it all to make emotionally intelligent connections.

_____

_____

_____

Sub-Category #2 Service, Compassion, Benevolence: operating with a sense of contribution; aiding, helping, coaching, and developing others; giving; operating to constructively contribute to the emotional states and benefits of others; recognizing needs, wants and desires.

Biblical case study: John 2:1–11 Wedding at Cana: Jesus turned water into wine.

At the conclusion of this miracle, John 2:11 says, *"This beginning of His signs Jesus did in Cana of Galilee, and manifested His glory, and His disciples believed in Him."* Notice in this Biblical story how Jesus responds with compassion to the wants and desires of the people around Him, particularly the exchange between Jesus and His Mother in John 2:3–5: *"When the wine was gone, Jesus's mother said to him, "They have no more wine." "Woman, why do you involve me?" Jesus replied. "My hour has not yet come." His mother said to the servants, "Do whatever he tells you."*

Where do you recognize Jesus's emotional intelligence in the Wedding of Cana scene as you reflect on the attributes associated with this subcategory?

Sub-Category #3 Holistic Communication: the ability to effectively send and receive information including emotional content; listening; engaging and connecting with others; sending and receiving verbal and nonverbal signals constructively.

Biblical case study: Luke 13:10–17: Jesus Heals on the Sabbath: Jesus healed a woman, who for 18 years, was afflicted with sickness caused by a spirit which did not allow her to stand straight up.

> The greatest teachers are those who guide others back to themselves as connected to God.

Jesus's action— *"Woman, you are set free from your infirmity." Then he put his hands on her, and immediately she straightened up and praised God"* (Luke 13:12–13).

In spite of the fact that onlookers condemned Jesus for healing on the Sabbath, Jesus always put people before things. Do you? When has Jesus connected with you and moved you to a place of physical, mental and or spiritual healing? When have you offered this gift to someone entrusted to your care? Explain.

....
....
....
....

Sub-Category #4 Situational Perceptual Awareness: recognizing and processing dynamic, shifting emotional data; adapting to situational variables and changes; understanding which factors count, how much and responding with reasonable behavior.

Biblical case study: John 8:1–11: Jesus Forgives: He had the Emotional Intelligence (EI) to change His behavior five times within minutes to address the drama of the woman charged with adultery. In the end, the mob dispersed, and Jesus extended forgiveness, mercy and grace to the woman.

> *"Woman, where are they? Has no one condemned you?"*
> *"No one, sir," she said.*
>
> *"Then neither do I condemn you,"* Jesus declared. *"Go now and leave your life of sin"* (John 8:10-11).

Jesus exercising His divine behavioral preference - mercy and grace. He was also aware of other people's emotions in the group and managed them well.

The greatest teachers are those who guide others back to themselves as connected to God.

Where in your life have you had the opportunity to offer mercy, and grace to someone who under a law or rule didn't deserve it?

....
....
....

The above account of Jesus's Social-Awareness, in a highly emotionally charged scene, is a "drop the mic" tribute to His brilliant emotional intelligence in action. *"Let any one of you who is without sin be the first to throw a stone at her"* (John 8:7).

Reflect again on the attributes associated with this 5th subcategory under Social-Awareness: recognizing and processing dynamic, shifting emotional data; adapting to situational variables and changes; understanding which factors count, how much and responding with reasonable behavior. What do you want to remember from this example as a leader who is seeking emotional intelligence in Christ?

NOTE: Reader, we will repeat this case study and others you are reading in this chapter, offering more details because they are powerful examples of Christ in action using both EIC and Biblical DISC awareness. Repetition of content leads to an increase in the ability to transfer and apply new learnings.

Sub-Category #5 Interpersonal Development: growing and nurturing constructive connections; setting the tone for long-term depth and breadth in relationships.

Biblical case study: John 4:1–26: Jesus and the Samaritan Woman: While alone, Jesus engaged in a conversation with a Samaritan woman who had been married five times and was currently living with yet another man.

Jesus's conversation began about water, then living water, then where all people groups will worship the living God. His final words were:

> *"Woman, believe Me, an hour is coming when neither in this mountain, nor in Jerusalem, shall you worship the*

Father…But an hour is coming and now is, when the true worshipers shall worship the Father in spirit and truth; for such people the Father seeks to be His worshipers. "God is spirit; and those who worship Him must worship in spirit and truth." The woman said to Him, "I know that Messiah is coming (He who is called Christ); when that One comes, He will declare all things to us.' Jesus said to her, 'I who speak to you am He" (John 4:23-26).

This is the first of 153 times in which Jesus used the words I AM to declare his identity. It was through this unnamed woman who gave testimony about Him that led the entire community to believe in Jesus as the Messiah resulting in eternal consequences. This subcategory under the 3rd trait of EIC: Social-Awareness focuses on setting the tone of relationships. Jesus was masterful at this ability.

In what ways do you set the tone of relationships? Do you listen to understand or to be understood? Do you meet people where they are, loving first and then leading? Give an example from your life when you got out of your own way and allowed the Holy Spirit to connect to someone who was not easy to connect with?

....
....
....
....

Relational Management

Take a moment to self-reflect on your EIC Relational Management results and the subcategories. If you have also taken the Biblical DISC Assessment, you will know your personality style and how your style intertwines with the subcategories.

Sub-Category #1 Developing Relationships, Getting Along with Others: cultivating, nurturing and maintaining long-term personal and professional relationships; having quality connections and friendships.

Biblical case study: John 21:1–17: Jesus and Peter: The case study shows Jesus affirming Peter in front of the other ten Apostles. Although Peter denied knowing Him three times when he publicly stated that would never happen, Jesus took the time to restore Peter as the leader of the Apostles.

Jesus asked Peter three times *"Do you love me?"* With Peter's humble responses, Jesus undid his three denials and outlined a four-point action plan in leading the Apostles.

> *"When they had finished eating, Jesus said to Simon Peter, "Simon son of John, do you love me more than these?" "Yes, Lord," he said, "you know that I love you." Jesus said, "Feed my lambs." Again Jesus said, "Simon son of John, do you love me?" He answered, "Yes, Lord, you know that I love you." Jesus said, "Take care of my sheep." The third time he said to him, "Simon son of John, do you love me?" Peter was hurt because Jesus asked him the third time, "Do you love me?" He said, "Lord, you know all things; you know that I love you." Jesus said, "Feed my sheep"* (John 21:15-17).

Jesus knows how important it is for Peter to be recognized as restored in front of his friends. You will learn more about Peter's DISC later in the book. One of Peter's biggest fears is rejection and Jesus, in His emotionally intelligent way, meets Peter in his fear. We naturally give out what we desire to receive. When you follow the emotionally intelligent lead of Christ you gain access into how other people perceive life in the midst of differences. The Holy Spirit is your virtual assistant when it comes to this ability: To see a circumstance from another person's perspective and DISC style and connect in the midst of it all.

Simply put, in what ways do you make God recognizable to other people?

When has God met you in your biggest fears in life? Describe the ways you meet other people when they are experiencing fear, doubt or worry. Give a recent example from your life when you stepped out of your own filters and were able to see a situation from another person's perspective which resulted in a positive connection. Your filters are your knowledge, experience and values that influence how you listen, think and communicate.[3] When you allow the Holy Spirit to access your filters your entire world opens up along with your ability to make Christ Connections.

....

....

....

....

Sub-Category #2 Leadership and Influence: operating with warmth, likability, presence, charisma, and approachability; paying attention and focusing on results; being involved, engaging, passionate and powerful; showing deliberate persuasion; delivering solutions and success to others.

Biblical case study: Genesis 18:1,10–12; Genesis 21:7: The Lord Visits Abraham and Sarah: The Lord visited Abraham & Sarah over dinner and predicted that within a year Sarah would have a son. Although Sarah laughed at the idea because of their old age, it happened as the Lord predicted.

The conclusion of this miracle: Sarah became pregnant and bore a son . . . and Abraham gave the name Isaac to the son Sarah bore him in his old age. The name Isaac means joyful laughter.

Warmth and likability walks hand-in-hand with a fun personality. God has a fun personality when it's needed to reach the heart of His children for His purposes. Children adored Jesus, evidence that Jesus has a fun personality. The definition of charisma is compelling charm that can inspire devotion in others. Describe ways your behaviors inspire devotion to God in others?

---

[3] Sherpa Executive Coaching, https://www.sherpacoaching.com/

Simply put, in what ways do you make God recognizable to other people?

Be specific. If you don't know, ask a few people who know you and record their feedback below:

....

....

....

....

Sub-Category #3 Change Catalyst and Response: recognizing the need for change and championing action; developing interpersonal skills and abilities; initiating growth and progress on an individual, team and organization levels; facilitating maturity and success; focusing on positive outcomes.

> Invite the Holy Spirit in to increase your emotional intelligence in Christ before you offer guidance that will initiate learning and growth.

Biblical case study: Read Exodus chapter 3 & 4: The Lord Calls Moses back to Egypt: The case study involves the Lord calling Moses to return to Egypt and bring the Hebrew nation out of slavery to a preordained, promised land. Moses initially declined the assignment with: *"Please, Lord, send someone else!"*

The Lord's Strategy—Answering each question Moses had with specific responses coupled with reassurances of support. When Moses raised the issue of being slow of tongue, the Lord suggested his brother Aaron who spoke well. It wasn't until he talked to his father-in-law, Jethro, did Moses assume ownership of the assignment.

The Lord continues to champion human potential initiating growth and progress in the lives of His people, including you. Increase the pause between your response to someone who could use some mentoring and your choice of interpersonal communication.

Invite the Holy Spirit in to increase your emotional intelligence in Christ before you offer guidance that will initiate learning and growth.

When have you called on the name of the Lord to help you help another person move beyond their own self-doubt as God did for Moses?

....

....

....

....

Sub-Category #4. Negotiation and Conflict Management: bargains with abundance thinking for mutual gains; copes with conflict through positive proactive and reactive techniques; effectively deals with difficult people and situations.

Biblical case study: Acts 9:1–22: Paul Meets Jesus: Paul was on his way to Damascus to arrest men and women of the Way for the purpose of bringing them back to Jerusalem for trial, resulting in death sentences. Jesus's intended role for Paul was to work with these people to spread the Gospel to the Gentiles. Paul's behavior could easily be classified as being a difficult person going in the wrong direction creating negative results.

Read through Acts 9:1–20

> *"Meanwhile, Saul was still breathing out murderous threats against the Lord's disciples. He went to the high priest and asked him for letters to the synagogues in Damascus, so that if he found any there who belonged to the Way, whether men or women, he might take them as prisoners to Jerusalem. As he neared Damascus on his journey, suddenly a light from heaven flashed around him. He fell to the ground and heard a voice say to him, "Saul, Saul, why do you persecute me?" "Who are you, Lord?" Saul asked. "I am Jesus, whom you are persecuting," he*

replied. "Now get up and go into the city, and you will be told what you must do." The men traveling with Saul stood there speechless; they heard the sound but did not see anyone. Saul got up from the ground, but when he opened his eyes he could see nothing. So they led him by the hand into Damascus. For three days he was blind, and did not eat or drink anything. In Damascus there was a disciple named Ananias. The Lord called to him in a vision, "Ananias!" "Yes, Lord," he answered. The Lord told him, "Go to the house of Judas on Straight Street and ask for a man from Tarsus named Saul, for he is praying. In a vision he has seen a man named Ananias come and place his hands on him to restore his sight." "Lord," Ananias answered, "I have heard many reports about this man and all the harm he has done to your holy people in Jerusalem. And he has come here with authority from the chief priests to arrest all who call on your name." But the Lord said to Ananias, "Go! This man is my chosen instrument to proclaim my name to the Gentiles and their kings and to the people of Israel. I will show him how much he must suffer for my name." Then Ananias went to the house and entered it. Placing his hands on Saul, he said, "Brother Saul, the Lord—Jesus, who appeared to you on the road as you were coming here—has sent me so that you may see again and be filled with the Holy Spirit." Immediately, something like scales fell from Saul's eyes, and he could see again. He got up and was baptized, and after taking some food, he regained his strength. Saul spent several days with the disciples in Damascus. At once he began to preach in the synagogues that Jesus is the Son of God."

Jesus's response to Paul was short and He allowed him to be blinded and physically helpless. Jesus then gave Paul brief instructions on what to do next. He then remained in a state of blindness for three days, praying to understand the meaning behind his condition. In a vision, Paul was made aware that a person named Ananias would restore his sight and give him additional instructions. These sequences of events were responsible in totally redirecting Paul's energies into powerfully proving that Jesus was the Christ.

God knew exactly what kind of encounter was needed in order to move Saul into a personal relationship with His Son, Jesus Christ: a face-to-face encounter. Talk about emotional intelligence in action. We will explore more specifically Saul/Paul's personal DISC style in the following chapters. For now, reflect on how Jesus met Saul right where he was and loved him enough not to leave him there.

When was the last time you encountered a difficult person going in the wrong direction? Did you cope with the conflict using positive proactive behavior or not? Read through Saul's encounter with Jesus in Acts 9:1–22 and reflect on what you want to remember the next time you come face-to-face with a difficult person and/or conflict situation. Which verse stands out to you the most? Why?

....

....

....

Sub-Category #5 Teamwork and Collaboration: builds bonds; transforms groups into teams; foster unified engaged efforts; generates collaboration, cooperation participation and high-quality results; nurtures esprit de corps and the ability to develop synergy, interpersonal emotional effectiveness.

Biblical case study: John 11:1–45: Jesus and Lazarus: Jesus made sure the Apostles knew that Lazarus had died so that they would witness and be unified in understanding Jesus's power over death and the reality of the resurrection. Jesus would also use His behavioral insights and emotional intelligence to comfort Martha and Mary according to their needs. Finally, among the crowd of witnesses many would believe in Jesus but sadly Jesus's actions would galvanize the chief priest and the Sanhedrin to plot Jesus's death.

Jesus's words to the Apostles: *"Lazarus is dead, and for your sake I am glad I was not there, so that you may believe"* (John 11:14–15).

Jesus's conversation with Martha following her statement: *"Lord, if you had been here my brother would not have died."*

Jesus said to her: *"I am the resurrection and the life. He who believes in me will live, even though he dies; and whoever lives and believes in me will never die. Do you believe this?"*

In this scene Jesus is adjusting His responses according to the person or people He is addressing. As He often did and continues to do, Jesus focuses on touching the lives of all concerned to draw them closer to God. The definition of Esprit de corps is the *common spirit existing in the members of a group and inspiring enthusiasm, devotion, and strong regard for the honor of the group.* Walking into a highly emotionally charged situation was common for Jesus. Notice how Jesus addresses each person in this scene with interpersonal emotional effectiveness: met each person (Mary and Martha) where they were and loved them enough not to leave them there . . . Jesus knew the crowd was watching closely and picked His words wisely so as to inspire the group into devotion.

Take a moment to reflect back over this past week. When was a time that you had the opportunity to create a collaborative environment for people to connect? How do you create enthusiasm in the lives of people around you? The expression will be unique to your specific DISC and EIC profile. The root of the word enthusiasm is entheos, which means "God within." How do you want that to play out in your relationships this week? What do you want to see more of? Less of?

You now have had the opportunity to explore the four behavior traits and subcategories for EIC. For clarity, throughout the book, you will notice we have personalized each of the above four EIC traits: Self-Awareness | Self-Management | Social-Awareness | Relational Management as follows using our own terminology and methodology:

- Personal Identity
- Self-Control
- Altruism
- Christ Connections

We reference the Biblical DISC® Assessment, developed by Ken Voges and a registered trademark of Lead Like Jesus and In His Grace, INC., which offers you insight into how you and other people operate. When it comes to specific behaviors in different situations, the Biblical EIQ Assessment, developed by Lead Like Jesus with Biblical interpretation from Ken Voges, gives you the ability to specifically connect with people in the midst of different DISC profiles.

We recommend taking both the Biblical DISC Assessment: https://bit.ly/3EomOBW and the Biblical EIQ assessment: https://bit.ly/39e3f0M. Clarity of focus leads to accuracy of response. As you learn your Biblical DISC profile, your typical go-to behaviors, you are then in a position to identify and adjust what behaviors make God recognizable in your leadership style and what behaviors do not make God recognizable. The Biblical EIQ feedback offers you the opportunity to identify and adjust behaviors in order to maximize your ability to make Christ Connections that will result in a positive impact personally and professionally.

KEN VOGES IS THE DEVELOPER OF THE ASSESSMENT SUMMARY YOU RECEIVE AFTER TAKING THE ASSESSMENTS: BIBLICAL DISC

The Biblical DISC Assessment, includes four different personality profiles. Throughout the book, you will notice different DISC profiles of certain people in the Scriptures which will give you insight into their character traits. What they needed most and how they communicated best. Jesus was masterful at His ability to adapt His behavior and His questions in order to touch the hearts of the people He encountered. He did this in such a powerful way that lives were changed instantly: the woman at the well, the feeding of 5,000 people, comforting Mary and Martha at Lazarus's grave site and the woman caught in adultery.

> Your number one mission here on earth is to learn how to make God recognizable by first loving Him with all of your heart, mind, soul and strength AND allowing yourself-to receive His transformational love for you through Christ, and then sharing that love with those around you.

The Biblical DISC profile assessment walks hand-in-hand with the Emotional Intelligence in Christ (EIC) profile assessment (Biblical EIC). The Biblical DISC summary helps you define and understand the needs of a person. The Biblical EIQ summary offers the specific strategies and actions you can take in order to effectively meet those needs.

Your number one mission here on earth is to learn how to make God recognizable by first loving Him with all of your heart, mind, soul and strength AND allowing yourself-to receive His transformational love for you through Christ, and then sharing that love with those around you.

When you understand what makes people tick, you can then meet them where they are just as Jesus did and then lead them out of fear into faith, just as Jesus did. The Biblical DISC gives you insight into the operating system of people, including yourself, and the EIC gives you a method to help champion that operating system in Christ. Jesus is our Master Teacher in terms of what this looks like in real time.

> "The DISC research evidence supports the conclusion
>
> that the most effective leaders
>
> are those who know themselves,
>
> recognize the demands of the situation
>
> and adjust or change their behavior
>
> so as to have the best chance to meet the
>
> needs of any given opportunity."
>
> *- Ken Voges, Creator of Biblical DISC™*

This book focuses on your emotional intelligence in Christ. Below is the drive-by version of what each of the 4 DISC traits look like, so that you will have some knowledge and context around each profile when we reference them throughout the book.

Defining Your DISC Styles[4]

D—Dominance Styles: Work toward achieving goals and results; they function best in an active and challenging environment. If they wore a t-shirt it would say: "Getter Done." D's are motivated by power and respond to the question: What action needs to be taken to get this done? They will lean into conflict rather than run from it. If there is a crowded movie theater and there are two seats smack in the middle, they have no problem saying: excuse me, pardon me all the way to their ideal seats.

I—Influencing Styles: Work toward relating to people through verbal persuasion; they function best in a friendly and favorable environment. I's are people, people. They are motivated by relationships. Their

---

[4] The following information is taken from the Biblical DISC(R), developed by Ken Voges and is a registered trademark of Lead Like Jesus and In His Grace, INC.

t-shirt would say: people before things. Naturally optimistic they are incredible storytellers, oftentimes adding information that captivates those who listen. When faced with conflict they would rather move away from it rather than head right into it. Amongst friends and colleagues, they might be nominated the social chairman.

S—Steadiness Styles: Work toward supporting and cooperating with others; they function best in a supportive and harmonious environment. They are motivated by the team. If a new initiative comes down the pipe at work their thought is: how is this going to impact the team? Their t-shirt would say: consider the needs of others better than your own. Like an "I" profile they too will rather run from conflict. If they got a bad review at work, they may have to take a personal day off to regroup whereas a "D" would say: that's their opinion doesn't mean it's right.

C—Conscientious Styles: Work toward doing things right and focus on details; they function best in a structured and orderly environment. You want the plane you are flying in to be built by a "C." They are motivated by the details and data. You never have to ask a "C" if they have overlooked something, they hold themselves at such a high level of perfectionism that they have already asked themselves that question many times in the process. Their t-shirt would say: Show me the data.

To sum up the differences between the four DISC styles let's use the plane metaphor:

D: the pilot, no fear will head straight into the storm

I: head of marketing and public relations

S: customer service on the plane and off

C: engineers who build the plane

Let's take a snapshot view of Jesus's ability to adapt to all four DISC Styles:

D: Jesus walks into the Temple, turns over tables, and calls people out: John 2:13–17.

I: Jesus turns water into wine at a huge social event, a wedding banquet, the first miracle: John 2:1–11

S: Jesus pulls together His A-team, trains and equips the team to go out and make God recognizable: Luke 10:1–12

C: Jesus continually spoke of the details that would take place throughout the gospels around His death and resurrection. He had a strategic plan that was detailed: Luke 13:33, Matthew 16:21, Mark 8:31.

Continually, throughout Jesus's mission on earth He did three things:

1. Jesus **responded** to the people around Him by meeting them where they were.
2. Jesus **related** to people with empathy yet did not allow them to stay in victimization. He used powerful coaching questions to get people unstuck: What do you want me to do for you? He asked the blind man, clearly Jesus saw that He was blind yet did not want to rob the man of the opportunity to take ownership of his situation and declare what he wanted. Jesus then validated the man by saying: *"Your faith has healed you."* Mark 10:50–52
3. Jesus **reinforced** the Great Commission to go forth and make disciples (followers of Christ) to the ends of the world. Everyone is included. Matthew 28:16–20. *Everyone is invited to throw off their cloak and release their grip on the shiny objects of the world and follow Jesus: "Follow Me"* (Mark 1:17) and over 22 more times throughout the Gospels.

If you have not already done so, we invite you to gain a deeper understanding around what makes you tick by taking the Biblical DISC Assessment that is included as a part of this book. Go to https://bit.ly/3EomOBW.

In the first two chapters, we have given you a brief overview of the Biblical DISC four profiles and the four phases of Emotional Intelligence in Christ (Biblical EIQ). As you connect your Biblical EIQ assessment results to your Biblical DISC findings, you will begin to understand the behavior you need to practice, inviting the strength and guidance of the Holy Spirit, in order to be emotionally intelligent in Christ.

In the following chapters, you will learn how to apply your learnings and transfer them to EIC behavior that positively impacts your ability to relate to others as Christ relates to you. As you go through each chapter, start to switch your thinking from **EIQ traits** to **EIC behaviors**, to begin your transformation.

Chapters 3, 4, 5 and 6 take you into a deeper dive around each of the four behaviors of EIC, Biblical examples, focused case studies, tools for application followed by coaching questions giving you the opportunity to personally apply what you have learned.

In chapter 7, you will explore the connection between Biblical DISC and EIC. Use your Biblical DISC profile and EIQ assessment to gain insight into what people need to be emotionally intelligent in Christ. Mastering EIC takes applying the EIC Method to meet those needs in a Christ-led way.

In chapter 8 you will learn the Chavous, Cummins, Miller, and Voges EIC Method:

EIC = ENCOUNTER + IDENTIFIED BEHAVIOR + COURSE CORRECT

This model provides you with a simple formula for your personal application of the four behaviors contained in EIC.

Before you read each chapter, we invite you to pause for a few moments and invite the Holy Spirit into your reading experience.

> Holy Spirit, I give You permission to move me to linger over the content in this chapter that You desire to use to draw me closer to the love and guidance of Christ. I seek to follow His lead into being more emotionally intelligent in Him today than yesterday for the sake of salvation of souls.

CHAPTER 3

BEHAVIOR 1: PERSONAL IDENTITY IN CHRIST (SELF-AWARENESS)

"I have been crucified with Christ and I no longer live, but Christ lives in me. The life I now live in the body, I live by faith in the Son of God, who loved me and gave himself-for me" (Galatians 2:20).

GET READY READER, you are about to enter into the longest chapter of this book. As mentioned earlier, this first phase of Emotional Intelligence in Christ sets up your ability to successfully engage in the other three EIC phases described in chapters 4, 5 and 6. Lean in and invite the Holy Spirit to nudge you when you come across information that will guide you into the experience of encountering Christ. This first phase is the cornerstone of your success when it comes to Emotional Intelligence in Christ. Let's jump in.

The First *Behavioral* Step into Emotional Intelligence in Christ: Personal Identity.

You will notice in this chapter as well as in chapters 4, 5 and 6 that we have separated the content into the following areas:

- Define the Trait
- Biblical Examples
- Focused Case Study

DEFINE THE TRAIT

Personal Identity: (Self-Awareness in Christ) *"I have been crucified with Christ and I no longer live, but Christ lives in me. The life I now live in the body, I live by faith in the Son of God, who loved me and gave himself-for me"* (Galatians 2:20).

> **Whose I am** focuses on your identity intrinsically within yourself-as connected to God in relationship. **Who I am** externally focuses on your identity as reflected by the outside world, making it vulnerable to rising and falling depending upon how the world judges you.

Whose am I? How does my relationship with Christ shape my understanding of myself? Your personal identity, when grounded in Christ, leads with a humble acknowledgment that your identity, worth and value flow directly from knowing yourself-to be loved and adored by God who has a good plan that overrides any emotional life "pop-ups." It reflects on *Whose I am* versus *who I am*.

Whose I am focuses on your identity intrinsically within yourself-as connected to God in relationship. "As a follower of Jesus, understanding who I am begins with understanding whose I am. Who I am is not externally focused, but internally received as a child of God and follower of Jesus. It seems strange to say Whose I am versus Who I am. Because of Jesus, my identity is forever changed to the righteousness of God. Similar to the example of the caterpillar which contains the DNA of the butterfly: we mature into who we already are, by God's grace and guidance. Scripture is full of descriptors of our identity: Dearly loved (Colossians 3:12), *forgiven* (Romans 4:7), *chosen* (John 15:9), *a royal priesthood* (1 Peter 2:9), *the apple of God's eye* (Psalm 17:8), *the light of the world (Matthew 5:14), heir with Jesus* (Romans 8:17), *friends* (John 15:14) *and many more. Knowing who I am changes everything. Just think: Right now, in this minute, you are chosen by God, loved with an everlasting love, forgiven, redeemed, and filled with His Spirit from the top of your head to your toes. Now that's who you are and there is no external situation that changes the fact of your identity. Our greatest challenge is not accepting and abiding in who we are. As leaders, we must help people understand the significance of the power within us because of who we are in Him."* —Phyllis Hendry, co-author of *Lead Like Jesus Revisited*

When your identity is linked to knowing that you belong to the Lover of your soul, Self-Awareness becomes free and flexible, knowing that all things do work together for an ultimate good to those who love God and whose identity is grounded in God. Love and confidence become your way along with the ability to discern what is of God and what is not. Paul beautifully summed up Self-Awareness, as alive in Christ in Galatians 2:20 when he said: "I have been put to death with Christ on the cross, so it's no longer I who live, but Christ who lives within me. This life I live, I live by faith alone in the Son of God who loved me and gave His life up for me."

Jesus is the perfect One for us to follow when it comes to establishing our personal identity in God for victory over the world and its desires. Jesus died to all that the world offered in order to save our souls. When He walked this earth, He was on a mission to restore lost identities that had been hijacked by the things that Satan attempted to tempt Him with in the desert (Luke 4:1–13): passion, possessions, popularity, and power. Jesus is still on a mission to restore lost identities. Perhaps it's yours that He is after?

As you explore this first and foundational phase of Emotional Intelligence in Christ: your personal identity, invite the wisdom of the Holy Spirit into your reflections on Jesus's life and ministry when He walked the earth.

What does Jesus want you to remember about who you are and why you are here? He was masterful at recovering identities lost to the world and restoring them to their rightful owner—their Creator. Jesus

Christ will change your life from the inside out and your encounter with His emotional intelligence will spill over into the lives of those He entrusted to your care. He is the ultimate emotionally intelligent One for all to follow. Are you ready for the journey back to yourself-as connected to Christ?

The focus of this chapter is on the first essential component of emotional intelligence: personal identity. We cannot give out effectively what we have not given attention to within ourselves. Therefore, our ability to effectively manage our relationships with those around us is directly proportional to our ability to manage our perceptions and emotions that flow from our personal identity.

What does God say? Below are three questions to ask yourself-along with Scriptures that offer you insight into the answers.

Whose am I? Scripture:

- John 1:12: To those who believe in His name are given the right to become the children of God.
- Romans 8:15–16: I have received a Spirit of sonship . . . Abba Father, this spirit testifies that I am a child of the living God.
- 1 Peter 2:9: I am part of a royal priesthood, a Holy Nation, a people belonging to God.

Why am I here? Scripture:

- 2 Corinthians 5:20–21: To make God recognizable in this world. I am Christ's ambassador as if God were making His appeal through me. For my sake, He made Him to be sin who did not sin that I might become the righteousness (the excellence) of God.
- 1 Peter 2:9: As a part of God's child and a Holy Nation, I am here to declare the praises of Him who called me out of darkness into light.

- Galatians 2:20: I have been put to death with Christ on the cross, so it's no longer I who live but Christ who lives within me this life I live by faith alone in Him who died for me. I am here to live by faith and allow Jesus to live within and through me.

What will it matter?

It will matter in all of eternity for the sake of the salvation of souls, including your own; your choice to live in, with and through Christ will always end in life.

As you reflect upon who you are in Christ and why you are here on earth, take your curiosity a little further and explore the amount of time you spend worrying about what other people think.

> Jesus modeled for you true inner freedom, as He was not confined by status or the opinions of other people. When He walked on earth, He had one source of authority in His life: His Father, our Father.

What emotions hold you back from your identity in Christ?

....
....
....
....

What knocks your lights out during the day? Those triggers that evoke a sense of self-doubt? The opinions of other people? Not completing your to-do list? Unresolved conflict?

....
....
....
....

Do you focus more on identifying yourself-with your struggle instead of declaring your victory over it in Christ? How do you know? What behaviors show up when you are identifying with the struggle (reflect on your Biblical DISC summary)?

What behaviors do you want to express more of that give witness to your identity in Christ? Ask the Holy Spirit for the strength to remain in Christ, take every thought captive, and for the ability to surrender your identity to Christ.

Jesus gives you a beautiful image in John 15 when He describes the vine and the branch, truly this is the perfect analogy for an emotionally intelligent personal identity: Remain, remain, remain in Christ so much so that your perception of YOU flows directly from Christ's perception of you and positively impacts the world around you.

> Dear Lord, too often we experience identity theft that results in behavior and emotions that do not make You recognizable in this world. Forgive us for following the shiny objects that end up imprisoning us in the vicious cycle of asserting our will over Your will, our thoughts over the Holy Scriptures and our emotions over the fruit of the Spirit: love, joy, peace, patience, kindness, goodness, and self-control. Break us free, Lord, from the sin that so easily entangles us and the yoke of slavery that restricts us in our small cocoon of fear, doubt, and worry. We want to fly with You to the places You have prepared for us to go. Dear Lord, override our EGO, just as You did for Peter, Paul, Zacchaeus and Thomas and set us free from the prison of self: I, me, my.

Behavior 1: Personal Identity in Christ (Self-Awareness)

In this chapter you will explore a 3-Step Prison Break to help you recover your personal identity in Christ, the first phase of emotional intelligence in Christ, the cornerstone of the other three phases of EIC. You will explore an experience and process of breaking out of behavior that compromises the person God is calling you to be. Jesus was the ultimate ERR Doctor, as you will see as we reflect on the lives of five people who were imprisoned by their lifestyle and/or doubt: Peter, Mary, Zacchaeus, Thomas and Paul and the FREEDOM they gained as a result of an Encounter (E) with Jesus which led to Repentance (R) and a Resurrection (R) of purpose and personal identity, they experienced a breakout of the cocoon of worldly restrictions and embraced the One who died to give them the ability to soar by knowing who they are in Christ.

Jesus modeled for you true inner freedom, as He was not confined by status or the opinions of other people. When He walked on earth, He had one source of authority in His life: His Father, our Father.

As a result of this singular flow of personal identity, Jesus models for us the way into freedom which comes from a personal, intimate relationship with our Father, God. Jesus spoke of this intimate union in John 14:10: "Don't you believe that I am in the Father, and that the Father is in me? The words I say to you I do not speak on my own authority. Rather, it is the Father, living in me, who is doing his work." Jesus's personal identity flowed directly from the Father in and through Him.

If you choose to stand firm as you ground your identity in Christ, to follow Jesus's lead on this first and vital phase of emotional intelligence in Christ, you too will experience the freedom that Jesus's death and resurrection made possible for you.

As Paul declared in Galatians 5:1: *"It is for freedom that Christ has set us free. Stand firm, then, and do not let yourselves be burdened again by a yoke of slavery."* What is the yoke of slavery? It's anything that you attach your sense of identity to outside of a personal relationship with your Father, through His Son Jesus.

Jesus adores you. He will respond to the smallest glance on your part and seed of desire to know Him. A simple prayer: *"Lord I want to know You, I want to know me through Your love, come into my heart and transform me into Your likeness,"* is enough of an invitation for Jesus to begin His work of resurrecting your identity in and through His presence within you. Jesus Christ will change your life from the inside out. *"As the Father has loved me, so have I loved you. Now remain in my love"* (John 15:9).

Once you have given Jesus the authority over your identity in life, you reconnect to the presence of God's love and purpose for you. Let's take a look at a miraculous wonder found in nature to help us better understand how intimate this connection between you and your God-infused purpose is in life.

The caterpillar has the DNA of a butterfly, yet the predators of the world too often snatch it up before it transforms and embraces its ability to fly. The world screams for our identity and God consistently whispers His love into our hearts to win it back.

You have the DNA of God as you are created in the image and likeness of God. You have the ability to soar through the storms of life, all things are possible for you when it comes to mastering your mind for transformation and revival in, through and with Jesus. Jesus meets you and escorts you back into a personal identity revival. He is the cornerstone and master teacher for all aspects of your emotional intelligence.

Too often you play small, fueling lack and scarcity thinking. Similar to Thomas's doubt that blocked his ability to trust and believe, you are often blinded by the trickery of smoke and mirrors that Satan uses to distract you from the way out of your slavery to fear, self-doubt, and worry.

Behavior 1: Personal Identity in Christ (Self-Awareness)

Similar to Peter's outbursts of anger and frustration, too often you can get spun into the cocoon of EGO: Edging God Out of your perspectives, conclusions, and plans, forgetting that the One who calls you is faithful, He will provide a way out as He did for Peter when He filled his empty net with fish. Jesus moved beyond Peter's frustration to the ultimate goal: to set him free from the restriction of his desires and unmet needs so that he could fly beyond himself-by grounding his identity in Christ. Jesus is all about identity recovery. Seeking out the lost, people who have had their identity hijacked by the world and its shiny objects. Perhaps this is you?

Anger often rears its ugly head in the behavior of stonewalling, defensive behavior, and unkind words (towards others and yourself). Frustration is fueled by the need to be right, liked and understood and chains you in the prison of the shadow side of your positionality and false beliefs. Have you had enough?

What predators are threatening your personal identity? Your ability to identify with Christ's strength and God's will for you in life? In Luke 4, the devil tempted Jesus unsuccessfully with the following shiny objects that are destined to perish with use, which by the way in our materialistic culture, identity theft runs rampant:

- Power
- Popularity
- Passion
- Position

Invite the strength of Jesus to help overcome the devil's enticing invitations which can imprison your hijacked identity in the world. Paul gives a warning worth leaning into in Colossians 2:20–22: *"If you have died with Christ to the spiritual forces of the world, why, as though you still belonged to the world, do you submit to its regulations: "Do not handle! Do not taste! Do not touch!"? These will all perish with use."*

Biblical Examples

Imagine a triangle and at the top of the triangle you have your Will, the left corner of the triangle represents your Mind, and the right corner of the triangle represents your Emotions. Your Will directly influences your Mind (your thoughts, perceptions, conclusions, assumptions, beliefs) which directly impacts your emotions (what you feel: sad, happy, angry, frustrated, all of which create your attitude, a fixed state of mind).

An emotion is your body's response to your thought life. Your attitude is your closest friend or worst enemy and you get to choose it. How? By surrendering it up to God for His will to be done in and through your life, exalting God only OR not. God has given us free will and you can choose to sit yourself-on the throne of your Will as was the case in the Garden of Eden: deception, confusion, accusation, and self-doubt all play in the space of a Will directed by self: Your Will => Mind => Emotions => Attitude.

You can also choose another way. The way of Jesus, the way of love, knowing oneself-and seeing oneself-through the eyes of the Lover of your soul. Remember, the world screams for your identity, God whispers and invites you to remember *Whose you are, why you are here* and *why your presence on earth matters.*

Five prominent players from the New Testament were all trapped in the cocoon of worldly strongholds, and as a result had their identity hijacked: hunger for power, popularity, passion, and position: Peter, Zacchaeus, Mary Magdalene, Thomas and Paul. They forgot they had wings to fly. Jesus, being the prison-releasing, chain- breaking, cocoon-freeing Savior, meets them in their restricted state of being, and sets them free. Jesus recovered their personal identity. Once they met the humble love and mercy of Christ, they relinquished control over their own Will and received the key that set them free: Surrendering their Will over to God's Will.

Let's take a closer look at each one of these five lives whose personal identity was recovered in Christ. As you explore each journey, notice who you identify with the most? The least? Observe where you recognize yourself-in each of the following lives, whose personal identity was transformed by an encounter with Christ infusing emotional intelligence into their thoughts, emotions, words, and actions:

Peter

In Luke 5:1–11, Peter encounters Jesus face-to-face. Peter is a self-motivated entrepreneur who is dedicated to revenue-producing behavior; however, when his labor does not produce the desired outcome, he is left wallowing in the cocoon of self-pity, victimization, and frustration. Can you relate? When was a time you cast your net out into the world only to pull in an empty net? Jesus ignored Peter's victimization and pity party and invited him to jump back in his boat.

The difference this time, as Peter cast his net, is monumental: rather than by his own will and sheer determination to produce a desired outcome, Peter was now accompanied by the King of Kings and Lord of Lords. Jesus was in the "BOAT" and initiated the catch and the outcome was more than Peter could have imagined.

Reflect upon a time in your life when you came out of a situation after giving it YOUR all, exhausted and defeated and you encountered Jesus. What was the outcome as a result of your encounter with Jesus? How did you repent from self-focus (I-centered Will)? What did you resurrect? For example, Peter resurrected an emotionally intelligent faith-filled attitude of trust as he laid his will down and surrendered to Jesus as he proclaimed: *get away from me LORD for I am a sinful man.* A monumental first step when it came to resurrecting his personal identity in Christ. A humble recognition of self-in the presence of the King of Kings and Lord of Lords.

Peter's encounter with Jesus resulted in repentance from self-focused efforts that set up camp on top of E.G.O: *I want this outcome for my own advancement and I didn't get what I wanted, so I am imprisoned in the cocoon of frustration.* His sense of self-was quickly absorbed into the presence of Christ, the way, the truth and the life (John 14:6) and his truest, purest identity took center stage: *"I have been crucified with Christ and I no longer live, but Christ lives in me. The life I now live in the body, I live by faith in the Son of God, who loved me and gave himself-for me"* (Galatians 2:20).

Zacchaeus

In Luke 19:1–9: Zacchaeus encounters Jesus. Zacchaeus had gumption, a shrewd or spirited initiative and resourcefulness. He wanted to see Jesus and knew he was too short in the midst of the crowds to make that happen, so he climbed a tree. As a result, Jesus recognized his gumption that overcame a physical limitation and Jesus chose to step into his life. He ate at his table, with his friends and won his heart over to repentance and a resurrected life. Zacchaeus was stuck in the cocoon of worldly power and possessions that damaged his moral compass. The love and acceptance from Jesus (the encounter), in the midst of his sinful, small, and restricted negative behaviors resulted in a prison break and resurrected personal identity.

Take a moment to reflect on the following excerpt taken from *Hearing His Whisper... With Every Storm Jesus Comes Too* (Edge God In, by Lauren E Miller): Journal Entry: May 20, 2001. This is a boots on the ground example of Jesus showcasing emotional intelligence in action. Jesus recognizes a need and leads with emotional intelligence, grounded in love, to meet that need:

Me: I used to think that I knew the perfect way to get to you, Lord. I found myself-judging others if they went another way. I am starting to see that every human being has something to teach me . . . each soul reveals new insight into you and me. Show me how to touch every soul with love.

Jesus: You cannot force yourself-into the human heart. The hearts of my children are won over through unconditional love that is patiently poured out over time into their souls. To do this, you must first enter into their experiences . . . what moves their heart, no matter how worldly it may seem to eyes that have been enlightened to heavenly things. In order to win the confidence of man's heart, you must first step into his world. Then you earn the right to speak the truth in love and he will listen because you have loved him where he is without judgment. Your love for them will increase within their heart the desire to do what is right in God's eyes.

Because God is love, he moves souls into his heart through love alone. Take Zacchaeus for example, one soul living in sin . . . I went to his house, ate his food at his table with his friends. I entered into his life experience with great love and acceptance. My love entering into his life exposed the dark deeds of his soul thereby leading him to repentance and reconciliation and a resurrected life purpose.

You must do the same to win hearts for me. It is pride and ego that keep you from stepping into the lives of those who are entranced by the things of the world . . . Do I not enter into your worldly experiences? Is it not my great love and mercy in spite of your acts of disobedience that continue to draw your heart into mine? Do the same for one another.

Love first, sometimes use words, then lead. Follow my example . . . meet everyone on the road just as the Father ran to meet the prodigal son. Go and meet others, love them, take time to listen, and experience their joys and sorrows . . . all with great love and mercy and in time you will earn the right to speak the truth in love. Through love and mercy their eyes will be opened to the condition of their soul . . . just as yours is.

Do not forget the depths from which you were saved so that pride will not draw you away from my love. It is the desire that I see . . . the desire, always over the actions . . . offer the same grace to the souls around you . . . see others for what they desire to be apart from all the pain that causes them to act out . . . just as I continue to see you.

Zacchaeus's encounter with Jesus's mercy, acceptance, and love for him, arrived right smack in the middle of deceitful living, resulting in his recovered identity and restoration. Zacchaeus's life was positively impacted along with the lives of those who surrounded him.

It's amazing the ripple effect that occurs when one's identity is restored in Christ.

Mary Magdalene

In John 20:11–18, Mary Magdalene, most likely called Magdalene because she was from the town of Magdala, a fishing town on the coast of Galilee, encounters her Savior. Luke 8:2–3 speaks of seven demons that Jesus cast out of Mary which led to her repentance and resurrected identity. She ended up following Jesus and traveling with Him and the 12 disciples from town to town. Jesus was after Mary, to recover her identity into His. He's after you, too.

In John 20:11–18, Mary is one of the first to witness the resurrection of Christ. She encounters the resurrected Jesus at the tomb and her faith is flipped from despair and sadness around death to joy and excitement around the resurrection. Because of her original encounter with Christ, through repentance of her former ways of living, Mary experienced a resurrected purpose and mission in life, her personal identity was restored.

Mary's identity went from being hijacked to being anchored in the Lover of her soul. Mary followed Jesus to the grave. In spite of her personal experience of deliverance, Mary experienced doubt even in the presence of the Lord, as she pleaded with the Risen Lord thinking He was the gardener to show her where Jesus was taken.

Interestingly, Mary's eyes were opened when Jesus called her name (personal identity). Once again, Jesus restored a lost identity to its rightful owner. Jesus saw Mary's need for deliverance and using emotional intelligence grounded in love, He met that need.

Doubting Thomas

In John 20:24–31, we meet Thomas, commonly known as "doubting Thomas." In spite of the evidence and eyewitness accounts of the resurrected Lord, Thomas defends his positionality, blocking his ability to believe. The result: no joy. His cocoon of doubt restricts his ability to grow wings and fly into faith.

> Know this, Satan is consistently prowling around trying to hijack your identity and the authority of God in your life.

Jesus crashed that party and offered the evidence Thomas needed to believe to override the statement of unbelief Thomas made in John 20:24: *"Unless I put my hand in his side and my fingers in the holes of his hands I will not believe."*

What ultimatums have you declared over your life?

"Unless I _____, I will not _____." For example: Unless I achieve this specific status, I will not feel successful . . . or enough. Unless I get married, I will not feel complete.

Thomas's encounter is worth your reflection as it touches upon a shared human experience: self-doubt, a big fat identity theft serpent. Satan has been at this since the garden: *"Did God really say that?"* (Genesis 3:1) and again in Luke 4:3, he actually tries to take a hit at Jesus's identity: *"If you are the Son of God."*

Know this, Satan is consistently prowling around trying to hijack your identity and the authority of God in your life.

He is the ultimate spin doctor as he comes up with one liners that twist your mind and compromise your emotions which all flow from a leak in your willpower to take every thought captive and make it obedient to Christ. (2 Corinthians 10:5)

Jesus's invitation to all of us began with His command to Thomas in John 20:27: *"Stop doubting and BELIEVE."* Give more authority to the strength of God's Holy Spirit within you than to your circumstance.

After Thomas encounters Jesus, in John 20:28, he falls to his knees in repentance: *"My Lord and my God."* Jesus did not have to spend time edifying Thomas in the midst of his doubt and yet He did it anyway as He once again, identified a need and used emotional intelligence grounded in love to meet that need. Jesus gave Thomas the validating evidence he needed to believe.

Jesus entered into Thomas's lack of faith and trust and pulled Thomas in, through, and out of his doubt. The result: Resurrected conviction and faith along with an anchored personal identity in Christ.

Thomas represents our shared doubt and lack of faith. Perhaps we can learn from his repentance and join the blessed group that Jesus referenced in John 20:29: *"Blessed are those who believe and do not need to see."*

What are you resisting in your life that is flowing from your own self-doubt:

- Belief that you are loved and adored by God?
- Worthy of God's forgiveness?
- Part of a bigger plan, orchestrated by the Lover of your soul?
- Perhaps you have not yet encountered the humble, persistent love of Jesus?

Invite Him into your heart and life today. Trust that God is good and has your best interests in mind. Self-doubt will hijack your ability to remember that your true personal identity lies within the presence of Christ within you. Jesus loves you enough not to leave you doubting your worth and value, as He did for Thomas, He does for you, modeling faith in action. Hope is a person, the person of Jesus Christ at the center of your sense of self, your personal identity.

Paul

Last but not least there is Paul, full of passion and conviction. Acts chapter 9 reveals the story of Paul's personal identity restored in Christ. Paul is the perfect example of a man who was imprisoned by his positionality, the drug of approval and identity theft. His cocoon of positionality was so tightly wound around his will that his moral compass was rocked. Killing Christians and destroying homes and families were just a few of the ramifications of his passion without Christ at the center of it. His identity was hijacked by his position of influencing power on the world. Is yours?

Paul's encounter with Christ offers us a crisp, clear witness of the transformation that can happen when the sinner meets the Savior, resulting in a 3-step prison break: An Encounter with Christ which leads to Repentance and a Resurrected purpose and passion for God's will that is grounded in a personal identity fueled by a personal relationship with Jesus Christ of Nazareth.

The prison metaphorically represents our enslavement to the world and its ways: popularity, passion, position, possessions. Do not touch, do not taste; these are all destined to perish with use (Colossians 2:21). Paul reminds the Galatians in chapter 5:1 that *"it is for freedom that Christ has set you free, stand firm then and do not allow yourself-[indicating a choice point that you have] to be burdened by the yoke of slavery."*

My coaching question to you, dear reader, is this: what have you *"allowed"* to hijack your

"I have been crucified with Christ and I no longer live, but Christ lives in me. The life I now live in the body, I live by faith in the Son of God, who loved me and gave himself-for me" (Galatians 2:20).

identity? The drug of approval? The disease to please? The need to be right? Liked? Understood? Lean into the Lover of your soul and *allow* Him to replace any misplaced desire with an undivided heart that seeks His kingship and authority within your heart, mind, will and emotions.

Filled with zeal, Saul (his "BC" name, Before Christ) was on the way to defend his positionality, as he was once again in route to kill more Christians and SHAZAM, Jesus jumped right between Saul's will and God's Will for Saul and knocked him to the ground. Perhaps it was the force of sin meeting the Savior . . . or the power of grafting a severed "shoot" (Paul) back into the Vine (Jesus). Either way, the force from Saul's face-to-face encounter with Christ was enough to rock Saul's entire trajectory of who he was, why he was here and why it mattered . . . in an instant Saul's personal identity went from being hijacked to recovered. He walked away with a new name in Christ: Paul.

Instantly, Jesus began to retrieve Paul's lost identity and restore it back to its original positionality as declared by Peter in 1 Peter 2:9: *"You are a royal priesthood, a holy nation, a people belonging to God for the purpose of declaring His praises to the ends of the world."* He did it for Paul and He will do it for you.

Paul thrust his will into his positionality and lost his identity in the world. Jesus was determined to get it back, He saw the need and used emotional intelligence, grounded in love, to meet that need. God is the hound from heaven and as the popular worship song by Cory Asbury declares about Jesus relentless pursuit of your soul: "No mountain you won't climb up, shadow you won't light up, coming after me . . . no wall you won't rip down, lie you won't tear down . . . coming after me."

This encounter, with the love of Christ, led Paul to declare the foundational verse for this first phase of "Emotional Intelligence in Christ":

"I have been crucified with Christ and I no longer live, but Christ lives in me. The life I now live in the body, I live by faith in the Son of God, who loved me and gave himself-for me" (Galatians 2:20).

You will have the opportunity to explore Paul's DISC pattern and how Jesus used it to step in with emotional intelligence to transform Paul's life.

FOCUSED CASE STUDY

As we have reflected on so far, Personal Identity is the 1st behavior of Emotional Intelligence in Christ. Let's shift our focus to one particular case study that powerfully showcases the Emotional Intelligence of Christ in action to recover the *personal identity* of a woman who lost herself-to the ways of the world. Jesus intentionally detoured to Samaria in order to make this encounter happen.

> A character trait of highly emotional intelligent people is the ability to see and respond to the desired state of being of others, often overlooking the bad behavior that is a result of past pain and false beliefs about oneself, Jesus was masterful at this.

Just as Jesus was after the identity restoration of the woman at the well, He desires to do the same for you. He adores you and is constantly looking for creative ways to win you back into communion with God, to share the gift of emotional intelligence through the presence of the Holy Spirit within you. Why? Because Jesus knows that love saves, judgment repels. He sees you for who you desire to be rather than how your behavior shows up.

A character trait of highly emotional intelligent people is the ability to see and respond to the desired state of being of others, often overlooking the bad behavior that is a result of past pain and false beliefs about oneself, Jesus was masterful at this.

One of His most powerful demonstrations of this was on the cross when Jesus said, *"Father forgive them, they know now what they do"* (Luke 23:34).

Thoughtfully read through the Scripture below and ask the Holy Spirit to speak into your identity, revealing to you what you have lost along the way that Jesus desires to restore today.

The Woman at the Well John 4:1-29

"Now Jesus learned that the Pharisees had heard that he was gaining and baptizing more disciples than John—although in fact it was not Jesus who baptized, but his disciples. So he left Judea and went back once more to Galilee.

Now he had to go through Samaria. So he came to a town in Samaria called Sychar, near the plot of ground Jacob had given to his son Joseph. Jacob's well was there, and Jesus, tired as he was from the journey, sat down by the well. It was about noon.

When a Samaritan woman came to draw water, Jesus said to her, "Will you give me a drink?" (His disciples had gone into the town to buy food.)

The Samaritan woman said to him, "You are a Jew and I am a Samaritan woman. How can you ask me for a drink?" (For Jews do not associate with Samaritans.)

Jesus answered her, "If you knew the gift of God and who it is that asks you for a drink, you would have asked him and he would have given you living water."

"Sir," the woman said, "you have nothing to draw with and the well is deep. Where can you get this living water? Are you greater than our father Jacob, who gave us the well and drank from it himself, as did also his sons and his livestock?"

Jesus answered, "Everyone who drinks this water will be thirsty again, but whoever drinks the water I give them will never thirst. Indeed, the water I give them will become in them a spring of water welling up to eternal life."

The woman said to him, "Sir, give me this water so that I won't get thirsty and have to keep coming here to draw water."

He told her, "Go, call your husband and come back."

"I have no husband," she replied.

Jesus said to her, "You are right when you say you have no husband. The fact is, you have had five husbands, and the man you now have is not your husband. What you have just said is quite true."

"Sir," the woman said, "I can see that you are a prophet. Our ancestors worshiped on this mountain, but you Jews claim that the place where we must worship is in Jerusalem."

"Woman," Jesus replied, "believe me, a time is coming when you will worship the Father neither on this mountain nor in Jerusalem. You Samaritans worship what you do not know; we worship what we do know, for salvation is from the Jews. Yet a time is coming and has now come when the true worshipers will worship the Father in the Spirit and in truth, for they are the kind of worshipers the Father seeks. God is spirit, and his worshipers must worship in the Spirit and in truth."

The woman said, "I know that Messiah" (called Christ) "is coming. When he comes, he will explain everything to us."

Then Jesus declared, "I, the one speaking to you—I am he."

Just then his disciples returned and were surprised to find him talking with a woman. But no one asked, "What do you want?" or "Why are you talking with her?" Then, leaving her water jar, the woman went back to the town and said to the people, *"Come, see a man who told me everything I ever did. Could this be the Messiah?" They came out of the town and made their way toward him."*

Let's take a look at some initial observations of the Woman at the Well in light of what we learned about the DISC profile in chapter two[5]

- She is free spirited while expressing strong, independent tendencies (perhaps an "I" on the DISC profile with some "D" tendencies).
- Married 5 times
- Living with a man who is not her husband
- Easily engaged in conversation with a stranger (typical of an "I" DISC profile as I's are motivated by relationships).
- Appears to have a quick and curious mind.

Jesus sees right to the heart of the woman and who she desires to be. Somewhere along the way, she forgot how much God loves and adores her just as she is. Jesus knows that it's an encounter with love that will transform her identity back to her creator. He also knows that judgment would hold her captive to a false identity, created by the assumptions and conclusions she has made about herself-based on the behavior of others.

> The first behavior of Emotional Intelligence in Christ is to guide people back to themselves as connected to God, restore people's identity in God.

Clearly, to Jesus, she represented a valuable human being. How do we know that she is valuable to Jesus? Jesus used the word *woman*, *GUNE*, four times to three ladies that Jesus valued. The word suggests a tone of respect or endearment or both. The first time Jesus used it was with his mother at the wedding in Cana: 'Dear *woman*, why do you involve me?" (John 2:4). The second was at the cross: 'Dear *woman*, here is your son, and to the disciple, 'Here is your mother' (John 19:26–27). The third time was the woman

---

5 Ken Voges, copyright, In His Grace, Inc., Houston Texas 1997):

at the well as Jesus declared: 'Believe me, *woman*, a time is coming when you will worship the Father neither on this mountain nor in Jerusalem' (John 4:21). The fourth time was the woman on trial for adultery, which we read about in chapter one from John 8:10–11: '*Woman*, where are they? Has no one condemned you?' "No one sir,' she said. 'Then neither do I condemn you.' Jesus declared, 'Go now and leave your life of sin.'

Jesus was and always is at work to seek and save the lost. He is the hound from heaven to recover God's children, those whose personal identity has been hijacked by the world around them. Those who have given power away to circumstances, people, and situations to define their sense of worth, value, and capability.

The woman at the well came face to face with the great "I AM." It is important to note here that Jesus declares for the first time in John 4:25–26 that He is the Messiah. Who does He declare it to? The woman who lost her identity in the struggle and Jesus came to restore it to its rightful creator. She declared to Jesus in their conversation that she knew that the Messiah was coming and that when He came, He would explain everything to her to which Jesus responded: *It's ME, I am the One you have been waiting for, the One who is your Savior, to save you and restore your identity.*

The first behavior of Emotional Intelligence in Christ is to guide people back to themselves as connected to God, restore people's identity in God.

We love other people well BECAUSE we have personally encountered the love of God: *"We love because God first loved us"* (1 John 4:19). Jesus did this masterfully as He met the woman where she was, declared where she had been without judgment knowing that the first step in recovering one's identity is ruthless honesty around the truth:

> The Lord does not look at the things that people look at. People look at the outer appearance, but the Lord looks at the heart (1 Samuel 16:7).

Yes, I have had five husbands and the man I'm currently living with is not my husband, yet you love and accept me anyway.

Jesus brought the very thing that she was running from in life smack into the middle of their sacred conversation knowing that it was an essential element needed for her healing and restoration: I SEE YOU AND YOU MATTER TO ME. This clarity of focus around her truth, in the presence of unconditional love unlocked her ability to encounter redemption and restoration: *You love me for who I desire to be and that is enough to set me free from all that I have given power over to . . . to define my worth, value and capability. Today, I take it back because I have encountered my Savior.* She is so moved by this encounter that she runs off and becomes an evangelist for Christ: *"Come and see the One who told me everything I ever did . . . could this be the Messiah?"* (John 4:29). What is so interesting about this response is that the people of the town listened to her.

The fact that she came to the well in the heat of the day rather than with the other women in the early morning hours reveals that she experienced rejection. There was something about her that had been transformed enough to override the judgment of her accusers. The people listened to a sinner who had just encountered her Savior.

Jesus also maintains emotional intelligence, grounded in love, when His disciples returned and were surprised that He was talking with a woman, not to mention a Samaritan woman. Samaritans from a Jewish perspective at that time were considered half-breeds. They worshiped Yaweh alongside other gods. From the disciple's perspective they were thinking: *What the heck Jesus, not only is she a woman but unclean from our perspective . . . What are you doing?* Jesus knew their thoughts and chose to ignore them. Whatever you starve of your attention will eventually die. There are other moments throughout the gospels when Jesus called His disciples out for their thoughts, this time, it was not a lesson for the disciples, it was all about recovering what was lost: the woman at the well.

Jesus was not confined by status or the opinions of other people. He and the Father were and always are on mission for the salvation of souls.

The Lord does not look at the things that people look at. People look at the outer appearance, but the Lord looks at the heart (1 Samuel 16:7).

This verse is another key truth when it comes to embracing emotional intelligence in Christ: when our identity is grounded in Christ, we get to see things as God sees them, including our sense of worth, value and capability.

Until we encounter Christ in the space of unconditional love that moves our hearts into the truth of who we are, we will stay stuck in our inability to move onto the second behavior in Emotional Intelligence in Christ: Self-control. As we encounter Christ in humble truth and honesty as the woman at the well did, we too resurrect confidence and love within our identity which gives us power and authority over our mind, will and emotions.

> This is a key factor when it comes to being self-aware in Christ, to think of ourselves as Jesus thinks of us (identity in Christ).

Take a moment and Reflect on the following questions:

Where do you recognize yourself-within this case study? Do you identify with the woman at the well? Perhaps you can relate to the people in the town who believed her enough that they made their way towards Jesus? Or maybe it's the disciples who had unresolved judgments within their hearts? Either way, Jesus is after you. He desires to reclaim your identity in Him.

As you reclaim your identity in Christ you become aware of who you are, or rather "Whose" you are which resurrects your Self-Awareness within to the One who created you. Your realistic self-appraisal, confidence and motivation come alive in the One who adores you. The Holy Spirit is the gift that Jesus left us to remind us of all that Jesus taught us. Reflect on the following Scriptures from 1 Corinthians 2:10–16 as you consider your own encounter with Emotional Intelligence in Christ and the ramifications of that encounter when it comes to spiritual wisdom:

> *"These are the things God has revealed to us by his Spirit. The Spirit searches all things, even the deep things of God. For who knows a person's thoughts except their own spirit within them? In the same way no one knows the thoughts of God except the Spirit of God. What we have received is not the spirit of the world, but the Spirit who is from God, so that we may understand what God has freely given us. This is what we speak, not in words taught us by human wisdom but in words taught by the Spirit, explaining spiritual realities with Spirit-taught words. The person without the Spirit does not accept the things that come from the Spirit of God but considers them foolishness and cannot understand them because they are discerned only through the Spirit. The person with the Spirit makes judgments about all things, but such a person is not subject to merely human judgments, for, "Who has known the mind of the Lord so as to instruct him?"* **But we have the mind of Christ.**"

The last verse is a game changer: *But we have the mind of Christ.* What? Yes it's true, when we believe in our heart and confess with our mouth that Jesus is Lord, we have the God-given ability through the same Spirit that raised Jesus Christ of Nazareth from the grave to think the way Jesus thinks.

This is a key factor when it comes to being self-aware in Christ, to think of ourselves as Jesus thinks of us (identity in Christ).

Can you imagine how powerful this knowledge is when it comes to mastering your ability to manage your emotions well for the sake of loving others better in life?

Making intentional Christ connections in the lives of the people He entrusted to your care? It's a game changer because it's an identity changer. The woman at the well thought that she *was* her struggle and Jesus restored who she really was: a child of God who encountered her Savior. This encounter spread like wildfire into the lives of those who were willing to hear and respond. In fact, later on in John 4:39–42 many of the Samaritans said that they came to believe that Jesus was the Messiah because she led them to Him:

> *"Many of the Samaritans from that town believed in him because of the woman's testimony, "He told me everything I ever did." So when the Samaritans came to him, they urged him to stay with them, and he stayed two days. And because of his words many more became believers. They said to the woman, "We no longer believe just because of what you said; now we have heard for ourselves, and we know that this man really is the Savior of the world."*

Jesus recognized a need and desire and He stepped in, fully confident of His identity as the Messiah to meet that need, the need for the Samaritan woman to remember her identity in Christ (Galatians 2:20). Confidence evokes confidence.

Do you know *who* you are, or rather *Whose* you are? Jesus showcased His confidence in Whose He was and is: The Son of God, the Messiah sent to take away the sins of the world and those who believe in Him even though they die, yet shall they live (John 3:16).

> In order to master Emotional Intelligence in Christ your first step occurs when you personally encounter Christ.

Jesus's identity was always grounded in God which allowed Him the emotional intelligence of Self-Awareness, giving Him the opportunities to make heart connections that changed lives forever. It all begins with an identity grounded in who God says you are: *"But you are a chosen people, a royal priesthood, a holy nation, God's special possession, that you may declare the praises of him who called you out of darkness into his wonderful light"* (1 Peter 2:9).

TOOLS FOR APPLICATION

In order to master Emotional Intelligence in Christ your first step occurs when you personally encounter Christ.

A transformation occurs within your mind, will and emotions as a result of the Pentecost experience of your choice to wake up to the presence of God's love for you through Christ and sealed with the Holy Spirit.

The tool below offers you a visual that captures the ramifications of a soul who has personally encountered the indwelling, living Lord Jesus Christ. This first step makes the following three steps possible when it comes to mastering Emotional Intelligence in Christ. With Him, it is possible, without Him it is not. Your awareness of your inner emotions, which are your body's response to your thought life, come alive when you come face-to-face with the Lover of your soul.

I am reminded of the final hours of a dear friend of mine who was dying of the same disease I conquered, advanced cancer. Three days before she transitioned into the arms of the Lord she shared with me that Jesus was appearing to her and sharing small truths that she wanted to pass along. The one I remember the most was this: *"when people are unkind it's simply because they have disconnected from their awareness of how much God loves and adores them, this creates turmoil within the mind and spills out into ugly behavior . . . pray for their souls that they encounter the love of God and experience the mind of Christ."*

THE SIX PHASE RIPPLE IMPACT FOR EMOTIONAL INTELLIGENCE IN CHRIST

The following excerpt[6] has been revised from 5 Minutes to Stress Relief and will give you a brief overview of a methodology taken from the field of neuro-linguistic programming (NLP). NLP helps you communicate better by showing you how your mind thinks along with using proven techniques that support your personal excellence.

The Six Phase Ripple Impact for Emotional Intelligence in Christ has its roots from a Neuro-Linguistic Programming (NLP) process which offers you, the reader, some fun insight into your greatest place of emotional empowerment: the presence of Christ within you.

SPIRIT OF CHRIST (HOLY SPIRIT) => IDENTITY => BELIEFS => CAPABILITIES => BEHAVIOR => ENVIRONMENT

Set up in a concentric circle format, with the Holy Spirit in the center (sitting on the throne of your heart) and the environment level in the furthest circle from the center, imagine dropping a stone in a still body of water. It took little effort to release the stone (symbolic of releasing your identity, sense of meaning and significance, into Christ) to put into motion the six circles of personal excellence and emotional intelligence in Christ. Flowing out from the Holy Spirit to the center to the environment.

> The choice to make a positive shift at the level of your soul, personally encountering the love of your Savior, creates a ripple effect, inspiring and transforming your identity, beliefs, capabilities, behavior, and environment.

If you create a positive shift in your spirit through a personal relationship with Jesus Christ, guided by the indwelling Holy Spirit, then each circle will experience a positive change, marked by emotional intelligence in Christ. As your thoughts become transformed by Christ's thoughts through the Holy Spirit dwelling within you,

---

6 Lauren E Miller, Career Press/New Page Books, 2013 pp 107–113

your emotions are directly impacted for good. Expanding your relationship with God, in a positive direction is the highest level of personal transformation.

The choice to make a positive shift at the level of your soul, personally encountering the love of your Savior, creates a ripple effect, inspiring and transforming your identity, beliefs, capabilities, behavior, and environment.

Every ripple in the concentric circle will affect itself-and every circle after it.

Think about letting go of all that you are into the hands and heart of Jesus Christ—a complete surrender and leaning into Jesus. Similar to letting go of a stone into a calm body of water and observing the ripple effect, the act of letting go of YOU into HIM results in a ripple effect of positivity that cascades through your identity, beliefs, capabilities, behavior, and environment.

As you personally encounter Jesus Christ and invite Him to be the Lord of your life: Three major components of emotional intelligence in Christ–your mind, will, and emotions–begin to experience transformation. When Jesus sits on the throne of your heart, you begin to seek out His wisdom, compassion, and insight in every thought which influences your emotions.

The former way of "doing you" begins to experience the journey of an interior extreme makeover. The fullness of life as described by Jesus and Paul start to become your reality:

> *"I have come that they may have life and have it to the full"* (John 10:10).
>
> *"Do not conform to this world but be transformed by the renewing of your mind"* (Romans 12:1-2).

Your capabilities and beliefs fall between your identity and your behaviors. Your environment is where your behavior happens. Your behavior is what you do, think, and say and is directly influenced by your identity: Who am I? Why am I here? What will it matter? We just explored what this looks like in the beginning of this chapter.

The behaviors you manifest in your life flow from the highest emotional intelligence level of your spirit as connected to Christ and your sense of identity. When you make a shift back into the center of YOU, as connected to the love of God, your environment will shift accordingly.

Simply put, your soul connection with God drives the rest of your ship in life, how you show up. When you are disconnected from a personal loving relationship with God—your highest source of guidance, wisdom, and love—you begin to fragment the ripple effect out into the world around you. You start to live from the inside out, rather than the outside in. You know you have been hijacked by the outer world when your emotions flare up and spill over into negative behavior. As you reclaim your identity in Christ with the help of the Holy Spirit, you return to inner peace and the fruits of the Holy Spirit become the boss of your emotions: love, joy, peace, patience, kindness, goodness, gentleness, and self-control. *"A man is enslaved to whatever has mastered him"* (2 Peter 1:19).

As you reflect on your own relationship with the world, what has mastered you in your life? Is it your environment? Opinions and reactions of other people? The need to be seen, acknowledged, and recognized? Perhaps it's a specific behavior? If you are seeking freedom from compulsive behavior, you may say, "I just can't help myself." This reveals a type of personal enslavement by allowing some food, substance, situation, or person to master them over time, which in some cases results in a biological addiction.

> The key to freedom in situations like this lies in your ability to accept where you are, accompanied with a desire for positive personal transformation and a choice to take a step in that direction.

The stress hormone is linked directly to your emotional state of mind and heart. Extended emotional stress often leads to personal enslavement, which usually walks hand-in-hand with unhealthy outlets.

The key to freedom in situations like this lies in your ability to accept where you are, accompanied with a desire for positive personal transformation and a choice to take a step in that direction.

Unfortunately, we often look for the living among the dead. Our search for identity gets kidnapped by the shiny objects of power, possessions, popularity, and passion. We rise and fall emotionally depending upon how the world judges us. Jesus is calling us back to the center of our success in life: our personal relationship with Him. He is all about simplicity for freedom which John the Baptist captured when he said, *"I must decrease, He must increase"* (John 3:30).

The Six Phase Ripple Impact for Emotional Intelligence in Christ

> As you resurrect your remembrance of the divine power that courses through your being, an exhilarating experience of detachment begins to emerge, along with peace and wisdom that passes all human understanding.

As you explore and expand your soul connection with God, the chains that hold you back from emotional intelligence in Christ will begin to lose their grip on you.

As you resurrect your remembrance of the divine power that courses through your being, an exhilarating experience of detachment begins to emerge, along with peace and wisdom that passes all human understanding.

With increased frequency, you will begin to experience moments that are free from your need to own, control, possess, analyze, and conclude, along with your need to know why things happen as they do and how things will turn out. You will begin to gravitate towards the experience of presence. Being here now will begin to take on a lighthearted playfulness towards the moment of life in front of your face. Jesus was not confined by status and the opinions of other people . . . He was emotionally free and calls you into the same freedom: *"It is for freedom that Christ has set you free, stand firm then and do not let yourselves be burdened again by the yoke of slavery"* (Galatians 5:1).

As you draw near to God at the beginning of each day and throughout your day, your authentic God-given nature begins to emerge on the front lines of your life. You are reminded of your expansive value, worth, and purpose. You will no longer rise and fall depending on how the world judges you. The stress you have experienced resulting from endless comparisons, jealousies, and moments of envy will no longer enslave you. Once again, you will gain inner freedom to be you, as you remember yourself-as loved unconditionally by God.

As you reflect on the Six Phase Ripple Impact for Emotional Intelligence in Christ, where do you recognize yourself? Do you allow your environment to impact your sense of identity? If so, how specifically does that happen for you? Clarity of focus leads to accuracy of response.

Have outside circumstances directly impacted your sense of worth and value? Perhaps your behavior has anchored bad habits that have casted a negative self-image and tarnished your sense of identity. Maybe you have been hijacked by the drug of approval along the way which has caused you to believe that you are not capable of achieving what you feel moved to go for in life and therefore self-doubt lingers at the heart of your identity.

> As you surrender your identity to God, you gain access to emotional intelligence in Christ which directly impacts your beliefs, capabilities, behavior, and environment.

Come back to the One who offers you emotional victory over the shouts of the world around you along with deliverance from the shadows that linger within your mind. Anchor your identity in the Spirit of Christ within you, herein lies your victory over emotional turmoil in life.

As you surrender your identity to God, you gain access to emotional intelligence in Christ which directly impacts your beliefs, capabilities, behavior, and environment.

Reflect on the following questions and explore times in your life that you overlooked the risen Lord calling you back to your personal identity in Him. When have you exercised your free will in a way that imprisons your mind and negatively spins your emotions? The 3-step prison break, discussed earlier in this chapter, is available to you every day.

ENCOUNTER THE SAVIOR => REPENTANCE => RESURRECTION OF YOUR IDENTITY IN CHRIST.

Reflect on the following questions:

When have you experienced an encounter with the Lord that resulted in repentance from negative behavior that compromised the person God is calling you to be?

....
....
....
....

What were the ramifications of your choice to explore a changed behavior that aligns with your identity in Christ?

....
....
....
....

Behavior 1: Personal Identity in Christ (Self-Awareness)

What behavior still blocks your ability to expand your personal identity in Christ? For example, the need to be right blocks empathy and compassion.

_____

_____

_____

Imagine and reflect for a moment on what it was like for Mary to be freed from seven demons. What a thick cocoon of restriction she must have felt. The Lord saw her ability to fly and set her free from bondage.

Similar to Thomas declaring doubt in his life, in what areas of your life are you imprisoned by doubt? What doubt are you declaring over your life? What specifically are you doubting? Where do you doubt? Who do you doubt? When do you doubt? What behavior occurs when you doubt?

_____

_____

_____

_____

Thomas shut down in spite of being surrounded by joy from the good news from Mary—He has risen. Misery LOVES company. Gossip evokes gossip. Doubt evokes doubt. Are you harboring doubt in your identity? Is it stunting the development of your wings so that you can experience a prison break and fly where God calls you to fly ... back into your personal identity in Christ as defined by God?

Take a moment to pray a deliverance prayer:

> "Dear Lord, in the name of Jesus Christ of Nazareth, by the blood of Christ, I bind, rebuke and cast out the spirit of doubt in my life, specifically casting out:_____
> (self-doubt, doubting you are with me, that you have plans

for me, that you love me). I bind, rebuke and cast out all Spirits associated with the spirit of doubt and declare Your victory over doubt in my life. I surrender all that I am to you. Fill me with your Holy Spirit." —*for more deliverance prayers explore Francis MacNutt and the Unbound Model by Neal Lazano.*

As a result of his encounter with Christ, Paul went on to be one of the most passionate and convicted followers of Christ to this day. Jesus's gift of freedom is not confined by time or intensity. Paul went from killing Christians to proclaiming Christ in a matter of days. Now that's a prison break worth reflecting upon.

Paul encountered Jesus, repented of his sin and entered into a resurrected life that was so radical and instant that Jesus's followers experienced fear when Paul knocked on their door after his conversion (Acts 16:23).

Later in Peter's ministry, Peter experienced a physical jailbreak (Acts 12:3–11) when an angel of the Lord entered his prison cell, released the chains that bound him and walked him out of prison. Are you sitting in the jail cell of your mind? Your own will? Your emotions? Invite the Holy Spirit to do for you what the Angel did for Peter: remove your chains and walk you out of bondage.

What would you imagine that would look like for you? What would you call your jail cell? Here are a few examples: Self-pity? Judgment? Positionality that creates ugly behavior against those who do not share your position? Fear of what people think? Doubt that God has your back and your best interests? Lack of trust? Lack of belief? Fear of failure? Selfishness? Greed? Control? What is the name of your prison? Your hijacked identity?

Encounter Christ through intentional prayer and reflection on God's Word throughout your day. Pick one of the five prominent Biblical characters we explored in this chapter each week. Reflect on their prison-break and how it relates to where you feel emotionally compromised today. Focus on their encounter with Christ and how it led to repentance: a conscious choice to turn away from a false identity into your identity in Christ.

What do you want to pivot away from in your life that is blocking your ability to see yourself-through the eyes of your Savior?

....
....
....

What do you want to expand in your life that supports your ability to step out of your will and into God's will for you?

....
....
....

Write a mission statement for your life with Christ that reflects your commitment to love the Lord with all of your heart, mind, soul, and strength and love your neighbor as yourself-(Mark 12:29–31). Invite Jesus into the center of your will, mind, and emotions. Reboot your identity as defined by God.

....
....
....

For example: I am committed to putting God's will above my own. I have been crucified with Christ on the cross, it's no longer about me, what I think, want, and need, it's about Jesus living in and through me for the glory of God. My authentic personal identity is found in Jesus alone. I want what He wants, when He wants it, and how He wants it. I am here in God's time for His purpose so that He can make His appeal through me for the sake of salvation of souls. Less of me and more of you, sweet Jesus, for Your glory . . . not mine. My joy and peace are complete as I surrender all that I am into all that Jesus IS. Just Jesus. The sweet union of the created one to its Creator. Authentic personal identity restored.

COACHING QUESTIONS

Who am I? Why am I here? What will it matter? Reference back to "Tools for Application" on page 70.

What do I know to be true about myself-as a result of knowing Christ and following His example? (For example: I am a sinner, I am forgiven, I am redeemed, I am loved, I am enough in Christ, I'm not alone and I am set free).

Who does God say I am in the Scriptures? Read John 1:12, Romans 8:15–16, 1 Peter 2:9, 2 Corinthians 5:20.

How does knowing who I am in Christ impact my sense of identity?

The tool I commit to apply in my life in order to expand the EIC behavior of Personal Identity is (review "Tools for Application" on page 70.)

Write down three specific behaviors that you imagine you will notice to be different as a result of applying EIC Personal Identity in Christ:

Prayer

Dear Lord, help me to see myself-as You see me. To know that my sense of safety is in direct proportion to how deeply I connect my worth and value to who You say I am. Help me to remember that I am Your ambassador in this world and that my ability to impact the lives of the people entrusted to my care flows directly from my connection with You. My identity and beliefs about myself-come from who You say that I am along with my sense of purpose. More of You, Lord, less of me. I give You permission to override me when I start to look for who I am outside of my relationship with You. With You, I lack nothing. I want to be aware of my emotions and be able to master them through You, for Your glory. Lead me into emotional intelligence in and through You. I want to see myself as You see me.

CHAPTER 4

BEHAVIOR 2: SELF-CONTROL (SELF-MANAGEMENT)

*"But the fruit of the Spirit is love, joy, peace, forbearance, kindness, goodness, faithfulness, gentleness, and **self-control**"* (Galatians 5:22–23).

*"Like a city whose walls are broken down is a man who lacks **self-control**"* (Proverbs 25:28).

Chapter Contents
- Define the Trait
- Biblical Examples
- Focused Case Study
- Tools for Application
- Coaching Questions
- Prayer

> Self-control is the ramification of surrender to the presence and authority of Jesus Christ of Nazareth in your life.

Define the Trait

SELF-CONTROL IS THE last fruit of the Spirit that resurrects the other fruits to the front line of our behaviors.

Self-control is the ramification of surrender to the presence and authority of Jesus Christ of Nazareth in your life.

The resulting relationship is a face-to-face encounter with the One who died to win you over to eternal love and security. Your awareness of the presence of Christ within you gives you the ability to be the boss of your emotions rather than allowing them to be the boss of you.

Self-management flows from knowing one's identity in Christ so profoundly that the useless trinkets and shiny objects of the world, which once gained free rent between your two ears and spilled out into your behavior, are stopped in their tracks. Self-discipline, trustworthiness, transparency, adaptability, and optimistic character emerges to the front lines of your ability to manage your emotions well. The trinkets of needing to be right, liked, understood, seen, acknowledged, and recognized to feel successful, valued, and enough in this world are replaced with a spirit of power, courage, self-control, and an overall feeling of peace despite external triggers.

In a calm, confident manner with the help of the Holy Spirit who dwells within you, you posture yourself-in the image of Christ, knowing that your place of victory over the triggers in the world lies in your ability to surrender all emotion over to the emotionally intelligent One. In this expansive choice point of managing your feelings, you remember that success is not defined by what you achieve but by the person you are while you complete that success.

> St. Paul defined this second step of emotional intelligence perfectly when he said in Galatians 5:6: *"The only thing that counts is faith expressing itself-through love."*

St. Paul defined this second step of emotional intelligence perfectly when he said in Galatians 5:6: *"The only thing that counts is faith expressing itself-through love."*

And when you don't feel you have enough love or faith, self-management in Christ pauses and asks the Emotionally Intelligent One: "I believe, Lord, help my unbelief, lack of love and faith . . . I want what You have; I permit You to override my impulse for negative emotions that spill out into negative behavior to make me emotionally intelligent in You."

To fully grasp the understanding of self-control, we must acknowledge that there exists a very real enemy of our souls. The evil one has a plan that he would like to impose on all of humanity. He intends to *"kill, steal, and destroy"* lives that should be Heaven bound (John 10:10). Satan attempts to accomplish this by creating division. We see that playing out in our everyday lives. Disunity, discord, mistrust, and anger abounds in the age we live in.

Nearly every sphere of daily life is plagued by dissonance and strife. From politics to healthcare, education, business, sports, and arts and entertainment, everywhere we turn there seems to be an "us versus them" way of thinking as opposed to a "we are in this together" mentality. Even the faith community is nonexempt from the pitfall of the denominational divide.

In the last few years, it appears that Satan is focusing his efforts to divide our world through his tool of offense. Offended people have a hard time looking in the mirror and accepting the blame, instead they choose to focus on everyone else. We seem to be a triggered culture that is standing at the ready to pull the verbal and sometimes physical "trigger" rather than seeking understanding and positive intentions in others. Forgiveness, essential to being forgiven for our own mistakes, seems to be unfashionable by today's measures.

Incivility appears to be all around us and even the world recognizes its path of destruction. Christine Porath, a researcher and Associate Professor of Management at the McDonough School of Business at Georgetown University, concludes that the primary reason that executives fail in the workforce is due to an insensitive, abrasive, or bullying leadership style. In Porath's popular TED Talk on "Why being respectful to your coworkers is good for business," the researcher concludes that rudeness impacts our emotions, motivation, performance, and the way that we ultimately treat others.

She presents well-tested research on the destructive impact of a culture rife with rudeness, disrespect, and lack of kindness. Incivility is like a virus that harms those directly impacted along with those who witness the poor conduct. Porath states that due to incivility in the workplace, 66% of those who experience or witness rude behavior cut back their efforts, 80% have documented lost work time, and 12% have walked away from their jobs entirely.

> The closer you draw into Christ's love, the more capable you will become at managing your emotions with the fruit of the Spirit: Self-Control.

Where is all of this turmoil coming from? It's a lack of self-control enabling a surrender to the schemes of the enemy. Division and offence are just part of the enemy's plans for destruction. Let's face it, we are witnessing firsthand the desires of the flesh showcased on center stage all around us. What part do you play in the area of self-control hijacked by your need to be right, liked and understood?

Each of us has our own screenplay that we direct by behaviors that play outside the arena of self-control. Your ability to manage your emotions well is in direct proportion to your identity being grounded in Christ, the first EIC behavioral trait discussed in chapter 3.

The closer you draw into Christ's love, the more capable you will become at managing your emotions with the fruit of the Spirit: Self-Control.

St. Augustine shared that his greatest victories came when he gave his spirit permission to guide his flesh. Too often the flesh guides the spirit. The outcome is beautifully described by Paul in his letter to the Galatians 5:19–21.

> *"The acts of the flesh are obvious: sexual immorality, impurity and debauchery; idolatry and witchcraft; hatred, discord, jealousy, fits of rage, selfish ambition, dissensions, factions and envy; drunkenness, orgies, and the like. I warn*

you, as I did before, that those who live like this will not inherit the kingdom of God."

Where do you recognize yourself-in the list of the flesh described by Paul above? The first step towards freedom from the flesh is ruthless honesty. Perhaps it's jealousy? Envy? Selfish ambition that has had its way with you in life. James says in James 3:16: *"For where you have envy and selfish ambition, there you find disorder and every evil practice."* Without self-control, capturing the ability to walk in emotional intelligence is like trying to catch a trout with your hands in a stream, you may grab it for a split second but then it quickly slips out of your hands.

In terms of emotional intelligence, self-control is part of self-management which also includes discipline, how we relate to goals, living by principles and personal values, and the ability to adapt to situations, relationships, and feelings.

Self-control provides the foundation for the other aspects of self-management to be successful. So, what exactly is self-control? The word most commonly used in the Bible for self-control, *Enkrateia*, is derived from the Greek language and means "self-mastery" or "power over oneself." *Enkrateia* is having command over one's will, control of appetites, and regulation of emotions and behavior. Self-control enables a person to delay gratification and ignore impulses.

The stronger a person's internal character becomes, the greater the ability to exert self-control over temptations. In other words, the more we grow in Christ, being like Him in character and doing the things that He did, the more self-control we will have over the temptations in our lives.

> So, self-control is a supernatural mastery over the mind, emotions, and will that come as a result of being transformed by the Spirit of the One who mastered every thought, feeling, and behavior perfectly.

When we "abide" in Jesus, according to John 15:5, we will bear much fruit. Great results personally and with others will flow out of our relationship with Jesus. Further, when we fail to "abide" or remain in Jesus, our source, Scripture says that we "can do nothing."

Galatians 5:22–23 is the fruit that Christians reap from living a life in Christ and being close to the vine that John 15:5 talks about. According to Pastor Bill Campbell of Life Bridge Church in Fort Wayne, IN, love, joy, and peace are the fruit that reflects the character of God. Additionally, patience, kindness, and goodness all exhibit His traits and qualities. Furthermore, faithfulness, gentleness, and self-control are all evidence of a transformed life.

So, self-control is a supernatural mastery over the mind, emotions, and will that come as a result of being transformed by the Spirit of the One who mastered every thought, feeling, and behavior perfectly.

So, if we remain in the vine and receive His fruit, then why do we still experience struggle, strife, pain, and sorrow? Doesn't the Bible teach us that God won't give us more than we can handle? Actually, the opposite is true. According to John 16:33, Jesus said *"I have told you these things, so that in me you may have peace. In this world you will have trouble. But take heart! I have overcome the world."*

We are guaranteed that by being close to Jesus, we will experience hardship. However, He promises to provide comfort and peace through His Spirit and the ability to overcome temptation with self-control. *"And God is faithful; he will not let you be tempted beyond what you can bear. But when you are tempted, he will also provide a way out so that you can endure it"* (1 Corinthians 10:13).

BIBLICAL EXAMPLES

There are countless examples of Christ exhibiting self-control along with sharing how to do this through him. Proverbs 25:28, tells us that, *"Like a city whose walls are broken through is a person who lacks self-control."*

This means without self-control or self-management, we are broken, ending up in ruin

> Self-control allows us to trust God and continue to do good in the midst of undesirable situations.

and decay. Samuel, Nehemiah, and Jesus's experience in the wilderness are three examples to help guide us into self-control or self-management. One invites us to trust the Lord, the other shows us how to do it even when it is hard, and the last one shows us how Jesus demonstrated it through His temptation in the wilderness.

In 1 Samuel 24 the connection is made between trusting in God and having self-control. Saul was after David, who spent many days and nights hiding from him as the story goes. After a point, Saul uncovered David's location and went into the cave where David was hiding. Saul had to use the bathroom, and David cut a piece of his garment instead of killing him. He did this by knowing His God and the judgment God had for Saul, not him.

> *"See, my father, look at this piece of your robe in my hand! I cut off the corner of your robe but did not kill you. See that there is nothing in my hand to indicate that I am guilty of wrongdoing or rebellion. I have not wronged you, but you are hunting me down to take my life. May the Lord judge between you and me. And may the Lord avenge the wrongs you have done to me, but my hand will not touch you"* (1 Samuel 24:11–12).

Vengeance is the Lord's (Romans 12:19). Let God do His work and resist the urge to take matters into your own hands.

Self-control allows us to trust God and continue to do good in the midst of undesirable situations.

David knew that God had a plan and trusted Him to see it through based on God's timing and not his. When presented with a situation where you are about to lose control, speak out loud 2 Timothy 1:7, *"For God hath not given us the spirit of fear; but of power, and of love, and of a sound mind."*

Nehemiah 4 also shares good teachings on how to use self-control even when it is hard to do. Nehemiah was called by God to rebuild the wall in Jerusalem after the Exodus. While rebuilding the wall, he was placed under attack. Instead of retaliation and fighting back, he stayed on the course of his mission. He strategically placed some of his men as guards and had the others keep working—what a testimony of faith, focus, and self-control. Proverbs 16:32 brings home this concept, *"Better a patient person than a warrior, one with self-control than one who takes a city."*

> A mastery of one's thoughts, emotions and behavior through self-control is a crucial element of being emotionally intelligent in Christ.

Jesus's experience in the wilderness is the last example of self-control in action. Jesus went into the wilderness for 40 days, and while there, Satan tested His self-control by offering Him control over the entire world. Jesus knew that God's Kingdom was the only kingdom and exercised self-control, one of the fruits of the Spirit. His love, patience, and goodness teach us all to be more like Him and less like Satan.

Know that to exercise self-control; you must be prepared for trials and temptation. Know that even though it won't be easy and frustrating at times, you have the power in Christ and are never alone in any battle that comes your way. With every emotional challenge, Jesus comes too.

FOCUSED CASE STUDY

A mastery of one's thoughts, emotions and behavior through self-control is a crucial element of being emotionally intelligent in Christ.

Again, being close to "the vine" enables us with the ability to have self-control over temptations just as Jesus did in the wilderness.

So, how did Jesus handle His thinking, feelings, and behavior leading up to His darkest of hours? The following case study of Jesus praying in the Garden of Gethsemane at night presents a riveting example of how Jesus had a mastery of Himself-during an intense situation marked by deep sorrow, frustrating friends, a cunning and deceptive ambush, a devastating betrayal, and a violent situation.[7]

The 26th chapter of Matthew describes the night of Jesus's betrayal by Judas in the Garden of Gethsemane. Jesus, our sinless Savior was also a suffering Savior. The night before His crucifixion, Jesus went to the garden with Peter, James and John, the disciples that were also present with Him at the transfiguration. They saw Him in glory and were about to see Him in absolute suffering. Sin and death, which transpired in a garden meant for pleasure, was atoned for once and for all by Jesus, who willingly gave up His life to endure suffering in a garden of agonizing pain and sorrow.

Matthew Henry in his commentary on this chapter states, "*The words used denote the most entire dejection, amazement, anguish, and horror of mind; the state of one surrounded with sorrows, overwhelmed with miseries, and almost swallowed up with terror and dismay. He now began to be sorrowful, and never ceased to be so till he said, 'It is finished.' He prayed that, if possible, the cup might pass from him. But he also showed his perfect readiness to bear the load of his sufferings; he was willing to submit to all for our redemption and salvation. According to this example of Christ, we must drink of the bitterest cup which God puts into our hands; though nature struggle, it must submit.*"

On the night Jesus was betrayed, He fully submitted His will to the Father so that He might complete His mission on earth. Jesus felt dejected while He prayed, so much so that He was *"overwhelmed with sorrow to the point of death"* (Matthew 26:38). His emotions must have been on overload when He asked *"Father, if it is possible, may this cup be taken from me"* (v. 39). Despite His feelings, Jesus acknowledged *"not as I will, but as you will."* He took control of His emotions, obeyed the Father, and submitted Himself-to complete the mission He set out for when He prayed for a second time saying, *"My Father, if it is not possible for this cup to be taken away unless I drink it, may your will*

---

7 Ken Voges, copyright, In His Grace, Inc., Houston Texas 1997

be done" (v. 42). Jesus demonstrated ultimate emotional self-control when He submitted to the will of the Father in the garden.

Jesus also stayed the course and avoided derailment from His mission when He chose not to be offended to the point of sin by Peter, James, and John sleeping in the garden or, especially, by Judas who went on to betray his Master.

> *"Then he returned to the disciples and said to them, "Are you still sleeping and resting? Look, the hour has come, and the Son of Man is delivered into the hands of sinners. Rise! Let us go! Here comes my betrayer!" While he was still speaking, Judas, one of the Twelve, arrived. With him was a large crowd armed with swords and clubs, sent from the chief priests and the elders of the people. Now the betrayer had arranged a signal with them: "The one I kiss is the man; arrest him." Going at once to Jesus, Judas said, "Greetings, Rabbi!" and kissed him. Jesus replied, "Do what you came for, friend." Then the men stepped forward, seized Jesus and arrested him"* (Matthew 26:45-50).

> God gave us the Holy Spirit, the ultimate gift to master self-control.

Jesus could have easily been offended to the point of rage when the arresting party came in the cloak of darkness rather than apprehending Him in daylight one of the many times He was publicly present. Jesus could have been so angered that he may have justifiably called down 72,000 angels to obliterate the soldiers and Judas. But He chose to remain controlled and complete His mission.

> *"Do you think I cannot call on my Father, and he will at once put at my disposal more than twelve legions of angels? But how then would the Scriptures be fulfilled that say it must happen in this way?" In that hour Jesus said to the crowd, "Am I leading a rebellion, that you have come out with swords and clubs to capture me? Every day I sat in*

the temple courts teaching, and you did not arrest me. But this has all taken place that the writings of the prophets might be fulfilled." Then all the disciples deserted him and fled" (Matthew 26:53-56).

TOOLS FOR APPLICATION

God gave us the Holy Spirit, the ultimate gift to master self-control.

> In gaining self-control and emotional intelligence in Christ, you need to be imitators of Jesus.

Galatians 5:23 shares that self-control is a product of having the Holy Spirit. Therefore, we must have the Holy Spirit before exercising any self-control. God has given us the option to choose to invite the Holy Spirit's strength to help us with self-control or not. Our choice will make all the difference in the outcomes we experience.

1 Peter 4:7 tells us, *"the end of all things is near. Therefore be alert and of sober mind so that you may pray."* Other interpretations invite us to be of sound mind, self-controlled, and sober. We must remember that the Holy Spirit directs us in all truths. When we surrender to God and let go of our flesh, that is where the true transformation begins.

As was stated earlier in this chapter, John 15:5 paints the perfect picture of abiding in Jesus and developing fruit in our lives. The Holy Spirit cultivates the fruit of self-control in our lives when we "remain close to the vine" by being like Jesus and doing what He did. Jesus said in John 5:19, *"Very truly I tell you, the Son can do nothing by himself; he can only do what he sees his Father doing, because whatever the Father does the son also does."*

In gaining self-control and emotional intelligence in Christ, you need to be imitators of Jesus.

Our friends at Lead Like Jesus, a global training and equipping ministry that teaches the leadership model of our Lord, have a very useful tool modeled after the habits that kept Jesus on track with His mission to glorify the Father in Heaven.

THE BEING HABITS[8]

Memory verse: *"But his delight is in the law of the Lord, and on his law he meditates day and night. He is like a tree planted by streams of water, which yields its fruit in season and whose leaf does not wither. Whatever he does prospers."* (Psalm 1:2–3).

The Recalibration Tools to Lead Like Jesus and Develop Self-Control

No matter how good the tools are, if you don't use them, they will not work. The daily pressures and concentration on the moment-by-moment duties can often isolate and distort a person's perspective and ability to focus. Jesus modeled certain habits for keeping focused and on track with His mission. We can implement these habits to grow closer "to the vine" and strengthen the muscle of self-control. The five of the habits Jesus modeled that are essential components of living, loving, and leading like Jesus are:

1. Solitude
2. Prayer
3. Study and application of Scripture
4. Accepting and responding to God's unconditional love
5. Involvement in supporting relationships

These habits reflect the central theme of all that Jesus sought to do—to know the will of God and to do the work that had been given Him to do. They were simple expressions of who He was and His intimacy with the Father. In your case, they must first take on the form of disciplines before they can become habits. Depending on your past experience and daily habits, it will take time for all of them

---

[8] The following tool, The Being Habits, is adapted from Lead Like Jesus: Beginning the Journey @2003. Used with permission.

to become an integrated part of your efforts to grow in self-control and lead like Jesus. All of them are powerful and transforming. All of them will feed and nourish your soul and your relationships.

The biggest temptation you face in making the journey from discipline to habit will be impatience for measurable and sustainable results. The immediate price to be paid for acquiring the habits of Jesus is time, effort, and trust in the process and in the One who says again *"Follow Me."* If you develop the relationship with Jesus through the Habits, they will truly become a lifestyle that serves you in all seasons of life.

Habit #1: The Habit of Experiencing Solitude

"Be still and know that I am God" (Psalm 46:10).

Jesus spent significant time alone away from human contact throughout his season of leadership. In solitude, He found what was essential to deal successfully with the trials and challenges that He faced. We can be very sure that what Jesus found useful for the conduct of His life in the Father will also be useful for us. In fact, He gave us many commands about the Habits.

What do we mean by solitude? Solitude is being completely alone with God away from all human contact. It is stepping outside the back door of your noisy demanding world of agendas and interaction with people to catch a breath of fresh air. It is being refreshed and restored by the internal rhythms of life that are going on all around you but are uninterested in who you are in the world or what's on your mind. It is to be challenged and comforted by the fact that the world doesn't depend on you to rotate on its axis and that you don't depend on your work in the world to provide meaning and value. It is resting in God's presence and pleasure. It is being alone without being lonely.

You can make better sense of the world, of yourself-and of others after a time alone with God. Without it you are playing a frantic game of hide and seek that can turn your goals in life and your leadership from "being more than conquerors" to just trying to make it through the day, the week, the month, and the year. Jesus is our example. Jesus often retreated to lonely places to be in solitude and prayer with the Father. How difficult we find it in our modern day to spend significant time with our Significant Other—God.

How much do you practice the habit of solitude—completely away from all human contact in contact with God? Evaluate your experience by answering the following questions:

How long has it been since you spent an hour in solitude?

How long has it been since you spent a day with God?

How much time have you spent in solitude with God in the past week?

Let's look at Jesus, our example, and our Lord. Even Jesus engaged in external solitude as a means of fortifying His inner peace and purpose.

Read Matthew 4:1–11 below when Jesus was preparing for the tests of leadership and public ministry. He spent forty days alone in the desert. As you read, compare Jesus's experience with any times of solitude you have spent before facing a new ministry or a critical crossroads in your life.

> *Then Jesus was led by the Spirit into the desert to be tempted by the devil. After fasting forty days and forty nights, he was hungry. The tempter came to him and said, "If you are the Son of God, tell these stones to become bread. Jesus answered, "It is written: 'Man does not live on bread alone, but on every word that comes from the mouth of God.'" Then the devil took him to the holy city and had him stand on the highest point of the temple. "If you are the Son of God," he said, "throw yourself-down. For it is written: He will command his angels concerning*

you, and they will lift you up in their hands, so that you will not strike your foot against a stone.'" Jesus answered him, "It is also written: 'Do not put the Lord your God to the test. Again, the devil took him to a very high mountain and showed him all the kingdoms of the world and their splendor. "All this I will give you," he said, "if you will bow down and worship me." Jesus said to him, "Away from me, Satan! For it is written: 'Worship the Lord your God, and serve him only.'" Then the devil left him, and angels came and attended him.

Describe a time when you spent significant time in solitude as you faced a ministry opportunity or a crossroads experience in life. Note the challenge you faced, how you spent your time in solitude and what the results were.

....
....
....
....

Immediately after humbling himself-by being baptized to "fulfill all righteousness," Jesus was led by the Holy Spirit into a time of prolonged solitude where He was tempted by the devil. In our humanness, it is easy to focus on what Jesus gave up during that time and miss what He received. In His time alone with God, He received the spiritual nurture and perspective that allowed Him to overcome the powerful and subtle temptations of the enemy for that time and gave Him a perspective for all His ministry. Although physically hungry after His prolonged fast, Jesus was spiritually at "the top of his game." Though sorely tempted in the three areas most devastating to a leader— instant gratification, recognition and power, Jesus used the power of God's Word against His adversary and won. Find time for some solitude today!

"Do not be anxious about anything, but in everything, by prayer and petition, with thanksgiving, present your requests to God. And the peace of God, which transcends all understanding, will guard your hearts and your minds in Christ Jesus" (Philippians 4:6–7).

Habit #2: The Habit of Prayer

> Prayer is an essential act of our "free will" that demonstrates whether we are really serious about living and leading like Jesus.

If there was one thing to know about a leader that would be most instructive about how and where they might take their followers, it would be their prayer life. To live, love and lead like Jesus, one must develop the instinctive habit of actively and constantly seeking to follow His model and His instructions on prayer and obedience.

Inviting God In is the only way to put ourselves in position for the heart transplant required to move from Edging God out to Exalting God Only.

Prayer is an essential act of our "free will" that demonstrates whether we are really serious about living and leading like Jesus.

Without it we will never open the way for the Holy Spirit to do His work in and through us. Seeking God's will through prayer, waiting in faith for an answer, acting in accordance with it and being at peace with the outcome, calls for a level of spiritual maturity that will keep anyone seeking to lead like Jesus in lifelong training. It will be the nature and object of our prayers that will determine whether they are to fortify an EGO-driven end or to glorify God.

The ACTS of Prayer

A simple acrostic—ACTS— can help you remember four basic parts of prayer. ACTs has helped many beginners in prayer and served as a compass for weather-beaten veterans. Try it for a few days.

1. **A**doration: All prayer should begin here—telling the Lord that you love Him and appreciate Him for who He is.

   "Yours, O Lord, is the greatness and power and the glory and the majesty and the splendor, for everything in heaven and earth is yours. Yours, O Lord, is the Kingdom; you are exalted as head over all" (1 Chronicles 29:11).

2. **C**onfession: Immediately when we come into the presence of a Holy God we sense our inadequacies and are convicted that we still fall short of God's glory. Therefore, our first response to meeting and adoring God is confession. Sometimes we have to confess before we express our adoration and love.

   "If we confess our sins He is faithful and just and will forgive us our sins and purify us from all unrighteousness" (1 John 1:9).

3. **T**hanksgiving: Thanksgiving is the heartfelt expression of gratitude to God for all He has done in creation, redemption, and in our lives. During this part of your prayer, thank God specifically for all that He did for you since the last time you talked. As the old hymn says, "Count your blessings. Name them one by one. Count your many blessings; see what God has done." What if tomorrow you only had the things that you thanked God for today? Toothpaste, air, water, clothes, family, job, and you name it. Heed the Scripture:

   "Sing and make music in your heart to the Lord, always giving thanks to God the Father for everything, in the name of our Lord Jesus Christ" (Ephesians 5:19-20).

4. **S**upplication: Finally, we get to the part of prayer where most of us start—asking. Supplication is just a big word

for asking for what you need. Start with prayers for others and then ask for your own needs to be met. It's okay to have a big "wish list." According to God's Word, we can ask with confidence.

"Ask and it will be given to you; seek and you will find; knock and the door will be opened to you" (Matthew 7:7).

Stop now and spend a few minutes in prayer using **ACTS**.

As you embark on this journey to develop self-control through practicing prayer, you may be facing some challenges. Let us examine Jesus's example as a model to follow. Nowhere in the Bible are the elements of what it means to pray like Jesus more powerfully provided for us than in the dark hours of the night before he was betrayed and when the temptation to abandon His mission were at an almost unbearable level.

Read the prayer of Jesus and answer the questions of where He prayed, why He prayed, His posture in prayer, His request, and the answer to His prayer.

"Then Jesus went with his disciples to a place called Gethsemane, and he said to them, "Sit here while I go over there and pray." He took Peter and the two sons of Zebedee along with him and he began to be sorrowful and troubled. Then he said to them, "My soul is overwhelmed with sorrow to the point of death. Stay here and keep watch with me." Going a little farther, he fell with his face to the ground and prayed, "My Father, if it is possible, may this cup be taken from me. Yet not as I will, but as you will." (Matthew 26:36–46)

1. Where did Jesus pray and why? _____

    He went off by Himself-for prayer. A troubled soul finds most ease when it is alone with God, who understands the broken language of sighs and groans. Being alone with

God, Jesus could freely pour His heart out to the Father without restraint. Christ has taught and modeled for us that secret prayer is to be done secretly.

2. What was His posture in prayer?

He fell on His face before His Father indicating the agony He was in, the extremity of His sorrow and His humility in prayer. At other times, Jesus prayed looking up to heaven, with His eyes open, or kneeling. The posture of the heart is more important than the posture of the body but prostrating ourselves before God helps our heart posture.

3. What did He ask in prayer?

Jesus asked; *"If it be possible, let this cup pass from me."* He was asking if He could avoid the sufferings He faced. But notice the way Jesus couched His request; *"If it be possible."* He knew the Father would only allow what was for His glory and Jesus's good. He trusted the Father and left the answer to Him when He said, *"Nevertheless, not as I will, but as thou wilt."* Even though Jesus had a sharp sense of the extreme bitterness of the sufferings He was to undergo, He freely subjugated His desire to the Father. He based His own willingness upon the Father's will.

4. What was the answer to His prayer?

His answer was the will of the Father would be done. The cup did not pass from Him, for He withdrew the petition, in deference to His Father's will. But He got an answer to His prayer. He was strengthened for the mission He had come to fulfill, *"An angel from heaven appeared to him and strengthened him"* (Luke 22:43).

> Leading like Jesus and developing self-control will call you to proceed in faith and trust in God's grace to provide you with the courage to finish the task and do the right thing.

Doing the right thing for the right reasons may require you to drink the bitter cup in the form of ridicule, rejection, and anger. Your human tendency will be to try to avoid the pain.

Leading like Jesus and developing self-control will call you to proceed in faith and trust in God's grace to provide you with the courage to finish the task and do the right thing.

Habit #3: The Habit of Applying Scripture

As you can see, each day we are building the Habits and showing their relationships. Today, we continue with Habit #1: Solitude, as it is linked to Habit #2: Prayer and Habit #3: Scripture. When God calls you to Himself-it is a call to solitude. You need the habits of prayer and Scripture as God's cell phone to help you talk to Him and hear from Him during your time of solitude. Solitude plus prayer will be incomplete if you do not hear from God through the Scripture. All of us know the value of Scripture. If not, just begin studying it and you soon will experience all the benefits of knowing and doing the Word of God.

Study God's Word

If you only used the Bible to study and apply the practical wisdom it contains about dealing with people and overcoming your own internal challenges, it would still stand absolutely alone as the greatest book ever written. But it is so much more. It is an intimate love letter written to you from your Father. Through it He invites you to experience daily new and exciting dimensions of His love.

Scriptures are God's holy Word from the holy God, delivered by holy men, to teach holy truths, and make people holy.

Read 2 Timothy 3:10–17 and answer the questions about God's Word.

> *"All Scripture is God-breathed and is useful for teaching, rebuking, correcting and training in righteousness, so that*

the man of God may be thoroughly equipped for every good work" (2 Timothy 3:16).

1. What is the origin of all Scripture? _____
   Scripture is given by inspiration of God and therefore is His Word. It is a divine revelation, which you may depend upon as infallibly true. The same Spirit that breathed reason into you breathes revelation to you through the Word.

2. What is it useful for? _____
   The study of Scripture is profitable for all the purposes of the Christian life. It teaches you the truth. It rebukes you when you are wrong. It corrects you when you stray. It trains you in righteous living.

3. What is the ultimate result? _____
   By Scripture, you are thoroughly equipped for every good work. Whatever duty you have to do, or service is required from you, you find help in the Scriptures to equip you to do it.

It is all well and good to know that the Bible is useful; it is reliable; and it is valuable. It is another thing to make it your own in a practical way. It is only profitable if you read it. In what ways can you make the Word of God more effective in your life as a leader?

_____

_____

Apply the Word To Your Life

The most effective way to get the Word into your life is to apply it. Delving into the Word and getting the Word into you are essential, but the only way to abide fully in the Word is to apply it to your life. Jesus told this story. *"Why do you call me 'Lord, Lord' and do not do what I say? I will show you what he is like who comes to me and hears my words and puts them into practice. He is like a man building a house, who dug down deep and laid the foundation on rock. When a flood came, the torrent struck that house but could not shake it, because it was well built. But the one who hears my words and does not put them into practice is like a man who built a house on the ground without a foundation. The moment the torrent struck that house, it collapsed and its destruction was complete"* (Luke 6:46-49). What was the difference between the two men who built the house? Both of them heard, but only one acted. Only that one was able to stand firm.

Here are five practical ways you can cultivate Habit #3: Applying Scripture. You already know them, but the question is, "Are you practicing and applying them?" If you are not, it will take some time for all of them to become habits. After each explanation, evaluate where you are with your own practical application, what you plan to do to make it a habit, and when you will set a target date for each one to be a habit. Give yourself-time to add one discipline to the other until all are a part of your life. You are in the process of becoming more like Jesus and it will be better for you to master one discipline at a time beginning with the one that most appeals to you. Then you can add another on your own schedule. We are not trying to teach you these skills but give you a manual to use in your development. You might want to imagine each finger representing one way beginning with your little finger on the first one.

1. Hear the Word
2. Read the Word
3. Study the Word
4. Memorize the Word
5. Meditate on the Word

1. Hear the Word
The simplest way to receive the Word is to hear it. Even a child or a person who cannot read can hear the Bible. *"If anyone has ears to*

hear, let him hear" (Mark 4:23). "Faith comes from hearing the message, and the message is heard through the word of Christ" (Romans 10:17).

Matthew 13:3–23 lists four kinds of hearers of the Word: the apathetic hearer who hears the Word but is not prepared to receive and understand it (v.19); the superficial hearer who receives the Word temporarily but does not let it take root in the heart (v. 20–21); the preoccupied hearer who receives the Word but lets the worries of this world and the desire for other things choke it out (v.22); and the reproducing hearer who receives the Word, understands it, bears fruit, and brings forth results (v.23). Which kind of hearer are you?

However, you choose to hear the Word if you don't find a way to capture it you will soon forget. For example, can you remember what was said the last time you heard the Word or a sermon? One way to apply what you hear is to ask yourself-the following questions and jot down the answers. You may want to record them in your personal journal or make a form to help you remember.

1. What did God say to me through this message?
2. How does my life measure up to this Word?
3. What actions will I take to bring my life in line with this Word?
4. What truth do I need to study further?
5. What truth can I share with another person?

My evaluation of how much hearing of the Word is a habit of my life: 1 2 3 4 5

My plan to make this a habit of my life:

....
....
....
....
....

My schedule for improving on this discipline:

....

....

....

2. Read the Word

The second way you learn God's Word is to read it. *"Blessed is the one who reads the words of this prophecy, and blessed are those who hear it and take to heart what is written in it, because the time is near"* (Revelation 1:3). Here are a few suggestions on how to read the Word so that you hear all God is saying to you in your Quiet Time.

- Allow enough time to read His Word reflectively. God told Joshua, *". . . meditate on it day and night, so that you may be careful to do everything written in it. Then you will be prosperous and successful"* (Joshua 1:8).

  Do not try to read so much Scripture at one time that you cannot meditate on its meaning and let God speak directly to you and your situation. Our memory verse for this week is, *"But his delight is in the law of the LORD, and on his law he meditates day and night. He is like a tree planted by streams of water, which yields its fruit in season and whose leaf does not wither"* (Psalm 1:2–3).

- Balance your reading of the Word. Jesus said, *"Everything must be fulfilled that is written about me in the Law of Moses, the Prophets, and the Psalms. Then He opened their minds so they could understand the Scriptures"* (Luke 24:44–45).

  These three designations of Scripture cover all the Old Testament which was the Bible Jesus used. Be sure to vary your reading so that all the counsel of God will be available to you. You may read the Bible from Genesis to Revelation over a year's time by reading three chapters a day and five on Sunday. Another plan is to each day read a chapter from the Old Testament and a chapter from the New Testament each day. You may prefer to read through a book of the Bible a chapter a day before moving to another book.

- Apply the Word to your life each day. Revelation 1:3 says, *"Blessed is the one who reads the words of this prophecy, and blessed are those who hear it and take to heart what is written in it, because the time is near."*

  When you take it to heart, ask God to show you what it means to you and for your life. Jesus promised that *"If you obey my commands, you will remain in my love, just as I have obeyed my Father's commands and remain in his love"* (John 15:10). Every time you apply the Word of God to your life you grow closer to Him. Every time you fail to apply it, you leave the Word, like scattered seed, beside the road where Satan can steal it. Once you have heard His Word you are prepared to respond to it in prayer and obedience. Jesus said, *"If anyone loves me, he will obey my teaching. My Father will love him, and we will come to him and make our home with him"* (John 14:23).

My evaluation of how much reading the Word is a habit of my life:

1 2 3 4 5

My plan to make this a habit of my life:

My schedule for improving on this discipline:

3. Study the Word

When you study the Word, you go deeper into it. *"The Bereans were of more noble character than the Thessalonians; for they received the message with great eagerness and examined the Scriptures every day to see if what Paul said was true"* (Acts 17:11).

> Scriptures are God's holy Word from the holy God, delivered by holy men, to teach holy truths, and make people holy.

With study, you begin to have more power in your handling of the Word. Bible study is an in-depth look into the Scripture, to learn and discover more than you would see in them in an overview or in a devotional reading. It involves comparing what the Bible says in one passage to other passages throughout the Bible. It may begin with a question and search the Bible for its answer. It often includes gaining additional information through commentaries and study helps.

My evaluation of how much Bible study is a habit of my life: 1 2 3 4 5

My plan to make this a habit of my life:

....

....

My schedule for improving on this discipline: ....

4. Memorize the Word

A deeper way to get the Word into your heart is to memorize it. When you remember the Word, it really lives in you, you live in it, and God's promises become your possessions. *"How can a young man keep his way pure? By living according to your word. I have hidden your word in my heart that I might not sin against you"* (Psalm 119:9, 11).

There are several reasons to memorize Scripture. In Matthew 4:1–11, the account of Christ's temptation in the wilderness, Jesus set the example. He used Scripture as the sword of the Spirit against Satan even when Satan tried to misuse Scripture as a part of the temptation. Memorizing Scripture helps you gain victory over sin. It also helps you answer when people have questions about your faith. *"Always be prepared to give an answer to everyone who asks you to give the reason for the hope that you have"* (1 Peter 3:15).

Being able to recite Scripture by heart helps you to meditate on it and gives you direction for your daily life at any moment. Most of all, the greatest benefit of memorizing Scripture comes from obedience to doing what God commands. *"These commandments that I give you today are to be upon your hearts"* (Deuteronomy 6:6).

Here are a dozen ways to memorize Scripture. Circle the numbers of the ones you already are using; draw a triangle around the number of the ones you want to improve on and put a box around the numbers of those you want to try.

How to Memorize Scripture[9]

1. Choose a verse that speaks to your need or which the Lord points out to you.
2. Understand the verse. Read it in context and in different translations.
3. Commit the verse to memory in your favorite translation. Divide it into natural, meaningful phrases and learn it word-by-word. If you learn it word-perfect in the beginning, it will be set in your memory, will be easier to review, will give you boldness when you are tempted, and will convince the person with whom you are sharing that he or she can trust your word. Memorize the verse reference and say it before and after the verse to fix it in your memory. Be ready if someone asks where it is in the Bible.
4. Develop some memory aids to help you remember the verse. For example, you might record it so you can listen to it. Leave a long pause after each verse so you

---

[9] Adopted from *The Disciples Cross: MasterLife Discipleship Training for Leaders*, pp.110–113

can practice quoting it. Then record the verse a second time so you can hear it again after you have quoted it without having to rewind it. Include the reference before and after.

5. Locate and underline the verse in your Bible to visualize it on the page.
6. Write the verse on a card or put it in your phone, including the Scripture reference and the topic it addresses. This allows you to relate the verse to a particular subject and enables you to find it when a need arises.
7. Place the written verse in prominent places so you can review it while you do other tasks. Put it over the kitchen sink, on the bathroom mirror, on your desk, on the dashboard of your car for reviewing at stoplights, or any place you will see it often.
8. Meditate on the verse savoring each word. Say it over and over emphasizing a different word each time. Turn the meaning around by adding a "not" to the verse. This will help you see the positive truth in context.
9. Use these activities to set a verse in your mind: see it in pictorial form; sing it making up your own tune; pray it back to God; practice it by making it a part of your life; and use it as often as possible.
10. Review, review, review. This is the most important secret of Scripture memorization. Review a new verse at least once a day for six weeks. Review the verse weekly for the next six weeks and then monthly for the rest of your life.
11. Have someone check quoting the verse or write the verse from memory and check it yourself.

12. Make Scripture memorization fun. Make a game of it. Get people to ask you any verse you have memorized at any time. This can be fun if a partner is also memorizing verses.

My evaluation of how much Scripture memory is a habit of my life:

1 2 3 4 5

My plan to make this a habit of my life:

....

....

My schedule for improving on this discipline: ....

5. Meditate on the Word

Another way you live in the Word and the Word lives in you is to think about it or meditate on it. *"His delight is in the law of the Lord, and on his law he meditates day and night"* (Psalm 1:2-3). Memorizing puts God's Word in your head. Meditating puts it in your heart.

You meditate on God's Word when you focus on a specific verse of Scripture such as Philippians 4:13, and chew on it and digest it until you have fully understood it. You may meditate a few minutes each day, concentrating on one verse a week. Select a verse you want to memorize or which has been a key verse in a passage you have just read. Ask the Holy Spirit for His revelation as you meditate. You may use some or all of these ideas:

Here are some practical ways to meditate on God's Word. Circle those you will try.

1. Read the verses before and after to establish the theme and setting. These will aid you in interpretation. Then you may write a summary of the passage.

2. Write the verse(s) in your own words. Say your paraphrase aloud.
3. Read the verse over and over again, emphasizing a different word each time you repeat it. For example, in the verse *"I can do all things through Christ who strengthens me"* (Philippians 4:13 KJV), first emphasize the word "I", then the word "can" and so on so that each word yields its full impact.
4. State the opposite meaning of the verse: e.g. "I cannot do anything if Christ does not strengthen me." What impact does the verse have now?
5. Write at least two important words from those you have emphasized in the verse. Ask these questions about the two words to relate the Scripture to your needs: What? Why? When? Where? Who? How?
6. Personalize the verse: Let the Holy Spirit apply the verse to a need, a challenge, an opportunity, or a failure in your life. What will you do about this verse as it relates to your life? Be specific.
7. Pray the verse back to God. Put your own name or situation in the verse.
8. Refer to other passages that emphasize the truth of the verse. List thoughts or ideas you might not understand or might have difficulty applying in your life. Seek out instruction or help in these areas.
9. Write a way you can use the verse to help another person.

My evaluation of how much meditation is a habit of my life:

....
....

1 2 3 4 5

My plan to make this a habit of my life:

....

....

My schedule for improving on this discipline: ....

> Your great challenge in developing self-control and leading like Jesus is that your human ego causes you to try to attain the worthiness of the unconditional love that is already yours.

Do not be overwhelmed by all the ways you can apply Scripture to your daily life. Begin to systematically master one skill at a time. As you grow in your application of the Word the other ways to use it will be more meaningful for you. If you need to go back and adjust your schedule to give yourself-more time please do. The direction you are going is more important than when you get there.

Habit #4: The Habit of Accepting and Abiding in God's Unconditional Love

"For God so loved the world that He gave His one and only Son, that whoever believes in Him shall not perish but have eternal life" (John 3:16).

Embracing the reality that God loves you

Your great challenge in developing self-control and leading like Jesus is that your human ego causes you to try to attain the worthiness of the unconditional love that is already yours.

It hurts your pride to accept that you cannot increase God's love for you by anything you do. He loves you totally and unconditionally as much today as He ever has or ever will. He cannot love you more; His love for you is perfect. It is breathtaking to even get a glimpse of how much He loves you and what it cost Him.

The implications of God's personal, unchanging, unrestrained, love for you and me are enormous. So enormous that it may seem easier to treat it as a concept that is beyond your comprehension and not even try to understand it. If you do, you leave the dearly purchased gift unopened and the joy of the giver unrealized.

The power of unconditional love is lived out in your relationships. For example, whenever we ask parents to raise their hands if they love their kids, all their hands go up. When we ask them if they love them only if they're successful, all the hands eventually go down. You love your kids unconditionally, right? If God's love for you was up for grabs based on your performance to the standards that His righteousness requires, you would never have another moment free from anxiety. What if you accept God's unconditional love for your life? What if you admit that you can't earn enough, achieve enough, or control enough to get any more love?

> Do you have enough faith in God's character and His promises to surrender to His love for you and give up control?

You already have all the love there is in and through Jesus! That is so powerful! Once you believe that you're perfectly, unconditionally loved, you won't get misled by earthly things. A teenager once said to the late missionary, Avery Willis, "I am afraid that if I really surrender to God that He will send me to Africa as a missionary." Avery replied, "If someone says that they will do anything you ask, would you punish them by making them do what they did not want to do? God loves you and He will only ask you to do what is for His glory and your good. Now He may have to change your heart so you are willing. Ask any missionary in Africa and he or she will tell you they are happier in the middle of God's love in Africa than they would be anywhere else in the world."

Do you have enough faith in God's character and His promises to surrender to His love for you and give up control?

Will you open your leadership to the influence of the love you have received? Check one of the following responses:

☐ Yes, I totally accept God's unconditional love for me and will live in that reality.
☐ Yes, I accept as true God's love for me, but I still think I must be worthy of it.
☐ I want to accept the reality that God loves me unconditionally but I'm having a hard time believing it.
☐ No, it is incomprehensible to me.

TO LEAD LIKE JESUS AND DEVELOP HIS SELF-CONTROL, YOU MUST LOVE HIM

Everything that you attempt in trying to lead like Jesus and develop His control, hangs in the balance of your response to the question that Jesus asked Peter, "Do you love me?" Your answer should not be given lightly because Jesus will take it seriously. Your answer will reveal your true motivations for all you have done. Like Peter all of us have given Jesus good reason to doubt our sincerity. We all fall short—sometimes in soul-shaming ways that we can hardly admit to ourselves let alone to the one we have failed.

Read John 21:15–19 and answer the question, in what ways did Jesus expect Peter to prove that He loved Him more than anything?

> *When they had finished eating, Jesus said to Simon Peter, "Simon son of John, do you truly love me more than these?" "Yes, Lord," he said, "you know that I love you." Jesus said, "Feed my lambs." Again Jesus said, "Simon son of John, do you truly love me?" He answered, "Yes, Lord, you know that I love you." Jesus said, "Take care of my sheep." The third time he said to him, "Simon son of John, do you love me?" Peter was hurt because Jesus asked him the third time, "Do you love me?" He said, "Lord, you know all things; you know that I love you." Jesus said, "Feed my sheep. I tell you the truth, when you were younger you*

dressed yourself-and went where you wanted; but when you are old you will stretch out your hands, and someone else will dress you and lead you where you do not want to go." Jesus said this to indicate the kind of death by which Peter would glorify God. Then he said to him, "Follow me!"

How did Jesus expect Peter to prove that He loved Him more than anything? ....

....

Do you love God enough to love His sheep—His lost sheep? Jesus had a right to suspect Peter's love after his denial at His trial. Jesus always has the right to ask the question, *"Do you love me?"* He did not ask Peter if he feared Him, respected Him, or admired Him, but He asked, *"Do you love me?"* Jesus wants to see evidence that you love Him. Jesus said, *"Inasmuch as you have done it to one of the least of these, you have done it unto me"* (Matthew 25:40). Jesus says that how you treat other people is how you treat Him.

What do you want to tell Jesus now about His unconditional love? What commitment will you make about loving Him unconditionally? Will you let Him love others unconditionally through you? Stop now and tell Him what is on your heart.

Habit #5: Maintaining Supportive Relationships

"As iron sharpens iron, so one man sharpens another"
(Proverbs 27:17).

Leadership is a very lonely business. When we rely on our own perspective of how we are doing, we are bound to slip into convenient rationalizations and blind spots that can quickly undermine our integrity and the trust of those who look to us for leadership.

Truth-Tellers

> Having truth-tellers in your life is probably the greatest resource for growth that you can have.

We all need trusted truth-tellers, preferably those not directly impacted by what we do, who can help us keep on course. If you can't name any active truth-tellers in your life or you have avoided or undervalued the ones you have, it's time to change.

Having truth-tellers in your life is probably the greatest resource for growth that you can have.

Too often in organizations, self-serving leaders cut off feedback by killing the messenger. Eventually the leader is fired, and although people had been available who could have given him or her helpful information, these leaders cut off the opportunity to grow. Feedback is a gift. If somebody gives you a gift, what do you say to them? "Thank you." Then you ask more questions to understand what is being said and why such as, "Where did you get it? Are there any special instructions to help me use it? Can you tell me more about it? Who else do I need to ask about it?"

Bring truth-tellers into your life, and they will tell you the truth if they know you'll listen. It doesn't mean you have to do everything that they say, but they want to be heard. And in the process if you'll share some of your vulnerability, then the give-and-take is fabulous.

> *"Two are better than one, because they have a good return for their work: if one falls down, his friend can help him up. But pity the man who falls and has no one to help him up.... Though one may be overpowered, two can defend themselves. A cord of three strands is not quickly broken"*
> (Ecclesiastes 4:9–10, 12).

Name some truth tellers in your personal life and in your leadership role:

Who would you like to choose to be a truth teller in your life?

Let me encourage you to contact that person and work out an accountability relationship with regular times of truth telling.

Being open to feedback from other people is not the only way to grow. Being willing to disclose vulnerabilities to other people is another. We're all vulnerable. We all fall short.

Don't be afraid to share your vulnerability. It's one of the most powerful things you can do to build a team and to build relationships with people you're leading.

> Don't be afraid to share your vulnerability. It's one of the most powerful things you can do to build a team and to build relationships with people you're leading.

They know you're not perfect, so don't act as if you were. More times than not they know it long before you reveal it.

Disclosing your vulnerabilities doesn't mean expressing all your inner thoughts. Rather, you want to share task–relevant information, struggles you're working on as a leader. If a truth–teller said that you're not a good listener, then what a wonderful thing to come in front of that team and share that. "Bill was kind enough to share feedback with me about my listening. I didn't realize that when you say things to me, I jump right on to my own agenda. But now I know and I would like to improve it, and the only way I can improve it is if you will help me." *"Wounds from a friend can be trusted, but an enemy multiplies kisses"* (Proverbs 27:6).

Name some times when you have been vulnerable as a leader and willing to share this with others. What was the result of your disclosure?

....

....

....

....

Small Group Accountability Fellowship

Throughout His earthly ministry, Jesus had all kinds of relationships with all kinds of people, but He maintained a special, intimate relationship with a small group of His disciples. To put things in perspective, Jesus had hundreds, or even thousands, of people flocking to Him everywhere He went. There were dozens of men and women who followed Him consistently from town to town. And yet He had twelve specially chosen disciples to whom He entrusted His mission, and three inner-circle confidants–Peter, James, and John–to lean on in crucial times. All of us need someone or several someones who love us unconditionally enough to still be our friend no matter what they learn about us.

In Mark 9:2–12, we are told that Jesus took Peter, James, and John with Him to a high mountain and revealed to them the full reality of His God nature on the Mount of Transfiguration.

> Jesus demonstrated peace most when everything around Him seemed to be in conflict.

There He instructed them to keep what they had observed in confidence. In Mark 14:33, Jesus again gathered the same three men to Himself-as He approached the crucifixion. Jesus demonstrated how much He valued the fellowship of those who knew Him best by taking them into the inner circle of His suffering in Gethsemane. As we commit to becoming more like Jesus in our leadership service, it is vital that we don't miss the important example Christ provided on how to combat the loneliness and isolation that can often be a part of being a leader.

If you are to maintain and grow in your daily walk as Jesus–like leaders, you need similar relationships. The temptations and challenges to be an ego–driven and fear–motivated leader are going to continue and probably intensify. The value of having a safe harbor relationship of support and accountability cannot be overemphasized.

> *"Let us consider how we may spur one another on toward love and good deeds. Let us not give up meeting together . . . but let us encourage one another"* (Hebrews 10:24-25).

Practicing the Habits Gives you Peace

Peace may sound like a strange characteristic in a leader. However, Jesus, the Prince of Peace, exhibited it throughout His ministry. Peace is an attractive trait in a leader and many leaders rise to power on promises of peace.

Jesus demonstrated peace most when everything around Him seemed to be in conflict.

People sense when a leader is in control of himself and has explicit faith in what he is doing.

Look at the following examples and match the response of Jesus to a difficult situation by writing the number of the event next to Jesus's response

1. During a storm at sea   .... Jesus withdrew to a mountain alone
2. When Jesus was on trial   .... Jesus told disciples to put up their swords
3. When He was accused of being demon possessed   .... Jesus calmly walked by a crowd
4. When Judas betrayed Him   .... Jesus taught calmly
5. When the people of Nazareth tried to throw Him over a cliff   .... Jesus called him a friend

6. When the soldiers came to arrest Him   .... Jesus was silent

7. When the people wanted to make Him King by force   .... Jesus was asleep

No wonder the *"People were overwhelmed with amazement." He has done everything well,' they said"* (Mark 7:37). Did you match the events in this order to which Jesus responded? 7, 6, 5, 3, 4, 2, 1. Even if you did not match them, you can see that Jesus demonstrated the quality of peace in all kinds of situations with different kinds of people.

Where did Jesus get this peace? He totally depended on the Father.

"Jesus gave them this answer: "I tell you the truth, the Son can do nothing by himself; he can do only what he sees his Father doing, because whatever the Father does the Son also does. For the Father loves the Son and shows him all he does. Yes, to your amazement he will show him even greater things than these" (John 5:19-20).

> Jesus said He gives peace that passes understanding because even in the midst of all kinds of conflict, you can have peace.

When the soldiers arrested Him in the garden, He told the disciples to put up their swords because, Jesus said, *"Do you think I cannot call on my Father, and he will at once put at my disposal more than twelve legions of angels?* (Matthew 26:53).

Where do you get such peace as a leader? From Jesus. He said, *"Peace I leave with you; my peace I give you. I do not give to you as the world gives. Do not let your hearts be troubled and do not be afraid"* (John 14:27). The world thinks peace is absence of conflict.

Jesus said He gives peace that passes understanding because even in the midst of all kinds of conflict, you can have peace.

Peace is a gift from God. *"I have told you these things, so that in me you may have peace. In this world you will have trouble. But take heart! I have overcome the world"* (John 16:33).

Doesn't it make you want to follow a leader like that? The same will be true with those who follow you. When everyone else is losing their head, they will look to see how the leader is reacting. The reason we included this tool as a means to develop self-control is because if you practice what we have been teaching you about the Habits you will develop a relationship with Jesus that will give you the fruit of the Spirit which includes and is anchored by self-control.

> "But the fruit of the Spirit is love, joy, peace, patience, kindness, goodness, faithfulness, gentleness and self-control. Against such things there is no law" (Galatians 5:22–23).

Whenever you realize you don't have peace and feel like your life is out of control, review the Habits to see if you are in tune with the Prince of Peace.

COACHING QUESTIONS

In this 2nd phase of EIC ask yourself:

When I notice strong negative emotions coming up inside me, what percentage of the time do I try to work through them myself?

....

....

....

....

What environments trigger a negative emotional response for me?

....

....

....

....

What do I want to remember about how Jesus handled His emotions when faced with potential triggers around Him?

_____
_____
_____

What was His intentional choice of response when He faced the devil in the wilderness in Luke 4?

_____
_____
_____

The tool I commit to apply in my life in order to expand the EIC behavior of Self-Control is (review "Tools for Application" on page 92.)

_____
_____
_____

Write down three specific behaviors that you imagine you will notice to be different as a result of applying EIC Self-Control in Christ:

_____
_____
_____

Prayer

Dear Jesus, Your self-control in the face of agony, betrayal, and personal danger inspires me to drink from the bitter cup that You did. I recognize that You faced suffering and sorrow to and through the point of death. The same enemy that tempted You in the wilderness is after my soul. Give me the strength that You demonstrated in your darkest hour to stay true to my mission and purpose of glorifying my Father in Heaven as You did. Only by staying close to You, the vine and the source, do I have the ability to resist temptation. Your Word says that when tempted, You will provide a way out so that I can endure. I stand on Your Word and submit to Your will. When the challenges in my day overwhelm me with negative thoughts and strong feelings, please guide me towards the right behavior. And, when I fail, please give me the grace to lovingly grow from my mistakes and exert mastery over my future thoughts, feelings, and behavior. I love You, Lord Jesus, and it is in Your holy, majestic, and almighty name I pray. Amen!

CHAPTER 5

BEHAVIOR 3: ALTRUISTIC ATTITUDE (SOCIAL-AWARENESS)

"When the Son of Man comes in his glory, and all the angels with him, he will sit on his glorious throne. All the nations will be gathered before him, and he will separate the people one from another as a shepherd separates the sheep from the goats. He will put the sheep on his right and the goats on his left. Then the King will say to those on his right, 'Come, you who are blessed by my Father; take your inheritance, the kingdom prepared for you since the creation of the world. For I was hungry and you gave me something to eat, I was thirsty and you gave me something to drink, I was a stranger and you invited me in, I needed clothes and you clothed me, I was sick and you looked after me, I was in prison and you came to visit me.'" (Matthew 25:31-36).

Chapter Contents
- Define the Trait
- Biblical Examples
- Focused Case Study
- Tools for Application
- Coaching Questions
- Prayer

Altruism is the unselfish concern for other people—doing things simply out of a desire to help, not because you feel obligated to out of guilt, shame, duty, loyalty, or religious reasons.

Behavior 3: Altruistic Attitude (Social-Awareness)

In this chapter, we will address Altruistic Behavior.

Altruism is the unselfish concern for other people—doing things simply out of a desire to help, not because you feel obligated to out of guilt, shame, duty, loyalty, or religious reasons.

It refers to behavior that benefits another individual at a cost to oneself. There are countless examples all around the world of altruistic behavior, involving people giving up their money, energy, time, and resources to help others in spite of themselves. These can be as simple as giving an umbrella to someone older when you see them standing in pouring rain without one or as complex as putting your life in danger to defend someone. Altruistic behavior is the act of giving up something or yourself-for the benefit of another.

So why would we bother to care about others versus ourselves?

If you look to science, you will find numerous studies have shown that altruism, and random acts of kindness, are good for our health and can measurably enhance your peace of mind. When we implement acts of kindness, it causes a release of hormones that contribute to our mood and overall well-being by boosting endorphins that promote a positive mindset. Our predisposition to help others is believed to have arisen via the association between altruism and pleasant emotions so when we behave altruistically, we are emotionally rewarded.

It is also believed that amongst diverse human populations, there is consistent support of kin selection. Kin selection occurs when an animal engages in self-sacrificial behavior that benefits the genetic fitness of its relatives. The theory of kin selection is one of the foundations of the modern study of social behavior, whose examples can be seen in food sharing, political alliances, and passing of wealth, to name a few. Science thus termed a phrase called prosocial behavior meaning

> In order to know the source of altruistic behavior or any of the EIC behaviors you must first know God and His Word.

behavior that benefits other people or society as a whole, acting out in our helping, sharing, donating, cooperating, or volunteering.

Although science works to study behaviors of the physical and natural world through observation and experiment, we as Christians go to the Source of everything including science for answers.

In order to know the source of altruistic behavior or any of the EIC behaviors you must first know God and His Word.

Genesis tells us that in the beginning, when God created heaven and the earth, the Spirit of God moved upon the face of the waters. God went further to create human beings with the deliberate intention of having us experience and express the love that exists between the Father, Son, and Holy Spirit.

Genesis 1:26 (KJV) says, *"And God said, let us make man in our image, after our likeness: and let them have dominion over the fish of the sea, and over the fowl of the air, and over the cattle, and over all the earth, and over every creeping thing that creepeth upon the earth."*

Throughout the Scriptures, "heart" is used to describe the personality of God's people. This heart, given to us by God during our creation, is responsible for our having the likeness of God, including His heart that is full of love, influencing our altruistic behavior. You will find several intellectual activities of the heart that are specifically mentioned in Scripture and one important one speaks to our thinking with our hearts.

Philippians 4:8 says, *"Finally, brothers and sisters, whatever is true, whatever is noble, whatever is right, whatever is pure, whatever is lovely, whatever is admirable—if anything is excellent or praiseworthy—think about such things."*

So, what does this look like as we communion with the larger body of Christ?

> The altruistic emotionally intelligent Christian gives generously of time and resources for no personal gain, and often at personal risk.

We, as individuals, contribute to the Christian ecosystem in a unique, selective, and special way. As immortal spirits, we are made in God's image, housed in the flesh, with His characteristics. This sets us apart from other animals because we have the remarkable ability to relate to God. This relatability is the source of our altruistic behavior. A further aspect of man's God-image is described in Genesis 1:28–29. A man was given authority over all living creatures and was to fill and subdue the earth. In His image, God has absolute control, and man is to exercise delegated control over his environment.

God tells us that this behavior is the attitude of Christ and obeying him is our ultimate reward.

In Philippians 2:5, God (through Paul) says, *"You must have the same attitude as Christ."*

This tells us that God's intention for us to be altruistic is by no accident. It is a natural tendency that He gave to humanity. Giving to others often feels good and can result in unexpected gains for the giver and was given to us by God. Compassion to pain, the need for help, children's excitement when sharing are just a few examples.

Altruism in the Bible is also the fundamental message of Jesus, teaching us to help others through sacrifice.

The altruistic emotionally intelligent Christian gives generously of time and resources for no personal gain, and often at personal risk.

In the overview, we suggested that being emotionally intelligent in Christ occurs when you establish a deeper relationship with Him. This is a significant theme of the Bible as far back as the Mosaic Law (Exodus 22:22–24, Deuteronomy 10:18, 14:28–29, 27:19), where the Bible records God's desire that His people care for the widows, the orphans, and the poor in their communities. God commanded that His people *"Love your*

> It is love that moves us into the realm of Emotional Intelligence in Christ, and altruism is love in action.

neighbor as yourself (Mark 12:31)," and this command takes an altruistic heart.

This means being more like Him so you can develop His attitude. Remember that Jesus pointed out that one of the greatest commands comes before the second greatest command–love the Lord your God with all of your heart, mind, soul, and strength, followed by loving your neighbor as yourself (Mark 12:30-31).

An essential reflection here is to fill up with the intimacy of God first. Then from that overflow of encountering God's love, you are in a position to love your neighbor in a healthy portion, without depleting yourself. Take time to ground yourself-and harness the power within your heart to achieve what is given to you. To deny ourselves in the context that Jesus speaks of, we must first experience the overwhelming, never-ending love of God.

It is love that moves us into the realm of emotional intelligence in Christ, and altruism is love in action.

We love because God first loved us, as the Apostle John says in 1 John 4:19.

To further this, let's look at the things that separate us from God. The "natural man" or sometimes "carnal mind" used in the Scriptures refers to something that separates us from God.

The person without the Spirit does not accept the things that come from the Spirit of God but considers them foolishness, and cannot understand them because they are discerned only through the Spirit. The person with the Spirit makes judgments about all things, but such a person is not subject to merely human judgments, for, "Who has known the mind of the Lord so as to instruct him?" But we have the mind of Christ (1 Corinthians 2:14-16).

It is easy to surrender to our "natural man" or ego. The ego is that part of our fleshly side that craves popularity, position, passion, and possessions. Ego has been commonly referenced as the acronym: Edging God Out. It craves the shiny objects of the world and is fueled by selfish ambitions and vain conceit. When we replace God as the one we worship, our source of security and self-worth, and as our audience, and judge of our life decisions, we end up craving the shiny objects that will never satisfy us.

The ego, by definition, is a person's sense of self-esteem or self-importance. It acts in "self-interested" or "selfish" or "egoistic" behavior that is motivated solely by the desire to benefit oneself. The *ego* is who we think we are. But who we *think* we are is not who we *really* are and is far from the nature of God. When the ego takes over, altruistic behavior is lost, and we lose sight of the teaching and love of Christ.

Your source, Jesus Christ of Nazareth, will help you yield to the ego and embrace the love needed for effective compassion and service and the power of the Holy Spirit in and through you. Mark 12:31 says, *"Love your neighbor as yourself."* This also means you will never love another any more than you love yourself-and you will only love yourself-when you know you are loved by God, which leads you to care for yourself.

> Remember that the whole is greater than the sum of its parts, and that each part must continually work toward the altruistic nature He desires for us.

Remember that we are an important element of Christ's Ecosystems, His community. The body of Christ ecosystems is made up of several different kinds of communities sharing resources that help each survive in a more cooperative environment. Ecosystems shouldn't work in silos but rather in unity towards God's strategy.

In the next chapter the idea of ecosystems and how they work toward the whole of God's Kingdom is explored in social management, but for now, concentrate your thoughts on the role you play individually to support the growth and strength of God's ecosystem as a whole.

Remember that the whole is greater than the sum of its parts, and that each part must continually work toward the altruistic nature He desires for us.

A Biblical Example

A great example of altruistic behavior in Christ is showcased in the famous Good Samaritan parable found in Luke 10:25–37:

> *"A man was going down from Jerusalem to Jericho when robbers attacked him. They stripped him of his clothes, beat him, and went away, leaving him half dead. A priest happened to be going down the same road, and when he saw the man, he passed by on the other side. So too, a Levite, when he came to the place and saw him, passed by on the other side. But a Samaritan, as he traveled, came where the man was; and when he saw him, he took pity on him. He went to him and bandaged his wounds, pouring on oil and wine. Then he put the man on his donkey, brought him to an inn, and took care of him. The next day, he took out two denarii and gave them to the innkeeper. 'Look after him,' he said, 'and when I return, I will reimburse you for any extra expense you may have.'"*

As you can see, the Good Samaritan had the altruistic spirit of God for his neighbor.

Jesus recognized that He could do nothing by Himself: *"Very truly, I tell you, the Son can do nothing by himself; he can do only what he sees his Father doing because whatever the Father does, the Son also does"* (John 5:19).

> Altruism, therefore, begins with God and is reflected in us when we mirror His goodness.

Any good we do in this world is a ramification of our being linked to the heart of our good God. Jesus expands on this concept in John 15:5 when He invites followers to remain in the vine: *"I am the vine; you are the branches. If you remain in me and I in you, you will bear much fruit; apart from me, you can do nothing."* He speaks of this relationship of remaining in Him throughout John 15. Jesus then invites us to consider the source of love more intimately in John 15:9–16:

> *"As the Father has loved me, so have I loved you. Now remain in my love. If you keep my commands, you will remain in my love, just as I have kept my Father's commands and remain in his love. I have told you this so that my joy may be in you and that your joy may be complete. My command is this: Love each other as I have loved you. Greater love has no one than this: to lay down one's life for one's friends. You are my friends if you do what I command. I no longer call you servants because a servant does not know his master's business. Instead, I have called you friends, for I have made known to you everything that I learned from my Father. You did not choose me, but I chose you and appointed you so that you might go and bear fruit—fruit that will last—and so that whatever you ask in my name, the Father will give you. This is my command: Love each other."*

Altruism therefore, begins with God and is reflected in us when we mirror His goodness.

Jesus is God's message to humanity. Jesus is the light of the world who clarifies the meaning and destiny of human existence.

Luke 10:27 says, *"Love the Lord your God with all your heart and with all your soul and with all your strength and with all your mind'; and, 'Love your neighbor as yourself."*

The above verse beautifully explains how altruism works. Selfless concern for other peoples is made possible through our personal experience with the love of God. God's way of giving is our only example of genuine altruism. Although it is impossible to be as perfect as God, we can develop His character by being gracious, generous, and lending to the needy without regret. When we practice being altruistic, we learn, in a small way, to be like both the Father and the Son. The Holy Spirit is the driving force from our personal relationship with Christ that creates that selfless concern for the well-being of others. Invite the Holy Spirit to help you to think less of yourself-and more of the people around you.

Have you ever noticed the joy, purpose, and peace you experience when you do a random act of kindness for another person? That is God's love in action, the simple definition of altruism and your greatest place of purpose.

Don't let the troubles of this world affect the sharing of God's love. Even with the current complexities of our global world, we can still be engaged with one another through altruistic behavior. Being truly altruistic takes us having the heart of Jesus and listening to His calling for you. It starts with a friendship with Jesus Christ. Status, other people's opinions, or judgment should not influence you, but rather look at the question of "What Would Jesus Do?" and act on it as He would.

To continue these examples, let's look at Daniel and how he exhibited the altruism of Jesus. In a brief historical summation of Daniel's life, you will see the significant influence that the climate of the time had on him. Nebuchadnezzar ruled Babylon from 605 to 562 BC and was an able but cruel ruler stopping at nothing for conquest. He put Jerusalem in horror and exiled the Israelites to Babylon. This new ruler took away Daniel's heritage, culture, and ability to worship by the laws of Moses. But this story shows how being altruistic happens in even the most difficult situations if you model the behavior of Jesus.

As the story proceeds, Daniel and his friends, Hananiah, Mishael, and Azariah, were taken captive and trained for the Babylon service as wise men for the King. Part of their training was induction into the society and thus eating food at the King's table. According to Jewish law, the Jews were forbidden from eating any unclean animals, including any meat offered to idols. While at the King's table, Daniel noticed what was being served.

Nebuchadnezzar's table contained both unclean animals and meat offered to idols. Daniel was now faced with a decision to compromise his integrity before God and conform to the King's command or stand on his commitment to God and face the wrath of the King, which would mean certain death.

> As this points out, we can exercise God's love and His altruistic leadership under the most challenging circumstances.

Daniel's decision is recorded in the text, *"But Daniel purposed in his heart that he would not defile himself with the portion of the king's meat, nor with the wine which he drank: therefore he requested of the prince of the eunuchs that he might not defile himself"* (Daniel 1:8).

Daniel decided to obey God rather than man but not by refusing to eat what was at the table of the King. He did this through altruistic behavior by not putting Ashpenaz, whose care he was placed under, in danger. Instead, Daniel used an altruistic leadership approach by respecting all involved and keeping his actions consequences with all in mind. His solution was to fast in faith from food for ten days, only drinking just water.

In the Scripture, it tells us that Daniel's and his friends "countenances were, at the end of the ten days, fairer and fatter in the flesh than all the children which did eat the portion of the king's meat" (Daniel 1:15).

As this points out, we can exercise God's love and His altruistic leadership under the most challenging circumstances.

Daniel's altruistic approach demonstrated concern and respect for both his immediate superior and his friends.

> Daniel's motivation started with a personal relationship with God. Because of that relationship, he was able to extend altruistic behavior to others.

There were many other examples of Daniel's altruistic leadership, but the most impressive thing to note is the motivation behind the behavior.

Daniel's motivation started with a personal relationship with God. Because of that relationship, he was able to extend altruistic behavior to others.

This altruistic love shouldn't be hard for us to find as it was the same love that God gave us through His Holy Spirit and embedded in our hearts.

Focused Case Study

As you have read, Altruistic Behavior is an essential behavior for being emotionally intelligent in Christ.

But what does it look like in action?

The following is a robust case study[10] that showcases the Emotional Intelligence of Christ in altruistic behavior during the death and resurrection of Lazarus. As we dig deeper into this case study, we will begin to notice the differences in Jesus's behavior as he individually spoke to both sisters on the death of their brother Lazarus:

Bethany, a small village, was home to Mary and Martha and their brother Lazarus. According to the Gospel (John 11), the miracle of Lazarus's resurrection took place there. Jesus loved Lazarus and his sisters. When Lazarus became sick, Mary and Martha sent a message to Jesus asking him to come to help, and when Jesus heard of Lazarus's death, he wept and was greatly saddened.

Although Lazarus had been entombed for four days by the time Jesus arrived at Bethany, he was raised by Jesus from the dead and emerged from the tomb wearing his burial clothes. This was the miracle of his resurrection witnessed by many Jews.

John 11:1–7; 12–15:

---

10 Ken Voges, copyright, In His Grace, Inc., Houston Texas 1997

> *"Now a man named Lazarus was sick. He was from Bethany, the village of Mary and her sister Martha. (This Mary, whose brother Lazarus now lay sick, was the same one who poured perfume on the Lord and wiped his feet with her hair.) So the sisters sent word to Jesus, "Lord, the one you love is sick." When he heard this, Jesus said, "This sickness will not end in death. No, it is for God's glory so that God's Son may be glorified through it." Now Jesus loved Martha and her sister and Lazarus. So when he heard that Lazarus was sick, he stayed where he was two more days, and then he said to his disciples, 'Let us go back to Judea.' His disciples replied, 'Lord, if he sleeps, he will get better.' Jesus had been speaking of his death, but his disciples thought he meant natural sleep. So then he told them plainly, 'Lazarus is dead, and for your sake I am glad I was not there, so that you may believe. But let us go to him.'*

Let's take a look at the Biblical DISC profiles of Martha and Mary

Martha a High D, was the oldest, meticulous, controlling homemaker and appears to be the owner of the family home. She was open to hospitality and welcomed Jesus whenever he was in town. Because of her High D, style she was heavily task driven.

> When applying the EIC methodology, we look at the encounter, identifying behavior and course correction.

Mary, a High S, was the middle sibling, quiet and empathetic. Because of her High S style, she was very feeling driven.

Lazarus was the youngest and a respected member of the community.

When applying the EIC methodology, we look at the encounter, identifying behavior and course correction.

EIC= ENCOUNTER + IDENTIFY BEHAVIOR + COURSE CORRECT

In looking at the encounter that Martha and Jesus had, the Scriptures tell us that as soon as Martha heard that Jesus was coming, she went to meet Him.

> *"Then Martha said to Jesus, 'Lord, if you had been here, my brother would not have died. But I know that even now, God will give you whatever you ask.' Jesus said to her, 'our brother will rise again"* (John 11:22-23).

This response is an example of how Jesus used the perfect Emotional Intelligence for Martha, a High D. His course correction was to respond with an action plan, and that was to ensure she knew that Jesus had this covered and Lazarus would resurrect.

If we now look at how the Father of Emotional Intelligence, Jesus, dealt with Mary, we will notice a quite different EIC response.

Jesus asked Martha to summon Mary. As soon as Mary heard this, she quickly got up and went to Him. When Mary came to Jesus, she fell at His feet and said the same thing her sister had said.

> *"After she had said this, she went back and called her sister Mary aside. 'The Teacher is here,' she said, 'and is asking for you.' When Mary heard this, she got up quickly and went to him. Now Jesus had not yet entered the village, but was still at the place where Martha had met him. When the Jews who had been with Mary in the house, comforting her, noticed how quickly she got up and went out, they followed her, supposing she was going to the tomb to mourn there. When Mary reached the place where Jesus was and saw him, she fell at his feet and said, 'Lord, if you had been here, my brother would not have died.' When Jesus saw her weeping, and the Jews who had come along with her also weeping, he was deeply moved in spirit and troubled. 'Where have you laid him?' He asked"* (John 11:28-34).

But Jesus handled His response to Mary differently based on her High S Style. He wept with Mary and related to her emotional state of being. In other words, He showed the same empathy and compassion for her and acted on it.

> As emotionally intelligent Christians, we must understand how to work as Jesus does to handle different personalities and situations.

As emotionally intelligent Christians, we must understand how to work as Jesus does to handle different personalities and situations.

We aren't made from the same cookie-cutter, so we all have different needs based on the work God has for us.

Our God is supportive and will always choose the correct response needed. Our job is to learn to model His altruistic behavior, so we can act not just out of concern for others but with the right actions that help support what a person is going through. The Holy Spirit is our virtual assistant when it comes to the ability to encounter the EIC wisdom within our hearts, identify the behavior that would best make God recognizable in the moment to the person in front of us, and act on it.

Tools for Application

In this section, we will suggest three powerful tools for developing an altruistic attitude: examining your motives, being Christ-filled, and mindful meditation. Applying these will help you immensely as you use the EIC methodology further detailed in chapter 8.

Examining Your Motives

The first helpful tool in your success toward EIC altruistic mastery involves examining your motives. A motive is a reason for doing something, especially one that is hidden or not obvious. By permitting yourself-to explore the obscure reasons for doing your acts of kindness towards another person, you open yourself-up to what the Psalmist invites us to do in Psalm 139:23–24, *"Search me, God, and know my heart; test me and know my anxious thoughts. See if there is any offensive way in me, and lead me in the way everlasting."*

As you invite the Holy Spirit into the workings of your mind, you are then in a position to shine the light of God's wisdom on thoughts that perhaps smuggle in motives that carry an attachment to elements of selfish ambition or vain conceit: *"Do nothing out of selfish ambition or vain conceit. Rather, in humility, value others above yourselves, not looking to your interests but each of you to the interests of the others"* (Philippians 2:3-4).

This conscious observation allows you to sift out the dirt while holding onto the gems of God's goodness and love for others. This, of course, is a job for the Holy Spirit: *"Holy Spirit, I permit You to sift my motives. Reveal to me any hidden agenda or selfish ambition that does not flow out of a pure heart. More of You and less of me."* Pray into your behavior the power found in declaring Philippians 2:3-4: *"Do nothing out of selfish ambition or vain conceit. Rather, in humility value others above yourselves, not looking to your own interests but each of you to the interests of the others."*

Perhaps this is what Jesus meant when He said: *"Blessed are the pure in heart, for they shall see God"* (Matthew 5:8). As you sift out the motives fueled by self-interest, you set yourself-free to offer a pure gift of selfless concern for another person, which in turn allows you to see God.

The next time you reach out to connect with someone, pause and examine your motives. Ask: what is my main desired outcome for connecting with this person? Do I have any ulterior motives that the Lord desires for me to examine? Invite the Holy Spirit within your motives: *Create in me a pure heart, oh Lord, that my motives are pure and my heart is set on You.*

> When you are Christ-filled, you can act on behaviors leading to positive relationships.

When was the last time you did something for someone yet had ulterior motives or selfish ambitions running under the radar? For example, you ask a coworker if they want an extra day off to relax and enjoy a long weekend, yet your real motive is this: you know the boss is going to be in town that day and you want to get a jump on a pitch before your coworker does.

Being Christ-Filled

A second tool in the application of an altruistic spirit is being Christ-Filled.

When you are Christ-filled, you can act on behaviors leading to positive relationships.

The Christ-filled Relationship Evaluator (C-FRE), developed by Dr. Estella Chavous, explains the need for Christians to learn, take, hear, observe, and do God's Word. Many times Christians are strong in faith but lack the strength to get through worldly challenges because of their lack of knowledge in God's Word.

> Giving the first fruits of your time and attention at the beginning of each day by inviting into your mind, will and emotions Christ's presence and guidance anchors your number one source for altruistic behavior.

Being altruistic can be supported by having a relationship with self, others, and first and foremost, Christ. An association of all three (God, self, others) involves developing the awareness, discernment, emotion, and renewal needed for effective Christ-filled relationships. Mastering Christ-filled Relationships can help build altruistism in self-and others and help to apply EIC effectively.

Giving the first fruits of your time and attention at the beginning of each day by inviting into your mind, will and emotions Christ's presence and guidance anchors your number one source for altruistic behavior.

You can't give out what you have not experienced. Begin each day by setting the emotional tone by connecting to Christ's love for you and surrendering yourself-to be used for His good purposes in other people's lives. Create mini-retreats for yourself-between each activity today and pray a Scripture into your mind, will and emotions: *Create within me a pure heart, oh Lord, and grant me a willing spirit to sustain me in this next hour that I would make You recognizable in my words, intonation and body language to the people I engage with.*

Take a moment to choose a Scripture that fills your heart and mind with a desire to be altruistic. For example, 1 John 4:19 *"We love because God first loved us."* Create a personal prayer from the Scripture you choose:

....

....

....

....

Meditation

The last and third tool is meditation. Christians often avoid meditation because they associate it with Eastern Religions. The book, *Let Meditation Mend You*, states that the Bible mentions the act of meditation 20 times and points out that the two Hebrew words for meditation, "Haga" (meaning, utter, or meditate) and "Sihach" (meaning to rehearse in one's mind or contemplate) is what we should be doing with God's Word (Drs. Chavous & Kambach, 2018).

> Meditation is the tool that lets you rehearse His Word in your heart and mind, getting fully in touch with the Holy Spirit.

Joshua 1:8 tells us the power of meditation, God's tool for instruction. *"This book of the law shall not depart out of thy mouth, but thou shalt meditate therein day and night that thou may observe to do according to all that is written for thy shall make thy way prosperous, and they shall have good success."*

You see, meditation is a powerful Biblical practice and can be used to focus deeper on God's Word and His altruistic behavior. As we meditate on God's altruistic spirit, we then can train our minds to see what He wants of us and for others. Meditation quiets your mind and enables you to be fully present in the moment. Instead of emptying our minds like other meditative practices, we as Christians fill it with His Word. Meditation will help us have the Mind of Christ by letting His Word enter into our hearts and minds.

> *"The person without the Spirit does not accept the things that come from the Spirit of God but considers them foolishness, and cannot understand them because they are discerned only through the Spirit. The person with the Spirit makes judgments about all things, but such a person is not subject to merely human judgments, for, "Who has known the mind of the Lord so as to instruct him?" But we have the mind of Christ"* (1 Corinthians 2:14–16).

As you see in Corinthians, those with the mind of Christ notice how Jesus models emotional intelligence through the power of the Holy Spirit.

Meditation is the tool that lets you rehearse His Word in your heart and mind, getting fully in touch with the Holy Spirit.

The next time you read through a passage or chapter in the Bible, read through it once. Read through it a second time and imagine what that scene or conversation must have been like, who do you identify most with in the Scripture passage? What questions do you imagine you would have had you been in that scene? Ask God those questions and be still before the Lord, listen to His response, imagine what He might say . . . go deeper in your ability to connect with the Scripture.

Journal your personal experience with the Scripture passages, meditate (think deeply and focus on) on what the Holy Spirit moves you to focus on. Ask: What do You want me to do with this Scripture today to model Jesus's altruistic behavior?

....
....
....

Coaching Questions

In this 3rd phase of EIC ask yourself:

What motives do I carry that block my ability to see life through another person's perspective?

....
....
....

How will Christ-Filled relationships help you master your altruistic nature?

....
....
....

How can meditating on God's Word help you adjust your acts of kindness to come from the heart and less from self?

....
....
....

The tool I commit to apply in my life in order to expand the EIC behavior of an Altruistic Attitude is (review "Tools for Application" on page 137).

_____

_____

_____

Write down three specific behaviors that you imagine you will notice to be different as a result of applying an Altruistic Attitude in Chris:

_____

_____

_____

Prayer

Heavenly Father, I come to You with a heart of gratefulness and thankfulness. You are constantly supplying all our needs even when we are not aware of it. We ask that You help us have the same altruistic heart You have, so we can model Your behavior to help others and build Your kingdom. We desire to be more like You in every way and live Your commandment to love thy neighbor as thyself. Thank You in advance for building this behavior in us and for the salvation You have given us.

"But I tell you that everyone will have to give account on the day of judgment for every empty word they have spoken" (Matthew 12:36).

CHAPTER 6

BEHAVIOR 4: CHRIST CONNECTIONS (RELATIONAL MANAGEMENT)

"And I saw the dead, great and small, standing before the throne, and books were opened. Another book was opened, which is the book of life. The dead were judged according to what they had done as recorded in the books" (Revelations 20:12).

CHAPTER CONTENTS
- Define the Trait
- Biblical Examples
- Focused Case Study
- Tools for Application
- Coaching Questions
- Prayer

EIC TRAIT DEFINED: CHRIST CONNECTIONS

IN THE PREVIOUS chapter, we introduced the concept of ecosystems and that the body of Christ ecosystems describes several different kinds of communities sharing resources that help us survive in a more cooperative environment. Christ connection behaviors play a vital part in the ecosystem of the body of Christ. Jesus's ministry focused on diverse community connections.

Living a Christ-filled social life keeps us away from working independently but more for the benefit of the whole.

> *"Our own body has many parts. When all these many parts are put together, they are only one body. The body of Christ is like this. It is the same way with us. Jews or those who are not Jews, men who are owned by someone or men who are free to do what they want to do, have all been baptized into the one body by the same Holy Spirit. We have all received the one Spirit"* (1 Corinthians 12:13).

Paul uses the body to illustrate how believers should be unified under one body, the body of Christ. Each individual part of the body is called to work together toward the social connections we have in our ecosystem. One of Satan's main strategies to destroy people is division. We have an abundance of theological paths and church models that affect our community. Jesus calls us all to follow Him.

> We can't make an authentic positive connection (void of selfish ambition and false motives) in relationships with other people unless we are personally connected to Christ within us.

In this final phase of EIC, Jesus first invites us into freedom in John 13:34–35: *"A new command I give you: Love one another. As I have loved you, so you must love one another. By this, everyone will know that you are my disciples if you love one another."*

We can't love other people without first encountering God's love for us through Christ (1 John 4:19) and the constant help of the Holy Spirit to remind our mind *Whose we are* in this world and why our hearts continue to beat.

We can't make an authentic positive connection (void of selfish ambition and false motives) in relationships with other people unless we are personally connected to Christ within us.

Jesus is our model and teacher for highly emotional intelligent relationships with one another.

In chapter three, we explored a ripple effect of EIC that first begins with encountering the Spirit of Christ. In this final phase of EIC, we are taking a deeper dive into the ramifications of that personal encounter with Christ in the lives of the people He entrusted to our care within the environment around us:

The Six Phase Ripple Impact for Emotional Intelligence in Christ

The Biblical DISC(R) assessment gives us insight into the specific behaviors that showcase the personality that God has blessed us with. In chapter 2, we briefly introduced the four DISC profiles. In this final phase of EIC, we are having a conversation around Christ Connections: in what ways are you aware of the emotions of other people, their DISC expressions and how well do you manage those emotions and expressions? Jesus was masterful at this, which you will see firsthand as we explore a case study later on in this chapter.

Below is a quick summary taken from Ken Voges's work on the Biblical DISC(R) of and how each DISC profile typically will solve problems. This is important to note at this point in the book because solving problems and decision making often involves other people: Christ Connections.

How you handle the emotions of other people in the midst of your connection is a game changer when it comes to your ability to manage the gifts and talents of people entrusted to your care. As you understand that not everyone sees situations the way you do or solves problems the way you do, you open yourself-up to seeing others as

Christ sees them: for who they desire to be rather than how their behavior shows up in the midst of strong emotions.

As you read through the following summary of the DISC, notice where you recognize yourself:

> **D's** are driven by control and the bottom line. High Ds solve problems like this: assess what's important => make a decision => move on with an action plan as they troubleshoot along the way. High Ds solve problems by debating your conclusions.
>
> **I's** are driven by feelings and relationships. High Is solve problems by hearing themselves speak in random thoughts. They verbally work through those thoughts and then SHAZAM, out comes a solution and it usually works.
>
> **S's** are driven by process and team. High Ss solve problems in this way: listen => process alone => visualize the solution => structure the process => account for contingencies => SHAZAM: institute a 3-cycle action plan.
>
> **C's** are driven by logic and data. This is how high Cs solve problems: collect the data => validate the data => organize the data => search for the flaw => reorganize the data => SHAZAM a plan of action. High Cs solve problems by continuing to ask validating questions.

Can you imagine the emotional flare ups that could occur as a high D works on decision making and problem solving with a high C? The D jumps in and out quickly with a solution before the C has finished collecting the essential data needed to organize and validate the data to make an effective decision.

> EIC provides the best methodology to manage diverse behaviors to strengthen the relationships with the people around us.

Bottom line, as Paul speaks about the body of Christ: *how can the eye say to the hand I don't need you?* Both offer essential ingredients for successful problem solving. The C can learn from the D how to stay out of the weeds. The D can learn from the C how to tune into important details that could result in more effective and sustainable outcomes. Paul sums this inclusive thinking up beautifully in 1 Corinthians 12:21–26:

> *"The eye cannot say to the hand, "I don't need you!" And the head cannot say to the feet, "I don't need you!" On the contrary, those parts of the body that seem to be weaker are indispensable, and the parts that we think are less honorable we treat with special honor. And the parts that are unpresentable are treated with special modesty, while our presentable parts need no special treatment. But God has put the body together, giving greater honor to the parts that lacked it, so that there should be no division in the body, but that its parts should have equal concern for each other. If one part suffers, every part suffers with it; if one part is honored, every part rejoices with it."*

EIC provides the best methodology to manage diverse behaviors to strengthen the relationships with the people around us.

A few coaching questions to ask yourself-at this point would be: Do my behaviors make God recognizable within my relationships? In what ways are they inclusive? Am I responding to Jesus's invitation to love my neighbor as myself-through behaviors that align with my encounter with Christ?

Paul knew he belonged to Christ when he wrote to the people in Corinth reminding them of the first phase of EIC: Personal Identity in Christ: *"We are therefore Christ's ambassadors, as though God were making his appeal through us. We implore you on Christ's behalf: Be reconciled to God.* (2 Corinthians 5:20).

Paul experienced a personal reconciliation with Christ and wanted everyone to experience that personal encounter with Jesus's love. Why?

> The power that flows from a Christ connection will positively transform your life and relationships. Jesus's love evokes more love.

The power that flows from a Christ connection will positively transform your life and relationships. Jesus's love evokes more love.

"*We love because God first loved us*" (1 John 4:19).

An emotionally intelligent relationship, as a follower of Jesus Christ of Nazareth, is only possible when we have personally encountered the Lord as Peter did in his own boat, Saul did on the road to Damascus, Zacchaeus did when Jesus entered his home for a meal, the adulterous woman did and walked away with a new start fueled by forgiveness and love.

The stories of people who encountered Jesus are numerous throughout the four gospels, and they all have three things in common:

1. A personal encounter with Christ's healing love, which met each person just as they were, right where they were in their life. They didn't have to change to encounter Jesus's love and forgiveness. Jesus's love and forgiveness positively changed them and their ability to connect with people.
2. A change of heart happened as a result of an encounter with Jesus. Each person who was open to receiving Jesus's love and healing was moved to repent: *to make a conscious choice to go in a different direction, in this case,*

to turn away from an offense against God towards the loving presence and forgiveness of God through Christ.

3. A changed relationship: with God, self, and *other people*. In this chapter we are focusing on other people in your life. A perfect example: after Saul encountered the love and forgiveness of Christ, instantly, he flipped from being an enemy of the followers of Jesus to be a devoted disciple and leader in their midst. His relationships with people converted from one built on selfish motives and ambitions to Christ-centered connections. His personal encounter with the love and forgiveness of Christ made all the difference in the relationships he fostered from that moment on.

> The way you proceed in this final phase of EIC is in direct proportion to your encounter with Christ's love and your willingness to allow Him to sit on the throne of your identity (phase one of EIC).

Let's take a deep dive and follow Jesus's emotionally intelligent lead as we explore how to connect with other people. This is the final phase of Emotional Intelligence in Christ, the fruit, so to speak, of your labor in the first three phases. As Paul so brilliantly wrote to the Galatians:

"Do not be deceived: God cannot be mocked. A man reaps what he sows. Whoever sows to please their flesh, from the flesh will reap destruction; whoever sows to please the Spirit, from the Spirit will reap eternal life. Let us not become weary in doing good, for at the proper time we will reap a harvest if we do not give up" (Galatians 6:7–9).

Now, remember Paul is talking about first-hand comparison when it comes to sowing to his flesh versus the spirit. He played on both sides. He knew firsthand the ramification of sowing to please the flesh and to please the Spirit. Simply put, he is a firsthand witness, therefore let us lean into the wisdom he gained from his "BC" days:

Behavior 4: Christ Connections (Relational Management)

Before he encountered Christ. He is now inviting us to give our spirit permission to guide our flesh into all things, especially our relationships with other people.

The way you proceed in this final phase of EIC is in direct proportion to your encounter with Christ's love and your willingness to allow Him to sit on the throne of your identity (phase one of EIC).

Let's pull back the curtain once again and follow the lead of our emotionally intelligent mentor Jesus Christ of Nazareth who consistently sowed to please the Spirit and as a result transformed the lives of all who were willing to believe.

Jesus did one consistent emotionally intelligent behavior that is worth our attention in the midst of a hurried culture: He allowed himself-to be interrupted for the sake of healing, restoring and loving people.

> Jesus did one consistent emotionally intelligent behavior that is worth our attention in the midst of a hurried culture: He allowed himself-to be interrupted for the sake of healing, restoring and loving people.

The result? He created connections that transformed lives forever.

Are you interruptible? Take a moment to pray in the Lord's strength and wisdom. Lean into the powerful emotionally intelligent behavior of interruptibility:

> Dear Lord, You allowed Yourself-to be interrupted for the sake of healing, encouragement, love, teachable moments and overall presence to those in need. Grant me the grace of the PAUSE to stop in the midst of all my doing and accomplishing to make myself-present to those divine appointments that allow You to be recognizable in my ability to listen, love, heal and edify those people who cross my path today. I give You permission to override my EGO and ignite my desire to surrender my agenda for the sake of one soul who needs a word of encouragement, an act of kindness, the gift of love on their journey of life. You

put people above things, over Your to-do lists and between Your travel itinerary, grant me the grace to do the same for the sake of salvation of souls, the one mission that unleashes eternity on earth. I also give You permission to interrupt me in the shadows. The place where I forget that You are bigger than circumstance and will bring about a greater good than had the trial never occurred. Interrupt me when I think I am my struggle and remind me of my identity and purpose in and through You.

In the famous Mary and Martha story in Luke 10:38–42 Jesus called Martha out in love: Martha, Martha, Martha . . . you are so caught up in all of your doing and achieving, rushing around . . . where are you going in such a hurry? You are missing the opportunity to reflect and act upon what is truly important: faith, expressing itself-through love. Love pauses. Love notices those in need. Love seeks out an opportunity to edify and encourage. Love puts the needs of another before its own. Love allows itself-to be interrupted for a greater good than the task at hand. Love returns 10-fold, abundant joy and peace to those who allow themselves to be interrupted for the sake of more love in the world.

In our society we are rushing around, so busy, we have forgotten our greatest source for joy and peace: loving and leading those around us from a place of presence, service, and humility. We have gone so far as to create barriers around ourselves to prevent interruptions so that we can accomplish what we need to accomplish. There is nothing wrong with healthy boundaries to accomplish high priorities in life. This is a behavior that offers a positive impact on business as well as effective management of a home.

The practice of preventing interruptions is good until you start to put things (accomplishments and to-do lists) above the opportunity to encourage, inspire and/or edify another human being in need that God has put in your path. This takes discernment, a highly linked trait to emotional intelligence. Jesus also interrupted people who were hijacked by their struggle: the woman caught in adultery, the woman at the well, the paralyzed man. He interrupts us when we are hiding in the shadow of our despair, judgments, positionality, fear, self-doubt, and worry.

Are you interruptible for Christ Connections in the midst of the hustle for God's love, healing, and restoration to step into the lives of the people around you?

BIBLICAL EXAMPLE IN JESUS'S LIFE

In the book of Luke, Jesus was interrupted in the midst of other tasks, including travel, approximately 23 times for the sake of making positive connections with people: Christ connections.

As you read through each passage, observe Jesus's interruptibility for the sake of human connection. Take the time to thoughtfully read through each passage and linger with it in the context of your life. Perhaps take one passage a day for 23 days to anchor in the art of interruptibility within your behavior to intentionally create room in your life for Christ connections. Write down what you notice coming up for you. Perhaps those areas where you desire to override your drive to get things done with a conscious choice to pause on your part and allow a Christ connection to emerge.

> Look for an opportunity today to do a random act of kindness and trust the results to Christ.

Biblical examples of Jesus interruptibility in the Gospel of Luke:

Luke 2:41: At the festival of Passover, Jesus stayed to learn and ask questions in His Father's House . . . His parents realized He was not with them and after 3 days found Him. As a young boy, Jesus paused to embrace the opportunity to listen, ask questions, and learn. How often do you listen, ask questions and learn in the midst of the hustle?

Luke 4:33–35: Jesus was teaching in the synagogue when a man possessed by the foul spirit of a demon interrupted Him with loud cries, yelling at Jesus: "I know who you are - the Holy One of God!" Jesus rebuked the demon after a fit and the man was restored to his right mind. Jesus was not only teaching the way of God, He acted it out and was unattached to His preaching and teaching, willing to be interrupted for a greater good. A powerful question to ask when interrupted: "Is this mine, or someone else's?" Sometimes an interruption is an opportunity to delegate to the point person of the need at hand OR remind the person of the resources they have to work through the issue and access solutions. Be willing to be used and remain curious.

Luke 4:38–44: While visiting Simon Peter's house, Jesus heals Simon Peter's mother-in-law. Instead of taking a moment to rest and retreat Jesus is constantly called back into the mission of selfless love and healing of others. Jesus prioritized meaningful, intentional connection over tasks at hand, do you?

Luke 5:1–11: Jesus was teaching by the lake. He paused and went fishing with Peter. The result of that pause led to one of the most powerful leaders of The Way who was willing to surrender everything for the sake of preaching the Gospel message, including his life. Sometimes we give more authority to the task at hand to define who we are than to the ONE who calls us to that task.

Luke 5:12–14: In one of the towns Jesus was preaching in, He encountered a man with leprosy who asked Jesus to heal him . . . Jesus PAUSED and healed him. The result? The news about Jesus spread like wildfire and huge crowds came to hear Him and experience healing.

Look for an opportunity today to do a random act of kindness and trust the results to Christ.

He is in the multi-level marketing business and will never be outdone in generosity.

Luke 5:17: As Jesus was teaching the Pharisees and teachers of the law, He was interrupted by men who lowered their paralyzed friend through the roof in front of Him. Can you imagine in the midst of an intense lecture, keynote or presentation being interrupted midstream? Do you desire the success of others around you as much as you desire your own?

Luke 6:6: Again, Jesus is in the midst of executing a lesson plan and is interruptible to heal a man with a shriveled hand on the Sabbath. Invite the Holy Spirit in to bump you out of selfish ambition and toss you into selflessness that will produce a harvest more than eye can see or ear can hear.

Luke 6:19: Jesus is surrounded by people who come from all over to hear him preach as well as to be healed, including those troubled by impure spirits . . . all were cured. Remember, our battle is not against flesh and blood but against the spiritual forces of evil waging war against our souls. Are you troubled by an impure spirit? Is God putting a person in your life who is troubled by an impure spirit manifesting in negative behavior? Be open to interruptions that offer the opportunity to sow seeds of hope, faith, and love.

Luke 7:2: As Jesus entered Capernaum, a centurion soldier sent elders to ask Jesus to come and heal his servant. Jesus went with them. The result? Faith unleashed to heal the servant without Jesus going to the soldier's home. This encounter stopped Jesus in His tracks. He marveled: which means Jesus was filled with wonder or astonishment: *"Dear Lord, move me into the kind of faith that the centurion soldier had. I want to fill You with wonder today because of my choice to pause, believe and take action grounded in faith for the good of the people You entrusted to my care."*

Luke 7:11: Jesus went to a town called Nain. As He approached the gate, He encountered a dead person being carried out. He was interruptible to pause and heal a distressed mother's son and flip her grief into rejoicing in God's favor. Look for the opportunity today to flip another person's frown upside down.

Luke 7:36: While dining at a Pharisee's home, Jesus was interrupted by a "sinful" woman who anoints His feet with her tears and receives forgiveness and freedom. What sin keeps talking to you? Guilt and shame are two serpents that the devil uses to keep you stuck. Jesus wants to set you free today. Invite Jesus in to do the same for you as He did for the woman–set you free.

Luke 8:23–27: Jesus was sleeping in the boat while His disciples battled a storm. Fear got the best of them and they woke Jesus. Jesus calmed the storm and said, *"Where is your faith" (Luke 8:25)*. Look for the opportunity to calm an emotional storm today with words of love and kindness.

Luke 8:26–39: Jesus lands the boat on His way to the region of Gerasenes. He is met by a demon-possessed man. He casts out a legion of evil spirits into the pigs and the man is freed. What negative emotion can you cast out in Jesus's name that is blocking your ability to make a Christ connection today?

Luke 8:40–56: On His journey, Jesus pauses to heal Jarius's daughter and a woman who was bleeding for 12 years. He was interrupted after being interrupted. How do you handle interruptions that continue to occur in your day? People before things lead to things that champion people.

> It is noted several times throughout the gospel message that Jesus was moved with compassion. Compassion means you are concerned about the suffering of other people.

Luke 9:37: Coming down off the mountain after the transfiguration Jesus pauses to respond to the plea of a man for healing of his demon possessed son. When was the last time you were worn out at the end of your day and you asked for God's strength to show up for the people entrusted to your care with love, patience and kindness?

Luke 13:10: While teaching in the synagogue on the Sabbath, a woman, a daughter of Abraham, who was crippled by an evil spirit for

18 years, bent over and could not stand moved Jesus with compassion and He paused and set her free from her infirmity.

It is noted several times throughout the gospel message that Jesus was moved with compassion. Compassion means you are concerned about the suffering of other people.

Are you? In what ways does your behavior put that concern into action?

Luke 14:2: While eating at the house of a prominent Pharisee, a man was suffering from dropsy. Again, it was the Sabbath. Jesus paused and healed him. Perhaps one of the most difficult times to allow ourselves to be interrupted is when we are taking time to push our own refresh button. Setting healthy boundaries can be accomplished in the love of Christ. Too often we will let our irritations spill over into our expressions or allow other people's irritations trigger us. Next time you are interrupted during your own time of refreshment invite the Holy Spirit into your intonation, body language and facial expressions to communicate with kindness. Make Christ recognizable.

Luke 18:15–17: Jesus allowed the children to jump into His conversation. The disciples tried to keep the children from Jesus and Jesus invited them closer. Why do you think Jesus said that unless you change and become like little children you will not enter the kingdom of God in Matthew 18:3? Are children interruptible?

Luke 18:35–42: As Jesus was on His way to Jericho a blind man was on the roadside begging . . ."Jesus, Son of David . . . have mercy on me!" The disciples rebuked him but Jesus stopped and invited the man to His side: "What do you want me to do for you?" The man replied, "Lord, I want to see." His sight was restored! Imagine Jesus asking you that question today: "What do you want me to do for you?" In light of our desire to master emotional intelligence in Christ within our relationships, in what ways would you respond to that question?

Luke 19:1–9: Jesus was interrupted by Zacchaeus the tax collector. He paused and went to his house, ate with his friends and as a result

Zacchaeus repented from his sinful ways and salvation entered his life. Jesus was constantly on the lookout to seek and save the lost. Whose life do you want to enter into and make Jesus recognizable to today?

Luke 21:1–4: Jesus paused and noticed the widow's humble offering . . . think small, not BIG . . . Jesus honors the small humble acts of love and kindness. Do more of that today.

Luke 23:26: Jesus paused in the midst of the crucifixion to speak to the women who were weeping. Who does that? Jesus does. Ask for the ability to love others well in the midst of your own pain. Don't waste your suffering, make it meaningful. Lift up your suffering for the sake of the salvation of souls and the suffering of others.

Luke 23:34: On the cross, Jesus paused and prayed for the people: *"Father, forgive them they don't know what they are doing."* A powerful prayer to explore: *Dear Lord, help me to see others for who they desire to be rather than how their behavior shows up. Give me the grace to know that bad behavior often walks hand-in-hand with personal pain.*

Luke 23:40–43: Jesus was interrupted on the cross by the criminal who said: *"Remember me, Jesus, when you enter your Kingdom."* Jesus showed compassion and love in the midst of His intense suffering: *"Today you will be with me in paradise."* Pray for those who push your buttons and persecute you. Ask God to give you an opportunity to love them as Jesus loves them. This is a powerful behavior that opens the door for Christ connections.

> Use words that build people up today. Meet people where they are and lead them to higher ground by maintaining a centered and objective manner. Listen to understand rather than to be understood.

Luke 24:13–33: Road to Emmaus. Jesus walked with the disciples and stayed with them. They did not recognize Him until He broke bread. After Jesus rose from the grave, He met the disciples where they were emotionally. He patiently walked them through what had just happened without shaming them for not having more faith.

Focused Case Study

You might remember that we used the Woman at The Well as a case study in Chapter 3 to showcase Jesus's identity, which was shared for the first time in John 4:25–26: *"The woman said, "I know that Messiah" (called Christ) "is coming. When he comes, he will explain everything to us." Then Jesus declared, "I, the one speaking to you—I am he."*

Just as Jesus's identity was grounded and connected in God, so too, the first step in Emotional Intelligence in Christ is to anchor and ground your personal identity in Christ (chapter 3). This choice allows you to be successful in the behaviors contained within the other three areas of Emotional Intelligence in Christ discussed in chapters 4: Self-Control, 5: Altruistic Attitude and 6: Christ Connections.

> In order to create Christ Connections in this final phase of Emotional Intelligence in Christ, it is essential to create safe space between the sender and receiver of communication.

Let's continue our conversation around the woman at the well case study in light of your ability to make Christ Connections pulling from Ken Voges's work on Biblical DISC profiles and the book *The 9 Arts of Spiritual Conversation* by Mary Schaller & John Crilly, the authors outline ways to engage in initial conversation that allows for one to create enough trust to move towards spiritual issues. It also gives you the ability to manage conversations with other people from a place of love as Jesus did so masterfully. They are:

Arts for Getting Ready for spiritual conversations:

- Noticing
- Praying
- Listening

Arts for Getting Started with spiritual conversations:
- Asking Questions
- Loving
- Welcoming

Arts for Keeping it going:
- Facilitating
- Serving Together
- Sharing (1.)

In order to create Christ Connections in this final phase of Emotional Intelligence in Christ, it is essential to create safe space between the sender and receiver of communication.

As you reflect back on Jesus's encounter with the woman at the well (John 4:4–26), you will notice how Jesus maintained a space of observation rather than judgment. He used at least three of the Arts mentioned above: Noticing, Asking Questions and Facilitating to communicate to the woman that He was the Messiah.

Jesus observed and *noticed* the woman was there to draw water. So, Jesus *asks a question* using a reference, water, that she was very familiar with. He requested: *"Will you give me a drink?"* (John 4:7). Jesus *facilitated* the conversation to a need for "Living Water" which led her to longing to meet the Messiah. It was at that point, Jesus first used these words: *"I, the one speaking to you, I am he"* (John 4:26). The conclusion: this woman went back to the village sharing her story of meeting the Messiah. It resulted in: *"Many of the Samaritans from the town believed in him because of the woman's testimony"* (John 4:39).

As you practice this final phase of EIC to create Christ Connections, look for opportunities to notice other people's unique operating systems (how they do life). Ask the Holy Spirit to give you good questions to learn more about the people He entrusted to your care. From those questions and what you learn, facilitate meaningful conversations and connection: Notice => Ask => Facilitate & Connect. Look for opportunities to make Christ Connections today.

Tools for Application

One of my favorite take-aways from my Master's program in Adult Education/Human Resources Development was The Ladder of Inference, created by Harvard Professor Chris Argyris. This ladder contains seven steps from what you see to what you do about it.

An inference is a conclusion reached based on evidence and reasoning. Too often when our emotions get caught between the observable data and our conclusions about that data, several unwelcomed guests take up free rent between our two ears: filters, assumptions, conclusions, and false beliefs. These unwelcomed tenants often create the reactive response of:

- Mind reading
- Fortune telling
- Catastrophizing
- All-or-nothing thinking
- Overgeneralization and/or selective attention.

Read through the list above and **Reflect on the following questions:** Where do you recognize yourself? What unwelcomed tenant frequents your mind? What is your go-to? Clarity of focus leads to accuracy of response.

> Jesus is our model when it comes to impulse control or self-control which is the second behavior of Emotional Intelligence in Christ.

Neuroscience refers to these reactive responses as bottom up thinking and produces only three choice points of response to a threatening situation: fight, flight, or freeze. When a person is in "top down" thinking, then unlimited solutions become available in the executive thinking part of the brain which fuels productive behavior. How interesting that the field of neuroscience acknowledges that the highest form of behavior flows from the "top down." We know that top down is our connection with God down through our mind, will and emotions.

Can you imagine waking up tomorrow morning and miraculously during the night God gave you the ability to separate observable data from the following steps that Professor Chris Argyris put into a ladder format? Guess what? He did give you the ability to stay off the stage of drama and stay in **Observable Data**, which is the first step on the Ladder of Inference, followed by:

- **Filters:** your knowledge, experience and values that influence how you listen, think, and communicate (*Source: Brenda Corbett & Judith Coleman, Sherpa Executive Coaching book: Be Don't Do, p 31*).
- **Assign Meaning:** based on the content you filter out, you are left with the meaning you make from what is left.
- **Assumptions:** thoughts you come up with not based on the facts. You create the story.
- **Conclusions:** blurring the lines between fact and story based on your filters and assumptions. Some behaviors that often accompany conclusions may be: stonewalling, blaming, complaining, justifying, defensiveness, ugly talk.
- **Beliefs:** based upon how you run up your ladder via your filters, assumptions, and the conclusions you make, based on that intel you create beliefs. A belief about yourself, a situation, person, or outcome.
  The beliefs you hold can directly impact your filters (selected data).
- **Actions:** Last but definitely not least, you take action based on the other five steps. This is the top of your ladder. The actions you take can directly impact the observable data. In neuro-linguistic programming (NLP), we refer to three possibilities that can occur

at this point: distorting, deleting, or generalizing the observable data in order to back up your view of reality. *Neurolinguistic Programming is a methodology used to shift thoughts and behaviors to help achieve desired outcomes.*

Which step on the Ladder of Inference do you relate to the most? The least?

One of the top qualities commonly associated with highly effective leaders is impulse control. Jesus was and is a highly effective leader. Why? Because He loves first, then leads and sometimes uses words.

> It's about being centered and objective in order to see what's really going on around you, listening to understand rather than to be understood.

Jesus is our model when it comes to impulse control or *self-control* which is the second behavior of Emotional Intelligence in Christ.

It's the ability to stay at the bottom of the ladder without getting spun up to the top. The biggest example occurred when Jesus suffered, was rejected by His closest friends, falsely accused and put to death on the cross. In spite of all of it, one of the last phrases that Jesus spoke on the cross was: *"Father forgive them, they do not know what they are doing"* (Luke 23:34).

Jesus never detoured from His mission to save souls, not once did He play the victim card or shrink back from the ultimate sacrifice needed to accomplish God's plan of salvation. He had clarity of focus for accuracy of behavioral response.

It's about being centered and objective in order to see what's really going on around you, listening to understand rather than to be understood.

Being able to separate fact from rumor, opinion, or gossip, commonly referred to as the FROG effect. In order to create intentional Christ Connections, our ability to remain in Christ (John 15) is essential. Without Christ within us, there are too many triggers that hijack our ability to connect.

What kind of leader are you when it comes to impulse control around your emotions? How well do you do at being centered and objective in the midst of strong emotions?

What action step do you want to commit to today based on what you have learned? Perhaps it will be to observe what triggers in your life result in climbing the Ladder of Inference and inviting the Holy Spirit into your weakness.

The Ladder of Inference tool is highly effective with the support of the Holy Spirit within your mind, will and emotions to help you create Christ Connections and avoid misunderstandings.

> Deep within the heart of mankind is a desire to be seen, accepted, and loved by God.

An excellent TedEd talk by Trevor Maber is available online entitled: *rethinking thinking* which will give you the opportunity to see the Ladder of Inference in action. Once you observe what happens in your mind, with the help of the Holy Spirit, you can then become the boss of your ladder moving forward. You will begin to intentionally stay in the observable data, resisting the urge to assume and conclude based on the meaning you create from your filters.

Jesus was observant and high-noticing with each person He encountered, this emotional intelligent trait opened up doors for profound connections, as it will for you as you model your behaviors after Christ.

Jesus loved and loves people right where they are without shrinking back from the opportunity to lead them out of captivity. For example, Jesus reflected back what He observed to the woman at the well in John 4:17: *"Jesus said to her, "You are right when you say you have no husband. The fact is, you have had five husbands, and the man you now have is not your husband. What you have just said is quite true."*

Deep within the heart of mankind is a desire to be seen, accepted, and loved by God.

When you allow yourself-to experience that encounter with Christ you are then moved to offer that same gift to the people around you. This is the ripple effect of emotional intelligence in Christ we explored in Chapter 3: first encounter and anchor your identity in Christ which spills out into your beliefs, capabilities, behavior, and environment. This final behavior in the Emotional Intelligence in Christ process is the ability to make Christ Connections within your environment: personally and professionally.

> Whenever you forget that you are here to make God recognizable to each person God entrusts to your care, it always becomes about YOU.

The Ladder of Inference is a tool to help support your ability to create clear conversations based upon different assumptions. Now moving forward, it will help you avoid misunderstandings by doing what Jesus did: keep your filters in check and stay in observable data. This allows Jesus's love to guide your perceptions and interactions with people around you.

Below is a summary of five steps to short circuit your ladder referenced by Trevor Maber in his TedEd talk with a Christ focus added:

1. Breathe out any frustration and breathe in the Holy Spirit.

2. Ask yourself: What beliefs are at play? Ask Jesus to help you see clearly and respond in love.
3. What data and observations did you filter out because of your beliefs and why?
4. Are your assumptions supported by facts? If you are wondering what someone is thinking or meaning by what they say, follow Jesus's lead and ask a clarifying question.
5. Would a different set of assumptions create different feelings? Result in new and better conclusions and actions. What would Jesus think and or conclude in this situation? Let the love of the Lord within your heart protect you from taking offense.

The next time you feel spun and disconnected because of what someone says or does, pause and notice where your focus is camping: on yourself-or Jesus? Focusing on self-sounds like this: *how I feel, what they said to me that I gave power away to that hurt my feelings.* A Jesus response sounds like this: *It's not about you. You are my ambassador and I am making my appeal through you. You are not your own ambassador making your appeal for you.*

> In order to master Emotional Intelligence in Christ your first step occurs when you personally encounter Christ.

Whenever you forget that you are here to make God recognizable to each person God entrusts to your care, it always becomes about YOU.

When we follow Jesus's lead into this 4th phase of Emotional Intelligence in Christ and remember that it's about Jesus's love through us, living and speaking through us, you will find it easier to release the tendency to take things personally. This is a grace, ask for it:

> Dear Lord, give me the grace to release all offense today so that You can use me to make Your appeal for love through me. I desire that all of my connections today are grounded in Your

loving and compassionate presence. Touch my heart so that my lips will witness to Your unconditional love.

Additional tools to explore to help improve your ability to make more Christ Connections today than yesterday

Identify specific areas in your life where you grip onto your agenda so tightly that you are unable to tune into the needs and perspectives of those around you:

- Do you feel frustrated when people interrupt you with a need that from the eternal perspective is bigger than the task at hand? For example, you are working on your computer and your child needs help with a question on homework, you say you will be right there and spend another ½ hour working on your computer OR your spouse lets you know that dinner is ready, you share that you will be right there and you continue to work on your task until dinner is cold, your spouse continues to remind you and your frustration grows.
- Have you ever been interrupted while resting and experienced resentment or anger? Consider Jesus's intense schedule packed with healing after healing, keynote presentations teaching on the Kingdom of God one after the other.
- When have you PAUSED for the sake of another in need and the result ended up edifying more than the person you helped? For example, you stop to help someone who has just dumped their purse upside down by accident as they are rushing to catch a flight. You stop and help. The result? The hurried mom of three young children made their flight which allowed them to be by the bedside of their Grandparent who was about to transition into Jesus's arms. God is the

best Multi-Level-Marketer when it comes to random acts of kindness.
- Do your actions align with what you value most in life? Do you value kindness? Do you value family? Do you value being an ambassador for Christ? Explore your behavior today and notice how your choice of response to interruptions align with what you value most . . . or not.

Ask for the grace to be attentive to the divine interruptions that God puts in your day that offer an opportunity to glorify God and express love in action or perhaps receive His love and forgiveness.

- Pause and ask, "Is this interruption an opportunity to make you recognizable in this person's life today?" To restore the dark side of my personality into His light? Perhaps it will be to simply remind the person of their ability to tune into creative solutions therefore edifying and recognizing their gifts and talents that too often get lost in the midst of high demands.

Highlight your favorite top three Scripture references from this chapter's Biblical examples from Jesus's life, the times He was interrupted in the Gospel of Luke and meditate on what the Holy Spirit is speaking to you about through those Scriptures. Ask how specifically you can shift from being achievement-oriented to people-oriented for the sake of the salvation of souls and making God recognizable to the people who interrupt you on your way . . . to being busy.

From the Scriptures that highlight Jesus being interruptible, which person do you identify with the most when it comes to hiding in the shadow of suffering? To be interruptible is essential to practice attentiveness to the longing of our Lord to have us choose life over death, light over darkness and healing over despair. Jesus thirsts for our attentiveness to His healing touch in our lives so that we can participate in the healing restoration in the lives of the people He entrusts to our care.

Too often busyness is linked to worth and value which results in a "if this happens" or "if I achieve this" . . . "then" THEN I will be enough . . . THEN I will feel successful . . . THEN I will feel safe and secure. As Jesus said, *"You fool, this very night your life will be demanded from you . . . who will get what you have prepared for yourself?"* (Luke 12:20). Stay awake, keep watch. Be attentive to the opportunities Jesus will flip in front of you today for the purpose of interrupting your plans to make room for His plans to love and lead well the souls He entrusted to your care.

> Be interruptible for those tasks that make God recognizable on earth.

Which game are you playing? The eternal or the finite game of life? The eternal game is God-focused and other people oriented. The eternal game of life offers many opportunities for learning and growth through a variety of interruptions and pauses to create Godly character for an ultimate good on earth far beyond self.

The finite game is self-oriented, fast and furious, pushy, demanding and insecure with little patience and a lot of frustration due to the inconvenience of being slowed down by interruptions. The choice is yours and what you choose will make ALL the difference in the outcome you experience when it comes to Christ Connections.

Be interruptible for those tasks that make God recognizable on earth.

Surrender your will to His, be willing to pause for His purpose to spread the gospel message by behaviors in social situations that make God recognizable in this world.

Coaching Questions

In this 4th phase of EIC ask yourself:

Reflecting on my last week, when did I allow myself-to be interrupted to make a Christ Connection? When didn't I allow myself-to be interrupted to make a Christ Connection? Explain.

....
....
....

Have I experienced a personal encounter with Christ? If so, what have I noticed to be different when it comes to my ability to relate to other people?

....
....
....

Do I listen to other people to understand or to be understood? Explain.

....
....
....

Have I given Jesus's presence in my life more authority than my need to be liked, right or understood?

....
....
....

When I communicate to connect with other people, do I ask the Holy Spirit to give me the words to say or do I speak out whatever my emotions move me to speak? What do I want to do more of? Less of? To make room in my connections with other people for Jesus's presence and wisdom?

....
....
....
....

The tool I commit to apply in my life in order to expand the EIC behavior of Christ Connections is (review "Tools for Application" on page 161).

....
....
....
....

Write down three specific behaviors that you imagine you will notice to be different as a result of intentionally pursuing Christ Connections.

....
....
....
....

Prayer

Dear God, fill me with attentiveness to Your plans over mine. Help me to release my grip on my own agenda to make room for Yours. You allowed Yourself-to be available to those in need and as a result, the words You spoke spread like wildfire across the land. Help me to love, listen and respond with Godly character that gives witness to my position as Your ambassador. Interrupt my day to make You recognizable to the people around me. Make Your appeal for love and healing through my ability to pause and respond to Your voice. Give me eyes so I can see everything that I've been missing because of my big, bright, shiny to-do list. I want to be interruptible for the sake of salvation of souls and for Your good work in this world. Use me to connect with people around me by making You recognizable.

CHAPTER 7

DISC MEETS EIC BIBLE CASE STUDIES

THE CONNECTION BETWEEN DISC AND EIC

"Many people have their own private motives for what they do, and they are not even aware of them. They seem to be quite content when things are done as they like, but if events take a different turn, they quickly become testy and withdrawn. Differences of thought and opinion lead to more than enough bickering among friends and neighbors, among religious and devout people. Old habits are hard to break, and no one is easily led beyond his own point of view. If you lean more on your own reason or diligence than on the strength of your life with Jesus Christ, you will have only a slim chance of becoming an enlightened person—and if you do, it will happen slowly indeed. God wants us to conform our lives perfectly to his will and to reach beyond our passions and prejudices through an intense love for Him." [11]

THE BIBLICAL DISC profile assessment offers you insight into what people need and Emotional Intelligence in Christ provides you with the method to meet those needs in a Christ-led way.

---

[11] Thomas A Kempis, *The Imitation of Christ, A Timeless Classic for Contemporary Readers*, William C. Creasy, (Notre Dame, IN: Ave Maria Press, 1989), 43.

> As a believer in Christ and follower of His emotionally intelligent way of interacting with people, you have access through the indwelling Holy Spirit to think and interact with people just as Jesus did.

Are you intrigued with how Jesus was able, and is able, to know the deeper needs of the people He encountered and whose needs He met?

As a believer in Christ and follower of His emotionally intelligent way of interacting with people, you have access through the indwelling Holy Spirit to think and interact with people just as Jesus did.

"We have the mind of Christ" (1 Corinthians 2:16).

"I have much more to say to you, more than you can now bear. But when he, the Spirit of truth, comes, he will guide you into all the truth. He will not speak on his own; he will speak only what he hears, and he will tell you what is yet to come. He will glorify me because it is from me that he will receive what he will make known to you. All that belongs to the Father is mine. That is why I said the Spirit will receive from me what he will make known to you" (John 16:12-15).

"Very truly I tell you, whoever believes in me will do the works I have been doing, and they will do even greater things than these, because I am going to the Father" (John 14:12).

3 R's of DISC Relationships: Respond | Relate | Reinforce

EIC guides our understanding of the brilliance of Jesus's mind and how He was able to connect with each person He encountered. He was masterful at His ability to make meaningful connections in the midst of a variety of different personality profiles that He encountered: Below is a summary taken from Ken Voges's Biblical DISC Assessment, p 24. How to Respond, Relate and Reinforce the needs of people with different DISC styles. This is a powerful resource to keep nearby in that it offers you quick insight into how different DISC profiles operate and how to best connect and communicate with each profile. Where do you recognize yourself? Others?

As is the case with Jesus's ability to adapt within each of the four EIC traits, so too, He was and is able to adapt to each person's DISC profile. The key takeaway here is that Jesus met people where they were, just as He does for us today. He leans into our core need and meets it. As a result, lives were transformed and identities restored.

DOMINANCE (D)

HOW TO RESPOND TO A HIGH D
- Be firm and direct
- Focus on actions and goals
- Confront to get his/her attention

HOW TO RELATE TO A HIGH D
- Be brief and to the point
- Explain "How to acheive goals" using logic with an action plan
- Allow time to consider your ideas

HOW TO REINFORCE THE HIGH D
- Repeat the plan of action, focusing on goals, objectives, and results
- Give bottom line instructions
- Get out of his/her way

INFLUENCING (I)

HOW TO RESPOND TO A HIGH I
- Be friendly and positive
- Allow for informal dialogue
- Allow time for stimulating and fun activities

HOW TO RELATE TO A HIGH I
- Use friendly voice tones
- Allow time for them to verbalize their feelings
- Help them transfer talk to an action plan

HOW TO REINFORCE THE HIGH I
- Offer positive encouragement and incentives for taking on tasks
- Help to organize an action plan
- Communicate positive recognition

STEADINESS (S)

HOW TO RESPOND TO A HIGH S
- Be non-threatening and patient
- Allow time to process and adjust to change
- Make allowances for family or team

HOW TO RELATE TO A HIGH S
- Use friendly tones when instructing
- Giver personal, nonverbal acceptance and assurances
- Allow time to process information

HOW TO REINFORCE THE HIGH S
- Repeat any instructions
- Provide hands-on reinforcement
- Be patient in allowing time to take ownership

CONSCIENTIOUS (C)

HOW TO RESPOND TO A HIGH C
- Be specific and accurate
- Make allowance for initial responeses to be cautions and/or negative
- Allow freedom to ask questions

HOW TO RELATE TO A HIGH C
- Answer questions in a patient and persistent manner
- Mix accurate data with assurances
- Allow time to validate information

HOW TO REINFORCE THE HIGH C
- Provide a step-by-step approach
- Provide reassurances of support
- Give permission to validate information with third party

The Three R's for All

JESUS ADAPTS TO DIFFERENT DISC PROFILES

Below is a snapshot of a few examples of Jesus's ability to adapt to the person and/or situation at hand in order to make the biggest positive impact in people's lives by opening up the powerful presence of God. This gives witness to the perfect Emotional Intelligence that Jesus modeled on earth.

BIBLICAL DISC® ASSESSMENT

Let's take a closer look at Jesus's behavior on the D-I-S-C profile traits, notice His ability to adapt to the DISC trait in order to connect and positively influence the people He encountered: (Reference page 33 of the Biblical DISC, Ken Voges).

It takes the ability to pull behaviors from all four categories: Personal Identity | Self-Control | Altruism | Christ Connections in order to meet and positively impact people who have different DISC traits. Observe Jesus's amazing ability in action to respond, relate and reinforce the people He encountered.

Notice which encounter you relate to the most. Which DISC profile best describes the ways you show up in relationships? You will notice we have included both high and low examples associated with each of the 4 DISC traits below:

High D Traits

Total dominance: Jesus had unlimited and complete control in exercising authority over situations and individuals. Jesus showcases His ability to remain calm in the midst of a potentially emotional situation. He uses the EIC traits of Personal Identity (knowing the power of God within Him is bigger than the circumstance), Self-Control (calmly posing a question to call out the demons). These are two traits that you, the reader, as a follower of Christ have the ability to carry out as well in emotionally driven situations:

Know the strength of God within you is greater than the drama outside of you (Personal Identity in Christ).

God gave you the second trait of EIC: Self-Control, ask the Holy Spirit to make it come alive when you find yourself-face-to-face with a situation that could easily hijack your emotions: *"For the Spirit God gave us does not make us timid, but gives us power, love and self-discipline"* (2 Timothy 1:7).

Read Luke 8:27–35:

> *"When Jesus stepped ashore, he was met by a demon-possessed man from the town. For a long time this man had not worn clothes or lived in a house, but had lived in the tombs. When he saw Jesus, he cried out and fell at his feet, shouting at the top of his voice, "What do you want with me, Jesus, Son of the Most High God? I beg you, don't torture me!" For Jesus had commanded the impure spirit to come out of the man. Many times it had seized him, and though he was chained hand and foot and kept under guard, he had broken his chains and had been driven by the demon into solitary places.*
>
> *Jesus asked him, "What is your name?"*
>
> *"Legion," he replied, because many demons had gone into him. And they begged Jesus repeatedly not to order them to go into the Abyss.*
>
> *A large herd of pigs was feeding there on the hillside. The demons begged Jesus to let them go into the pigs, and he gave them permission. When the demons came out of the man, they went into the pigs, and the herd rushed down the steep bank into the lake and drowned.*
>
> *When those tending the pigs saw what had happened, they ran off and reported this in the town and countryside, and the people went out to see what had happened. When*

they came to Jesus, they found the man from whom the demons had gone out, sitting at Jesus's feet, dressed and in his right mind; and they were afraid."

As powerful as the demons were against the man in the passage, how did their behavior change when encountering Jesus? On a scale of 1 to 10, how would you rank Jesus's dominance factor? Explain.

....
....
....
....

Low D Traits

Total submission: Jesus demonstrates the ability to completely give up control in order to fulfill someone else's plan, desires or wishes, God's plan for salvation. Jesus exhibits the EIC trait of Personal Identity which gives Him the strength to carry out God's will in the midst of painful circumstances. Read Matthew 26:47–56:

"While he was still speaking, Judas, one of the Twelve, arrived. With him was a large crowd armed with swords and clubs, sent from the chief priests and the elders of the people. Now the betrayer had arranged a signal with them: "The one I kiss is the man; arrest him." Going at once to Jesus, Judas said, "Greetings, Rabbi!" and kissed him.

Jesus replied, "Do what you came for, friend."

Then the men stepped forward, seized Jesus and arrested him. With that, one of Jesus's companions reached for his sword, drew it out and struck the servant of the high priest, cutting off his ear.

"Put your sword back in its place," Jesus said to him, "for all who draw the sword will die by the sword. Do you think I cannot call on my Father, and he will at once put at my

disposal more than twelve legions of angels? But how then would the Scriptures be fulfilled that say it must happen in this way?"

In that hour Jesus said to the crowd, "Am I leading a rebellion, that you have come out with swords and clubs to capture me? Every day I sat in the temple courts teaching, and you did not arrest me. But this has all taken place that the writings of the prophets might be fulfilled." Then all the disciples deserted him and fled."

If Jesus chose to call on 72,000 angels to defend Him, what do you think the outcome might be with the group wanting to arrest Him? What score would you give Him for restraint? Explain.

....
....
....
....

High I Traits

Socially Interactive: Jesus has the ability to discern the needs of others with not only verbal affirmation and encouragement, but also seeking to meet their physical, emotional, and spiritual needs. He exhibits the EIC traits of Personal Identity and Altruism. He knows whose Son He is and what that power is capable of accomplishing in the midst of being aware of the needs of the people around Him (EIC trait of Altruism), including the learning opportunity for the disciples to bring what they have and He will multiply it. Read Matthew 14:13–21:

"When Jesus heard what had happened, he withdrew by boat privately to a solitary place. Hearing of this, the crowds followed him on foot from the towns. When Jesus landed and saw a large crowd, he had compassion on them and healed their sick.

> *As evening approached, the disciples came to him and said, "This is a remote place, and it's already getting late. Send the crowds away, so they can go to the villages and buy themselves some food."*
>
> *Jesus replied, "They do not need to go away. You give them something to eat."*
>
> *"We have here only five loaves of bread and two fish," they answered.*
>
> *"Bring them here to me," he said. And he directed the people to sit down on the grass. Taking the five loaves and the two fish and looking up to heaven, he gave thanks and broke the loaves. Then he gave them to the disciples, and the disciples gave them to the people. They all ate and were satisfied, and the disciples picked up twelve basketfuls of broken pieces that were left over. The number of those who ate was about five thousand men, besides women and children."*

How would you rate Jesus's response to the needs of the multitude of people in the passage? Explain.

....
....
....
....

Low I Traits

Seeking extreme isolation: Jesus took the time to be alone to recharge, reflect and redirect His energies in meeting the more strategic challenges ahead. Do you? Read John 6:14–15:

> *"After the people saw the sign Jesus performed, they began to say, 'Surely this is the Prophet who is to come into the world.' Jesus, knowing that they intended to come and*

make him king by force, withdrew again to a mountain by himself."

And Mark 6:45:

"Immediately Jesus made his disciples get into the boat and go on ahead of him to Bethsaida, while he dismissed the crowd."

Did the positive reaction of the people to Jesus's actions surprise you? Was it about to get out of hand? The proper response was to shut things down. However, considering the High I tendency to accept and embrace positive social pressure, this would have been very difficult to do. How well did Jesus do in handling this? Jesus clearly exhibits the EIC trait of Self-Control.

High S Traits

Undeserved patience: Jesus is masterful when it comes to the projection of unconditional love to an individual who has an unteachable moment. During this moment when Peter insisted that he would not deny Jesus, Jesus exhibited the EIC trait of Altruism (Social-Awareness) and Christ Connections (Relational Management). Jesus recognized Peter's weakness before Peter did and began to pray for him, knowing that Peter's weakness would result in Godly character which walks through the archway of humility. Jesus knew Peter needed a dose of humility to relate to the people He entrusted to his care. Jesus was aware of what Peter would do under social pressure and emotionally managed the moment well by speaking the truth in love.

Read Mark 14:27–29:

> "You will all fall away," Jesus told them, "for it is written: 'I will strike the shepherd, and the sheep will be scattered.' But after I have risen, I will go ahead of you into Galilee." Peter declared, "Even if all fall away, I will not."

Read Luke 22:31–34:

> "Simon, Simon, Satan has asked to sift all of you as wheat. But I have prayed for you, Simon, that your faith may not fail. And when you have turned back, strengthen your brothers."
>
> But he replied, "Lord, I am ready to go with you to prison and to death."
>
> Jesus answered, "I tell you, Peter, before the rooster crows today, you will deny three times that you know me."

How confident was Peter in projecting his prideful commitments to Jesus? How would you rank Jesus's patience? Being unable to get through to Peter, what did Jesus default to? How would you respond?

....
....
....
....

Low S Traits

Intense confrontation: Jesus also knew when it was time to take aggressive action against a policy that is totally contrary to moral and religious principles. Jesus stands for truth and showcases the EIC trait of Altruism, selfless concern for the wellbeing of others. Jesus knows what entrapments hold people captive and was and is committed to setting us free by pointing them out. It was often said of Jesus that He was not confined by status or the opinions of other people. This is a combination of Personal Identity and Altruism (Social-Awareness). When you are attached to the opinions of other people and/or status then intense confrontation is too often avoided for fear of what people will think. Jesus lives outside of that fear as He speaks the truth with courage and love. How do you handle confrontation when truth is on the line?

Read Mark 11:15–18:

> *On reaching Jerusalem, Jesus entered the temple courts and began driving out those who were buying and selling there. He overturned the tables of the money changers and the benches of those selling doves, and would not allow anyone to carry merchandise through the temple courts. And as he taught them, he said, "Is it not written: 'My house will be called a house of prayer for all nations'? But you have made it 'a den of robbers.'"*
>
> *The chief priests and the teachers of the law heard this and began looking for a way to kill him, for they feared him, because the whole crowd was amazed at his teaching.*

How patient was Jesus with the money changers? Who and what was Jesus defending? Was it justified and did it have consequences?

Low C Traits

(Note: low traits are listed first on purpose)

Rebellious, defiant: Jesus knows when to take public action to challenge, confront and offer correction to policies that are wrong and detrimental to the health of an individual or culture. Again, Jesus showcases the EIC trait of Altruism (Social-Awareness) along with Christ Connections (Relational Management). Jesus is always going for the bigger lesson that will ultimately set a person or group of people free from the entrapments of the world. Even if this means standing up in the midst of an angry and disapproving crowd. When was the last time you stood up for truth for the sake of another person or group of people knowing that it would not be received well?

....
....
....
....

Read Mark 3:1–6:

> *"Another time Jesus went into the synagogue, and a man with a shriveled hand was there. Some of them were looking for a reason to accuse Jesus, so they watched him closely to see if he would heal him on the Sabbath. Jesus said to the man with the shriveled hand, "Stand up in front of everyone."*
>
> *Then Jesus asked them, "Which is lawful on the Sabbath: to do good or to do evil, to save life or to kill?" But they remained silent.*
>
> *He looked around at them in anger and, deeply distressed at their stubborn hearts, said to the man, "Stretch out your hand." He stretched it out, and his hand was completely restored. Then the Pharisees went out and began to plot with the Herodians how they might kill Jesus."*

Christ Connections: The ability to connect to others as Christ connects to us: through the archway of unconditional love for God and people.

Where, what and how did Jesus choose to challenge religious leadership? How would you rank Jesus's emotional intensity? Were there consequences to His actions and was Jesus willing to accept them?

....

....

....

....

High C Traits

Sacrificial compliance to a plan: Jesus died to save. He gave up His ultimate rights for the benefit of someone else . . . all of humanity, including you, the reader. This is the ultimate example of all four phases of EIC: Personal Identity, Self-Control, Altruism for the ultimate ramification that continues to live out today:

Christ Connections: The ability to connect to others as Christ connects to us: through the archway of unconditional love for God and people.

Read Exodus 32:31–32 about Moses:

> *So Moses went back to the Lord and said, "Oh, what a great sin these people have committed! They have made themselves gods of gold. But now, please forgive their sin—but if not, then blot me out of the book you have written."*
>
> *The Lord replied to Moses, "Whoever has sinned against me I will blot out of my book. Now go, lead the people to the place I spoke of, and my angel will go before you. However, when the time comes for me to punish, I will punish them for their sin."*

Now read Matthew 26:39–44 about Jesus:

> *"Going a little farther, he fell with his face to the ground and prayed, "My Father, if it is possible, may this cup be taken from me. Yet not as I will, but as you will."*

> *Then he returned to his disciples and found them sleeping. "Couldn't you men keep watch with me for one hour?" he asked Peter. "Watch and pray so that you will not fall into temptation. The spirit is willing, but the flesh is weak."*
>
> *He went away a second time and prayed, "My Father, if it is not possible for this cup to be taken away unless I drink it, may your will be done."*
>
> *When he came back, he again found them sleeping, because their eyes were heavy. So he left them and went away once more and prayed the third time, saying the same thing."*

Who was the first recorded example of a person willing to give his life for the sins of others? _____

What was the Lord's response? _____

Who was the second person to give His life for the sins of others?

_____

What was God's response to Jesus's willingness to die? _____

_____

What was the consequence for us? _____

_____

Application: Reflect on the questions listed above. Consider Jesus's perfect example in adapting His behavior to meet the needs of others.

How Fear Impacts Your DISC

Fear is an emotion that Satan uses to spin us out of God's strength and peace.

> Fear is an emotion that Satan uses to spin us out of God's strength and peace.

Fear is the emotional ramification of a faith crisis. We are all vulnerable to getting hijacked by the serpent of fear from time to time, particularly when it comes to relationships: interpersonal (relating and communicating with people) and intrapersonal (interior thoughts within your own mind).

> *"For the Spirit God gave us does not make us timid,= [fearful] but gives us power, love and self-discipline"* (2 Timothy 1:7).

Second degree black belts in World Tae Kwon Do, often train outside the ring for hours at a time to up their skill set in the ring when face-to-face with their opponent. Understanding your unique tendency towards fear that is linked to your DISC profile offers you the opportunity to up your skill set outside the ring so that when you come face to face with your opponent fear in the ring, you can equip your mind and mouth for a victory. *"Do not conform to this world but be transformed by the renewing of your mind"* (Romans 12:2).

> When you give more authority to the love of God within you than to the emotion of fear, peace and confidence that God is bigger than your circumstance sinks into your emotions, restoring a peace that passes all human understanding.

The ultimate weapon to use in the ring of life when you face fear is found in 1 John 4:18: *"Perfect love casts out all fear."* Yes, it's true,

When you give more authority to the love of God within you than to the emotion of fear, peace and confidence that God is bigger than your circumstance sinks into your emotions, restoring a peace that passes all human understanding.

The result? Emotional Intelligence in Christ, which offers you the opportunity to connect in the midst of disconnect and conflict. Jesus was masterful at this.

Take a look at the fear tendencies associated with the different DISC styles. Where do you recognize yourself?

	D	**I**	**S**	**C**
FEAR	Losing	Rejection	Change	Being wrong
FEAR RESPONSE	Anger	Blame	Non-participation	Criticism
TENSION FEAR	Demanding	Attacks	Compiles	Avoids conflict
PROLONGED FEAR	Withhold contact	Shift blame	Passive/ Aggressive	Demand details

Case Studies

As you read through the following case studies, where do you recognize yourself? Other people in your life? Explore the combination of the Biblical DISC, identifying the needs of people and how to meet those needs using Emotional Intelligence in Christ.

God is the spark behind the Biblical DISC.

> When you combine your DISC style with Emotional Intelligence in Christ you now have a way to connect with people where they are along with the ability to love them enough not to leave them there.

When you combine your DISC style with Emotional Intelligence in Christ you now have a way to connect with people where they are along with the ability to love them enough not to leave them there.

This is all possible through the guidance and help of the Holy Spirit within you. As you will notice, throughout the Bible, this is how God loves His people, including you.

Let's take a closer look at Abraham:

Abraham (Abram): High S . . . extremely low D. Abraham fears change. God knows that which is why He gives Abraham plenty of time to process. God's relationship with Abram is all God. Looking at the Three R's of DISC Relationships on page "3 R's of DISC

Relationships: Respond | Relate | Reinforce" on page 174, what do we know about High S's: *Respond* by making allowances for family and or team. *Relate* by giving time to process and *Reinforce* by allowing time to take ownership.

First thing God told Abraham was to leave his family and go to the land I am telling you about (Genesis 12:1–20). Abraham started along and he took his dad with him. God told him again to leave his family and go to the land . . . what did he do? He took Lot. It took 40 years for Abraham to finally align to God's will . . . this is no shocker to God as He knows how Abraham is wired.

Abraham also got in a lot of trouble because his wife looked good. Low D's don't like conflict so they will tell a lie: *"You're my sister"* (Genesis 20:2). God took care of him again. King Abimelech had a bad dream: *"I'm a dead man if I touch her . . . leave now"* (Genesis 20:3). So, Pharaoh sent Abraham away with a ton of gifts.

Abraham did the wrong thing and he was blessed anyway. Finally, after 60–70 years Abraham listened and God told him the rest of the story. God knows that S's are tactical learners: *Walk through the land.* S's have to have 3 repeats of process instructions before they can finally take hold of the real plan and who they are again, God is connecting to Abraham in an emotionally intelligent way, knowing that one of his fear tendencies is linked to change. S's are also concerned with how their actions will affect the people around them. God was patient with Abraham knowing he needed to experience repetition of the process before he understood and took action.

Now let's shift to the New Testament and take a look at the brilliance of God's emotional intelligent encounters in the midst of different DISC profiles. Below are 4 people who struggled with their own fears and still carried out God's plan: Mary, the Mother of Jesus, Peter and Paul.

MARY the Mother of Jesus: Fast forwarding 1500 years, Mary shows up as a High C, High S and low D. To override her fear tendencies, God offers her some time to adjust, ask questions and validate the information with specific details. She is sweet, devout and perhaps a little hard on herself. The Angel Gabriel talked to Mary in Luke 1:28: *"Greetings, you who are highly favored! The Lord is with you."* Knowing that High S's Respond (3 R's) well to non-threatening words with a kind tone, God approached Mary in this way along with *Relating* to her with personal assurances. When Mary was troubled, the angel *Reinforced* her by providing reassurances of support in Luke 1:30–33: *"Do not be afraid, Mary; you have found favor with God. You will conceive and give birth to a son, and you are to call him Jesus. He will be great and will be called the Son of the Most High. The Lord God will give him the throne of his father David, and he will reign over Jacob's descendants forever; his kingdom will never end."*

Knowing that High C's need detail, Gabriel was sent to give her what God knew she needed in order to buy into His will for mankind through Mary's Fiat (her YES to the request from God, which shows her complete surrender through humility to God's will). As a high C, Mary needs more information and asks in Luke 1:34: *"How will this be,"* Mary asked the angel, *"since I am a virgin?"* The Angel gives her what she needs in Luke 1:35–37: *"The Holy Spirit will come on you, and the power of the Most High will overshadow you. So the holy one to be born will be called the Son of God. Even Elizabeth, your relative is going to have a child in her old age, and she who was said to be unable to conceive is in her sixth month. For no word from God will ever fail."* Elizabeth is with child and the shadow of the Most High will come over you and you will give birth to the Son of God. High C's need validation and reassurance.

Review the Three R's: "3 R's of DISC Relationships: Respond | Relate | Reinforce" on page 174 and you will notice how our emotionally intelligent God *Responded, Related and Reinforced* Mary as a High C and High S in a way that she felt safe and connected to God's will.

Once Mary received her validation and reassurance, she accepted God's will for her life in Luke 1:38: *"I am the Lord's servant," Mary answered. "May your word to me be fulfilled." Then the angel left her."*

What was the next thing Mary did? She went to Judah to be with Elizabeth who was six months pregnant so that she could see the fulfillment of the *validation and reassurance*, which is essential for a High C/S: hands on reinforcement. Math equation: 6 + 3 = 9 months. Luke 1:39–45 shows Mary's choice to validate what the angel had told her: *"At that time Mary got ready and hurried to a town in the hill country of Judea, where she entered Zechariah's home and greeted Elizabeth. When Elizabeth heard Mary's greeting, the baby leaped in her womb, and Elizabeth was filled with the Holy Spirit. In a loud voice she exclaimed: "Blessed are you among women, and blessed is the child you will bear! But why am I so favored, that the mother of my Lord should come to me? As soon as the sound of your greeting reached my ears, the baby in my womb leaped for joy. Blessed is she who has believed that the Lord would fulfill his promises to her!"*

> Just as God gifted Mary with a unique personal operating system, God has gifted you with the unique DISC profile as well, that you have for a reason, to accomplish His good works that He has prepared in advance for you to do in this world (Ephesians 2:10).

Mary stayed with Elizabeth an additional three months bringing Mary to the validation she needed to see Elizabeth give birth to John . . . validation that she needed that backs up what Gabriel said. How emotionally intelligent of God to set this up for a teenage girl knowing that she needed validation in order to have the faith. Did that stop her from putting things in a box that she didn't understand? Yes. Later when Jesus was born, Mary treasured all these things within her heart. Pondered (Greek translation . . . organizing all of your thoughts into a logical sequence to make sense of it.) Mary *pondered* her entire life. Pondered: to play out mental gymnastics, putting everything in a logical order.

Just as God gifted Mary with a unique personal operating system, God has gifted you with the unique DISC profile as well, that you have for a reason, to accomplish His good works that He has prepared in advance for you to do in this world (Ephesians 2:10).

Peter: I/D: The I/D's gift is to be in the secular community. They have a gift, an instinct to know when to ask for the close. Peter's fear tendency is loss of control and rejection. Notice how the Holy Spirit can flip a fear into a strength behavior. When the Holy Spirit is in charge of that they can sell Acts 2 and 3: the greatest number of people coming to a saving knowledge of Christ . . . Peter went ahead and presented the gospel: he understood the need of the crowd (Biblical DISC). He also knew what to tell the people that would meet their needs (EIC) and then offer the invitation. Peter, filled with the Holy Spirit, took control of the crowd without any fear of rejection. Peter's best presentation is when he is in front of the Sanhedrin (Read Acts 4), who, by the way, are ready to kill him. He is selling something they hate. Peter's High D kicks into action. What do we know from the Three R's of DISC Relationships with High D/I? High D's *Respond* by taking action around goals; they *Relate* by achieving goals using logic with an action plan; and they *Reinforce* by giving bottom line instructions.

> The Holy Spirit is truly our virtual assistant when it comes to following Jesus's lead around how to positively inspire people with different DISC profiles using Emotional Intelligence in Christ.

When you discover your DISC style know this: you give out what comes naturally to you. As a high D, Peter is action plan focused so He shines when given the opportunity to put his calling into action and would expect others to do the same if he is not emotionally intelligent, his behavior will be intimidating to someone who is a high I or S. Key element about Peter's presentation in Acts 4 is that he is filled with the Holy Spirit.

The Holy Spirit is truly our virtual assistant when it comes to following Jesus's lead around how to positively inspire people with different DISC profiles using Emotional Intelligence in Christ.

They ask him the question: By what power do you do these things? Peter, filled with the Holy Spirit masterfully, as is common for the D/I combination, puts them on trial. The result? They threw him out of the room. Then one of their own men, Gamaliel, the most respected of the Pharisees said, *"I advise you: Leave these men alone! Let them go! For if their purpose or activity is of human origin, it will fail. But if it is from God, you will not be able to stop these men; you will only find yourselves fighting against God"* (Acts 5:38-39).

> Without Christ at the center of your Personal Identity, the ability to manage your emotions well is difficult if not impossible.

Now, let's take a deeper dive into the one person that was completely hijacked by the world, which makes him very relatable. He encountered Christ, which changed his behavior and led to a complete course correction. After his encounter with Christ, he became an ambassador for Christ, transforming lives by preaching the gospel message. He experienced firsthand the emotional intelligence of Christ after Jesus had died and risen from the grave. This is a cool thought here, because that is the space that you are currently in: A.D. If Jesus did it for Paul, He can do it for you.

The Apostle Paul

(Positive & Negative sides of High D/C behavior)

Strength: Outstanding problem solver

Problem Solving Strategies: Debate everyone's conclusions

Wants: Influence & Control

Fears: Loss of Influence & Control

Fear controlled response: Anger, Aggressive action

Negative Self-Management response of Paul

Without Christ at the center of your Personal Identity, the ability to manage your emotions well is difficult if not impossible.

Persons with the D/C pattern fear not being sufficiently influential. This fear may relate to present circumstances, or it may relate to the future. They may also be fearful that their influence and eminence will erode in fields which change rapidly in response to new knowledge and skills.[12] When confrontations are necessary, they take up the challenge.[13]

The Apostle Paul's flesh side of Emotional Intelligence

> "I (Paul) persecuted the followers of this Way to their death, arresting both men and women and throwing them into prison, as the high priest and all the Council can themselves testify. I even obtained letters from them to their associates in Damascus and went there to bring these people as prisoners to Jerusalem to be punished."[14]

Jesus's EIC Christ Connections/Relational Management Strategies in responding to Paul's flesh actions

> "And it came about that as he journeyed, he was approaching Damascus, and suddenly a light from heaven flashed around him; and he fell to the ground, and heard a voice saying to him, 'Saul, Saul, why are you persecuting Me?'

---

12 Library of Classical Profiles Patterns John Geier, Dorothy Downey, Performax Systems International, January 1979, Volume V, page 25
13 Ibid page 16
14 Acts 22:4–5

And he said, 'Who art Thou, Lord?' and He said, 'I am Jesus whom you are persecuting, but rise and enter the city, and it shall be told to you what you must do.'

And Saul got up from the ground, and though his eyes were open, he could see nothing; and leading him by the hand, they brought him into Damascus. The men traveling with Saul stood there speechless; they heard the sound but did not see anyone. Saul got up from the ground, but when he opened his eyes he could see nothing. So they led him by the hand into Damascus. For three days he was blind, and did not eat or drink anything.

In Damascus there was a disciple named Ananias. The Lord called to him in a vision, 'Ananias!' 'Yes, Lord,' he answered.

The Lord told him, "Go to the house of Judas on Straight Street and ask for a man from Tarsus named Saul, for he is praying. In a vision he has seen a man named Ananias come and place his hands on him to restore his sight." And Ananias departed and entered the house, and after laying his hands on him said, 'Brother Saul, the Lord Jesus, who appeared to you on the road by which you were coming, has sent me so that you may regain your sight, and be filled with the Holy Spirit.'

And immediately there fell from his eyes something like scales, and he regained his sight, and he arose and was baptized; and he took food and was strengthened. Now for several days he was with the disciples who were at Damascus, and immediately he began to proclaim Jesus in the synagogues, saying, 'He is the Son of God.' ...

Yet Saul grew more and more powerful and baffled the Jews living in Damascus by proving that Jesus is the Messiah.[15]

---

15 Acts 9:1–18, 22

How to Respond, Relate and Reinforce a High D DISC

How to Respond to a High D

1. Be firm and direct
2. Focus on actions and goals
3. Caring confrontation may be necessary to get their attention

How to Relate to a High D

1. Be brief and to the point
2. Explain "How to achieve goals" using logic with an action plan
3. Allow time to consider your ideas

How to Reinforce the High D

1. Repeat the plan of action focusing on goals, objectives, & results
2. Give bottom-line instructions
3. Get out of the way[16]

After reviewing the High D Environmental Strategies of the three Rs above, reread the Acts 9 encounter of Jesus and Paul. Write down any points that validate Jesus's actions. Does 20th century DISC behavioral science appear to parallel Jesus's actions? ....

....
....
....
....

---

16 Biblical DISC™, page 24

Positive EIC Self-Control response of Paul

Measuring the Maturity of High D profiles

Embracing weakness over pride and control.

> "Therefore, in order to keep me from becoming conceited, I was given a thorn in my flesh, a messenger of Satan, to torment me. Three times I pleaded with the Lord to take it away from me. But he said to me, 'My grace is sufficient for you, for my power is made perfect in weakness.' Therefore, I will boast all the more gladly about my weaknesses, so that Christ's power may rest on me. That is why, for Christ's sake, I delight in weaknesses, in insults, in hardships, in persecutions, in difficulties. For when I am weak, then I am strong." [17]

Based on his profile, how difficult would it have been for Paul to come to this conclusion? In what way does his testimony validate positive Self-Management?[18]

JESUS IS OUR EIC MENTOR

The Holy Spirit is Our Virtual Assistant

> "It is for freedom that Christ has set you free, stand firm and do not allow yourself-to be burdened by the yoke of comparisons, jealousy or taking offense in the midst of conflict or different personalities and emotional expressions" (Galatians 5:1).

Follow God's lead, through Christ, and learn how to maintain emotional intelligence in the midst of different DISC styles.

---

17 II Cor. 12:7–10
18 Ken Voges, PowerPoint slides © copyrighted 2017, Biblical DISC™ Assessment

Follow God's lead, through Christ, and learn how to maintain emotional intelligence in the midst of different DISC styles.

Jesus is the ultimate mentor when it comes to reading people, meeting them where they are and then using emotional intelligence to meet their needs. In the next chapter, you will be able to see how this connection between DISC and EIC offers the perfect combination to fulfill the second greatest commandment: Love your neighbor as yourself. Identifying the needs of the people entrusted to your care and using the emotional intelligence in Christ to meet those needs: Personal Identity in Christ | Self-Control | Altruism | Christ Connections.

CHAPTER 8

APPLYING THE CHAVOUS/ CUMMINS/MILLER/ VOGES EIC METHOD

"Look to yourself, and beware of judging what others do. In judging others a person works to no purpose, often makes mistakes, and easily does the wrong thing, but in judging and analyzing ourselves, we always work to our own advantage. Our judgments are often based on our personal likes and dislikes; consequently, our private prejudices can easily overshadow our sound thinking. If we would always have our attention focused on God and if we would long for him alone, we would not be so easily upset when others do not accept what we have to say. But often something lurks within us, or intrudes from outside of us, which draws us along with it."[19]

ARE YOU READY to apply your knowledge of EIC? In this chapter, you will be introduced to a powerful method to help build your EIC! Looking back on previous chapters, you received assessment results, worked through EIC examples and case studies, and learned about tools and resources that can help you develop your Emotional Intelligence In Christ. The intention is that you gain a better awareness

---

19 Thomas A Kempis, *The Imitation of Christ, A Timeless Classic for Contemporary Readers*, William C. Creasy, (Notre Dame, IN: Ave Maria Press, 1989), 43.

of your behaviors, and the coaching questions help you reflect and journal your thoughts and actions plans for each. Get ready to bring together all that you have learned.

> As you understand each aspect of the EIC Method, you have the opportunity to grow in your EIC and the love God wants us to share and develop within you to share with others.

Emotional Intelligence in Christ is the activation of the Holy Spirit within you to discern and manage personal emotions and behavior in a way that honors God by loving others well as Jesus did.

The Chavous/Cummins/Miller/Voges EIC Method will advance you to become even more emotionally intelligent in Christ by learning to recognize the encounter, identified behaviors, and how to course-correct when needed. The information below explains the EIC Method, designed to help you take a deeper dive into the actions and reactions that flow from a personal connection with Christ.

As you understand each aspect of the EIC Method, you have the opportunity to grow in your EIC and the love God wants us to share and develop within you to share with others.

EIC = ENCOUNTER + IDENTIFIED BEHAVIOR + COURSE CORRECT

E: Encounter

The first element is the Encounter. An EIC encounter is expected, unlike the traditional definition of an encounter, which states it is unexpected. All encounters in this context are Christ ones, and because of this, no encounter happens by accident. We see this throughout Jesus's entire ministry, where he encounters people not by accident but by Godly design. Christ encounters happen all the time and are to be accepted with an open heart.

Have you ever been on a peaceful walk and ran into a person you've been avoiding due to an emotionally intense discussion? Perhaps on a trip to the grocery store, you come face-to-face with a colleague with whom you've had a conflict, or on a quick trip to the carwash, you end up in an encounter where you are asked to be a witness for Christ's love? He is constantly after you, giving you opportunities to face your emotions and connect to His courageous Spirit within you. He wants to give you the opportunity to overcome uncomfortable emotions with His power, love, and self-discipline: *"For the Spirit God gave us does not make us timid, but gives us power, love and self-discipline"* (1 Timothy 1:7). Christ encounters happen in all degrees, situations and are predestined.

Ephesians 1:11 says, *". . . in him we have obtained an inheritance, having been predestined according to His purpose who works all things according to the counsel of his will."* This means that Christ encounters happen by plan.

The first element in EIC is to understand and access the encounter before you take any action. *We love because God first loved us* (1 John 4:19). Through a personal encounter with God's love for you, with, in and through Jesus Christ, the Holy Spirit takes up residence within you and begins the mighty work of God in your life. Your behavior begins a transformation from the inside out. It's an interior extreme makeover that can't help but positively impact the lives of people around you. *"I have been crucified with Christ and I no longer live, but Christ lives in me. The life I now live in the body, I live by faith in the Son of God, who loved me and gave himself-for me"* (Galatians 2:20).

I: Identified Behavior

The next element in EIC is identifying the emotions around the behaviors associated with the encounter you have with another person. This involves an analysis of the behavior through: (1) understanding the unique personality style of the person, (2) understanding your unique personality, and (3) understanding each of your motivations.

The best way to understand behavior is through the Biblical DISC^(R) Assessment. Biblical DISC was introduced in previous chapters throughout the book to help you understand the personality traits of yourself-and others. It is a crucial factor in uncovering behavior. Motivation is also important because it is a complicated matching of actions and reactions between biological, environmental, cognitive, and emotional components.

Colossians 3:23 tells us that *"Whatever you do, work at it with all your heart, as working for the Lord, not for human masters."* This means that our motivation behind our actions and reactions should be that of the Lord's, which alone should make us think twice before we react.

> In this phase of EIC, course correction plays a considerable role in your goal of being Emotional Intelligent in Christ.

Galatians 5:22–23 says: *"But the fruit of the Spirit is love, joy, peace, forbearance, kindness, goodness, faithfulness, gentleness and self-control. Against such things there is no law."* The Holy Spirit is truly our virtual assistant when it comes to identifying behaviors that do not align with the person God has created us to be. Before you jump into your day, pause and offer up a simple prayer.

> Holy Spirit I give You permission to bump me when my behavior is flowing from my fleshy desires and false motives. Increase my ability to hear and respond to the voice of Christ within me that says: "this is the way, walk in it." Help me to expand the gap between what is happening outside of me and my choice of response to it. I want to pause and tune into Your guidance for me today before choosing a behavioral response.

To open up our hearts to identifying different behaviors, we must first take on the Spirit of God's behavior. Once accomplished, we have solved the identity of behavior in the EIC Method, allowing us to move to course correction.

C: Course Correct

The final element is course correction which can take shape in many forms.

In this phase of EIC, course correction plays a considerable role in your goal of being Emotional Intelligent in Christ.

There are many strategies and plans you can use for course correction depending on if you want to change, modify, or continue your behavior. The key is ensuring that your action plan involves Christ-centered activities to address the diverse situations you will come across. Surrender yourself-to God, ask for His guidance before acting on the behavior you have identified in yourself-and others.

John 16:13 says, *"I have much more to say to you, more than you can now bear. But when he, the Spirit of truth, comes, he will guide you into all truth. He will not speak on his own; he will speak only what he hears, and he will tell you what is yet to come. I tell you the truth; you will weep and mourn while the world rejoices."*

When you apply course correction, give the Holy Spirit permission to lead you down the right path, the sequence of activities, the speed, and the direction you should take to move forward in a way that aligns with God's will for you and those around you. As you learned in Chapter 7, Ken Voges provides the 3Rs (Respond, Relate, Reinforce) to address personality types in the Biblical DISC$^{(R)}$. This approach is one of the strategies you can apply to manage course correction within the EIC Method.

THE APPLICATION OF THE EIC METHOD

The EIC Method is a simple one and can be applied to any behavior with God's guidance. This chapter features six reference Scriptures with nine case studies chosen from five encounters in the Bible.

Scripture Study Reference 1: The Burning Bush

- EIC Case Study 1: Moses (burning bush)
- EIC Case Study 2: Aaron (burning bush)

Scripture Study Reference 2: The Golden Calf

- EIC Case Study 3: Aaron (golden calf)
- EIC Case Study 4: EIC of God towards Aaron—Through the Empowerment of Moses (golden calf)

Scripture Study Reference 3: Death and Resurrection of Lazarus

Jesus's response to our behaviors

- EIC Case Study 5: Martha (death of Lazarus)
- EIC Case Study 6: Mary (death of Lazarus)

Scripture Study Reference/Practice EIC method 4: At the Home of Martha and Mary

- EIC Case Study 7: EIC of Jesus toward Martha and Mary (death of Lazarus)

Scripture Study Reference 5: Jesus and the Miraculous Catch of Fish

- EIC Case Study 8: Peter (Jesus, the miraculous catch)

Scripture Study Reference 6: Sanhedrin Story

- EIC Case Study 9: Peter (Sanhedrin Story)

As you take a deeper dive into the case studies, pay close attention to the personality of the character's behavior. Throughout these case studies, you will be assessing the case study, determining the Biblical DISC Style, and then applying the EIC Method. As you know, we identified four Emotionally Intelligent in Christ behaviors: Personal Identity (Self-Awareness), Self-Control (Self-Management), Altruistic Attitude (Social-Awareness), and Christ Connections (Relational Management).

As you apply the EIC Method in excerpts taken from each case study, think about the *encounter, identified behavior (s), and course correction* that was or should be applied. Mastery of this will help you use the EIC Method in real-world scenarios and those you encounter.

As you learned, DISC helps you identify the behavior, and EIC enables you to correct it. In chapter 7, we shared how "Ds" jump in, and "Is" talk out, "Ss" need time to think, and "Cs" want data to analyze and validate. It is important to pay close attention to each DISC personality in each case study, empowering you with a DISC and EIC's strong marriage.

Let's put this EIC Method in action using our first case story on Moses. In each case study, we will look at the EIC of the character(s) and observe the EIC God, which is the behavior we want to model continually. In reference study four, you will be able to put into practice all that you've learned.

Scripture Study Reference 1: Moses and the Burning Bush (Exodus 3)

"Now Moses was tending the flock of Jethro, his father-in-law, the priest of Midian, and he led the flock to the far side of the wilderness and came to Horeb, the mountain of God. There the angel of the Lord appeared to him in flames of fire from within a bush. Moses saw that though the bush was on fire it did not burn up. So Moses thought, "I will go over and see this strange sight—why the bush does not burn up."

When the Lord saw that he had gone over to look, God called to him from within the bush, "Moses! Moses!"

And Moses said, "Here I am."

"Do not come any closer," God said. "Take off your sandals, for the place where you are standing is holy ground." Then he said, "I am the God of your father,[a] the God of Abraham, the God of Isaac and the God of Jacob." At this, Moses hid his face, because he was afraid to look at God.

The Lord said, "I have indeed seen the misery of my people in Egypt. I have heard them crying out because of their slave drivers, and I am concerned about their suffering. So I have come down to rescue them from the hand of the Egyptians and to bring them up out of that land into a good and spacious land, a land flowing with milk and honey—the home of the Canaanites, Hittites, Amorites, Perizzites, Hivites and Jebusites. And now the cry of the Israelites has reached me, and I have seen the way the Egyptians are oppressing them. So now, go. I am sending you to Pharaoh to bring my people the Israelites out of Egypt."

But Moses said to God, "Who am I that I should go to Pharaoh and bring the Israelites out of Egypt?"

And God said, "I will be with you. And this will be the sign to you that it is I who have sent you: When you have brought the people out of Egypt, you[b] will worship God on this mountain."

Moses said to God, "Suppose I go to the Israelites and say to them, 'The God of your fathers has sent me to you,' and they ask me, 'What is his name?' Then what shall I tell them?"

God said to Moses, "I AM WHO I AM. This is what you are to say to the Israelites: 'I AM has sent me to you.'"

God also said to Moses, "Say to the Israelites, 'The Lord, the God of your fathers—the God of Abraham, the God of Isaac and the God of Jacob—has sent me to you.'

"This is my name forever, the name you shall call me from generation to generation.

"Go, assemble the elders of Israel and say to them, 'The Lord, the God of your fathers—the God of Abraham, Isaac and Jacob—appeared to me and said: I have watched over you and have seen what has been done to you in Egypt. And I have promised to bring you up out of your misery in Egypt into the land of the Canaanites, Hittites, Amorites, Perizzites, Hivites and Jebusites—a land flowing with milk and honey.'

"The elders of Israel will listen to you. Then you and the elders are to go to the king of Egypt and say to him, 'The Lord, the God of the Hebrews, has met with us. Let us take a three-day journey into the wilderness to offer sacrifices to the Lord our God.' But I know that the king of Egypt will not let you go unless a mighty hand compels him. So I will stretch out my hand and strike the Egyptians with all the wonders that I will perform among them. After that, he will let you go.

"And I will make the Egyptians favorably disposed toward this people, so that when you leave you will not go empty-handed. Every woman is to ask her neighbor and any woman living in her house for articles of silver and gold and for clothing, which you will put on your sons and daughters. And so you will plunder the Egyptians."

EIC Case Study 1: Moses (burning bush)

CASE STUDY HIGHLIGHTS

- Moses is timid and resists, citing his lack of eloquence and abilities, and refuses to go.
- Moses seeks approval from his father in-law Jethro by asking his permission to go. *"Let me return to my own people in Egypt to see if any of them are still alive."* Jethro said, *"Go, and I wish you well."*
- Moses asks God what His name is?

DISC STYLE

- Moses is a "C" in DISC.
- Moses is logic-driven when it comes to solving problems. This style asks lots of validating questions, collects, validates, and organizes data. In doing so they search for flaws and logically reorganize to get to the final result.

EIC Method Application

E: Encounter

The encounter starts with God appearing to Moses in flames of fire from within a burning bush and speaking to him about going back to Egypt to return the Israelites to Canaan to accomplish this task.

I: Identified Behavior(s)

There are four EIC Behaviors: Personal Identity (Self-Awareness), Self-Control (Self-Management), Altruistic Attitude (Social-Awareness), and Christ Connections (Relational Management) that Moses demonstrated at the Burning Bush.

Moses displayed the two EIC behaviors of *Altruistic Attitude (Social-Awareness) and Christ Connections (Relational Management)* in dynamic ways as his ministry unfolds. Throughout his life, he displayed a selfless attitude. An illustration of this was Moses's quick reaction to defend the people when God had decided to destroy the idol-worshipping Nation of Israel at the foot of the mountain.

He had a real Christ Connection throughout his life and was the stepping stone in restoring God's kingdom's authority over the whole earth. Moses clearly displayed both of these behaviors, modeling the behavior of Christ. Let's examine how his EIC behavior is presented in Self-Identity and Self-Control.

Personal Identity (Self-Awareness)

The case study showed that when God asked Moses to accept His calling for him, Moses lacked his personal identity. Although God knew his abilities, Moses's deficiency in understanding "self" resulted in his not seeing that his worth and value were enough to carry out the mission God's presented. He went into his "C" style, trying to apply logic to the situation instead of looking within himself-to see the capabilities that God had given him. He even went so far as to ask that God ask his brother because he felt he was a better leader than himself. Remembering that the "C" personality trait is to seek validation, Moses exemplifies this perfectly by seeking validation for his father-in-law Jethro to follow God's direction. Once Jethro said, *"Go, and I wish you well,"* Moses had the confirmation he needed to fulfill the mission of Christ.

Self-Control (Self-Management)

Moses also lacked Self-Control. In the case study, you will see that he did not surrender to the presence and authority of God. Instead, he questions God's sovereignty and

> When we stay in God's Word, He will give us the discernment of thoughts and intentions of the heart, giving us the ability to work in His power and love and without fear.

his abilities to do as instructed. When you encounter a High C, like Moses, they think methodically, paying close attention to detail, and need time to process when making decisions. In this case, God didn't allow that processing time as He sees and knows our capabilities before we do. To master any new behavior, it's important to remember that Christ is by our side to help us manage our emotions. With Moses, his hesitation was fear and lack of confidence, as he doubted that God can make a way when from our human perspective, there is no way.

C: Course Correct

So, how do we course correct the Self-identity and Self-control behaviors that Moses lacked? Let's look at the 3 R's.

CONSCIENTIOUS (C)

HOW TO RESPOND TO A HIGH C
- Be specific and accurate
- Make allowance for initial responeses to be cautions and/or negative
- Allow freedom to ask questions

HOW TO RELATE TO A HIGH C
- Answer questions in a patient and persistent manner
- Mix accurate data with assurances
- Allow time to validate information

HOW TO REINFORCE THE HIGH C
- Provide a step-by-step approach
- Provide reassurances of support
- Give permission to validate information with third party

The Three R's for Conscientious

Using the 3Rs we see how God gave Moses the opportunity to Respond, Relate and Reinforce based on his "C" DISC tendencies. God compassionately meets Moses where he is and loves him enough not to leave him there:

Respond: Moses's lack of Self-Identity and Self-Management led him to seek reassurance for specific answers to his questions and concerns, which is why he responded to God in the way he did.

> It takes us surrendering ourselves to God and asking for His guidance on processing the behavior we have identified or exhibited.

Relate: Because Moses wanted answers, he mixed data with reassurances and sought third-party validation from Jethro.

Reinforce: Moses needed reassurance and support, and God gave this to him, allowing him to validate assertiveness and give him the resources he needed.

This case study is a testament to us working to be Christ-like and letting the Holy Spirit ease our concerns.

It takes us surrendering ourselves to God and asking for His guidance on processing the behavior we have identified or exhibited.

Moses resisted God and let fear come in. We consistently demonstrate this behavior, sometimes in our not knowing the next step or when asked to take on a challenge. *When this happens, pause and pray for the grace to accept what God has called you to do, ask for His guidance.* We do not know what form God will appear to us or how He will speak, but God does get His intentions to us when we ask, seek and knock . . . the door will open according to God's ultimate purpose for our lives. Staying in His Word and listening to whatever He says to us is the key.

> *"For the word of God is living and powerful, and sharper than any two-edged sword, piercing even to the division of soul and spirit, and of joints and marrow, and is a discerner of the thoughts and intents of the heart"* (Hebrews 4:12).

When we stay in God's Word, He will give us the discernment of thoughts and intentions of the heart, giving us the ability to work in His power and love and without fear.

EIC Case Study 2: God EIC toward Aaron (burning bush)

CASE STUDY HIGHLIGHTS

- God is concerned for the suffering of the Israelites, and He appears to Moses in the form of a burning bush.
- God is angered but encourages Moses, by using the resource Moses had in his hand: a staff. God also instructed Moses to take his brother, Aaron, with him as an aid. God is all about using the resources we have and multiplying them for His glory and our strength. Jesus fed 5,000 people, not counting women and children on five loaves of bread and two fish (Matthew 14:13–21).
- God speaks to Moses, informing him of His plan to return the Israelites to Canaan, asking Moses back to help accomplish this task.

DISC STYLE

- God is all Styles as He is the Creator

EIC Application

E: Encounter

God got Moses' attention using a burning bush. As soon as Moses stepped closer He began to speak to him. Oftentimes God will do the same for us. He gets our attention and then begins to speak and guide us. God is concerned about His people's suffering in Egypt and lays out His plan to Moses to return the Israelites to Canaan —to *"a land flowing with milk and honey"* (3:8). God sends Moses back to Egypt to accomplish this task. Moses is timid and resists, citing his lack of eloquence and abilities, and refuses to go. God is angered but encourages Moses, by transforming his staff into a snake in Exodus

4:2–4: *"Then the Lord said to him, "What is that in your hand?" "A staff," he replied. The Lord said, "Throw it on the ground." Moses threw it on the ground and it became a snake, and he ran from it. Then the Lord said to him, "Reach out your hand and take it by the tail." So Moses reached out and took hold of the snake and it turned back into a staff in his hand."* God performed miracles to validate the encounter and the call for Moses (high C's need validation). Knowing that Moses questioned his ability to be an eloquent speaker, God instructed Moses to take his brother, Aaron, with him in Exodus 4:13–14: *"But Moses said, "Pardon your servant, Lord. Please send someone else." Then the Lord's anger burned against Moses and he said, "What about your brother, Aaron the Levite? I know he can speak well. He is already on his way to meet you, and he will be glad to see you."* God is always one step ahead of the fears that hold us captive in life. When Moses asks God what his name is, God replies, *"I AM WHO I AM"* (3:14).

I: Identified Behavior

Personal Identity (Self-Awareness):

God was confident in His self-identity, telling Moses who He was when asked, He replied, *"I AM WHO I AM."* He also knew the right words of reassurance to use to let Moses be able to identify His God.

God reminds Moses of who He is in Exodus 20: *I am the LORD your God, who brought you out of Egypt, out of the land of slavery. You shall have no other gods before me. You shall not make for yourself an idol in the form of anything in heaven above or on the earth beneath or in the waters below.*

Through the four emotionally intelligent attributes below you will notice how God speaks to and directs us into the people He created us to be, just as He did for Moses: Self-Control (Self-Management).

God showed self-control several times. An example was when Moses questioned who God was and resisted His order to lead His people out of captivity. Although this angered God, He didn't act on that anger by lashing out instead, He knew what Moses needed to accept the challenge: encouragement and support. Jeremiah 17:10 says, *"I the Lord search the heart and examine the mind to reward each person according to their conduct, according to what their deeds deserve."*

He knows the conduct that Moses has in his heart and mind.

Altruistic Attitude (Social-Awareness):

God encourages Moses, by asking him to use the staff in his hand to perform the miracle of turning it into a snake. This increased Moses' trust factor which opened his heart to God's instructions.

Christ Connections (Relational Management):

God brings together the right connections. Knowing both Aaron and Moses, He knew the roles each would play in the mission He brought to them. Aaron was to support Moses and Moses Aaron.

C: Course Correct

> We must always remember that GOD understands our behavioral needs perfectly.

God applied eight of the bullet points from the CONSCIENCIOUS (C) chart "Conscientious Chart" (shown on page 210) in Exodus 3 & 4. As you read through the Scripture text, you will notice the course corrections God applied based on Moses' "C" DISC Style.

Response: God was specific and accurate with Moses and made allowances for his questioning his calling.

Relate: God allowed time for Moses to validate information even with the third-party validation of Jethro.

Reinforce: God gave Moses permission to validate and gave him reassurances in the support that Aaron would supply. He also let Moses know that He would be with him.

It is our role to model the behavior of Christ as was demonstrated in how He handled Moses. In the Old Testament, God is unique, sovereign, and unchanging. His unchanging nature is hinted at by his name "YAHWEH," meaning "to be," which is similar to the title God uses with Moses, *"I AM WHO I AM."* God's willingness to cause momentous events to teach a lesson is shown in His reaction to Moses' resistance. He gives us what is needed to course correct, providing the tools and resources to do so. His ability to empower us with the proper guidance and direction.

We must always remember that GOD understands our behavioral needs perfectly.

Furthermore, God provides us with case studies in His Holy Scriptures on how personal and unique He can be. Understanding of the DISC model unlocks these strategies so that we can determine how to *"Love one another"* (John 13:34–45). This coupled with the EIC model can help you work through life's most difficult challenges.

Scripture Study Reference 2: The Golden Calf (Exodus 32)

> *"When the people saw that Moses was so long in coming down from the mountain, they gathered around Aaron and said, "Come, make us gods who will go before us. As for this fellow Moses who brought us up out of Egypt, we don't know what has happened to him."*
>
> *Aaron answered them, "Take off the gold earrings that your wives, your sons and your daughters are wearing, and bring them to me." So all the people took off their earrings and brought them to Aaron. He took what they handed him and made it into an idol cast in the shape of a calf, fashioning it with a tool. Then they said, "These are your gods, Israel, who brought you up out of Egypt."*

When Aaron saw this, he built an altar in front of the calf and announced, "Tomorrow there will be a festival to the Lord." So the next day the people rose early and sacrificed burnt offerings and presented fellowship offerings. Afterward they sat down to eat and drink and got up to indulge in revelry.

Then the Lord said to Moses, "Go down, because your people, whom you brought up out of Egypt, have become corrupt. They have been quick to turn away from what I commanded them and have made themselves an idol cast in the shape of a calf. They have bowed down to it and sacrificed to it and have said, 'These are your gods, Israel, who brought you up out of Egypt.'

"I have seen these people," the Lord said to Moses, "and they are a stiff-necked people. Now leave me alone so that my anger may burn against them and that I may destroy them. Then I will make you into a great nation."

But Moses sought the favor of the Lord his God. "Lord," he said, "why should your anger burn against your people, whom you brought out of Egypt with great power and a mighty hand? Why should the Egyptians say, 'It was with evil intent that he brought them out, to kill them in the mountains and to wipe them off the face of the earth'? Turn from your fierce anger; relent and do not bring disaster on your people. Remember your servants Abraham, Isaac and Israel, to whom you swore by your own self: 'I will make your descendants as numerous as the stars in the sky and I will give your descendants all this land I promised them, and it will be their inheritance forever.'" Then the Lord relented and did not bring on his people the disaster he had threatened.

Moses turned and went down the mountain with the two tablets of the covenant law in his hands. They were inscribed on both sides, front and back. The tablets were the work of God; the writing was the writing of God, engraved on the tablets.

When Joshua heard the noise of the people shouting, he said to Moses, "There is the sound of war in the camp."

Moses replied:

"It is not the sound of victory, it is not the sound of defeat; it is the sound of singing that I hear."

When Moses approached the camp and saw the calf and the dancing, his anger burned and he threw the tablets out of his hands, breaking them to pieces at the foot of the mountain. And he took the calf the people had made and burned it in the fire; then he ground it to powder, scattered it on the water and made the Israelites drink it.

He said to Aaron, "What did these people do to you, that you led them into such great sin?"

"Do not be angry, my lord," Aaron answered. "You know how prone these people are to evil. They said to me, 'Make us gods who will go before us. As for this fellow Moses who brought us up out of Egypt, we don't know what has happened to him.' So I told them, 'Whoever has any gold jewelry, take it off.' Then they gave me the gold, and I threw it into the fire, and out came this calf!"

Moses saw that the people were running wild and that Aaron had let them get out of control and so become a laughingstock to their enemies. So he stood at the entrance to the camp and said, "Whoever is for the Lord, come to me." And all the Levites rallied to him.

Then he said to them, "This is what the Lord, the God of Israel, says: 'Each man strap a sword to his side. Go back and forth through the camp from one end to the other, each killing his brother and friend and neighbor.'" The Levites did as Moses commanded, and that day about three thousand of the people died. Then Moses said, "You have been set apart to the Lord today, for you were against your own sons and brothers, and he has blessed you this day."

The next day Moses said to the people, "You have committed a great sin. But now I will go up to the Lord; perhaps I can make atonement for your sin."

So Moses went back to the Lord and said, "Oh, what a great sin these people have committed! They have made themselves gods of gold. But now, please forgive their sin—but if not, then blot me out of the book you have written."

The Lord replied to Moses, "Whoever has sinned against me I will blot out of my book. Now go, lead the people to the place I spoke of, and my angel will go before you. However, when the time comes for me to punish, I will punish them for their sin."

And the Lord struck the people with a plague because of what they did with the calf Aaron had made."

EIC Case Study 3: Aaron (golden calf)

CASE STUDY HIGHLIGHTS

- Aaron is entrusted to watch the flock while Moses is getting the Ten Commandments
- Aaron's leadership is tested when asked to create a graven image of a golden calf and break a commandment (Exodus 20:3–5)
- Aaron succumbed to the pressures of the people causing the Hebrew nation to engage in a great sin of worship and sacrifice to an idol

- When Aaron is confronted by Moses, he shifts the blame on the people

DISC STYLE

- Aaron is an "I" in DISC
- Aaron is highly vulnerable to social pressure. This style is feeling driven and confronted with "why" questions. This leads them to either deny responsibility or shift the blame

EIC Application

Encounter

While Moses received the Ten Commandments, Aaron surrendered to peer pressure helping the impatient Israelites collect gold to build a golden calf to worship. Aaron's Biblical DISC trait of an "I" affected his actions on handling group pressure, interpretation of God's commandment, and taking responsibility for his leadership direction. The I's biggest fear is rejection which makes them vulnerable to peer pressure.

Identified behavior

Social-Awareness/Altruistic Attitude

In this particular case study, Aaron didn't demonstrate behaviors of Social-Awareness (Altruistic Attitude). Although his "I" trait of being outgoing and enthusiastic enhanced his ability to trigger action and activities in others, his acts to support the people weren't driven by altruistic behavior but more by giving in to the pressure surrounding him. The behavioral focus for this case study is in Self-Awareness (Personal Identity), Self-Control (Self-Management), and Relational Management (Christ Connection), affecting the way Aaron led during Moses' absence.

Personal Identity/Self-Awareness & Self-Control/Self-Management & Christ Connections/Relational Management

Aaron was very people-oriented and had strong communication skills. It wasn't surprising that Moses left Aaron in charge during his absence due to the leadership skills he processed. In Relational Management, Aaron was confident; his social and interactive style was likely why the Israelites felt he was approachable and could share their demands with him. In Self-Awareness, Aaron had a problem of constantly looking for approval. The fear of rejection was one motivating factor behind Aaron helping support the building and worship of the golden calf. His social management was good on the one hand but needed work on the other. He had a charismatic leadership style but caved under pressure. Aaron also lacked Christ Connection in that he didn't fully understand he was to enforce the Ten Commandments entrusted to him by Moses. He instead succumbed to the pressures of the people causing the Hebrew nation to engage in a great sin involving the first commandment.

Course Correct

Using the 3Rs we see that:

Response: Although Aaron was friendly and upbeat, he was very susceptible to social pressure. When correcting him publicly, he initially needed friendly tones.

Relate: Aaron needed to be empowered with the right action plan but supported with an accountability partner when encountering crisis management situations.

Reinforce: To avoid the shift blame/denial response, Aaron needed positive, public recognition and private understanding of his feelings.

The portrayal of Aaron seems like that of a conflicted personality. His one personality was a faithful companion to his brother Moses in Egypt, attempting to impress Pharaoh with magical signs. Still, at Mt Sinai, he exhibited a different personality. At the same time

> # INFLUENCING (I)
>
> **HOW TO RESPOND TO A HIGH I**
> - Be friendly and positive
> - Allow for informal dialogue
> - Allow time for stimulating and fun activities
>
> **HOW TO RELATE TO A HIGH I**
> - Use friendly voice tones
> - Allow time for them to verbalize their feelings
> - Help them transfer talk to an action plan
>
> **HOW TO REINFORCE THE HIGH I**
> - Offer positive encouragement and incentives for taking on tasks
> - Help to organize an action plan
> - Communicate positive recognition

The 3 Rs for Influencing

Moses received the Ten Commandments, Aaron surrendered to peer pressure and helped the impatient Israelites collect gold to build a golden calf to worship.

Aaron wasn't conflicted but instead displayed the Biblical DISC trait of an "I." When Aaron was presented with managing the Israelites, they instead talked him into building an idol, losing focus. This loss of focus is typical for the "I" DISC style as they solve problems by bringing in thoughts, new thoughts, and newer thoughts that are sometimes unrelated to solving the problem. In the case of Aaron, he acted on the wrong thinking, which was to support the Israelites building of an idol, not remembering what he was commissioned to do.

Aaron also let fear take over. When we live in fear, it drives us to the deception of thinking, in this case, the worshiping of idols. Isaiah 41:10 says: *"So do not fear, for I am with you; do not be dismayed, for I am your God. I will strengthen you and help you; I will uphold you with my righteous right hand."*

Aaron needed to realize as we all must, that God has us covered in every situation and will meet all of our needs no matter how demanding or impossible they seem.

EIC Case Study 4: EIC of God towards Aaron—God empowerment of Moses (golden calf)

CASE STUDY HIGHLIGHTS

- God was angered with Aaron and the Israelites and wanted to destroy them for the building of the golden calf.
- God knew the problems of the Israelites and counseled Moses on them, letting him know that they were stiff-necked people.
- God empowered Moses to handle the situation, knowing his heart and leadership style.

DISC Style

- God is all Styles as He is the Creator and can empower us with the ability to connect to different DISC styles to make Christ Connections

EIC Application

Encounter

God empowered and counseled Moses to handle the wrong action of Aaron and the Israelites. Moses understood God's mission and wanted to fulfill it even with their sins against God. Moses, through God, worked to find a resolution to the situation, acting on God's EIC.

Identified behavior(s)

This case study is an example of how Moses modeled all the four identified behaviors of Personal Identity (Self-Awareness), Self-Control (Self-Management), Altruistic Attitude (Social-Awareness), and Christ Connections (Relational Management).

> It takes humility and trust in God's support and protection to step up and own your part in undesirable outcomes.

Moses's personal identity (Self-Awareness) expressed itself-as a gifted, well-trained person, but his true greatness came from his personal experience and relationship with God. Moses Christ Connections or Relational Management helped him stand firm when needed to honor God's calling. He was also gentle when he asked for the forgiveness of the Israelites sin against God. Moses, through God, was able to maintain Personal Identity/Self-Awareness throughout his leadership and use the right amount of Self-Control.

One of the most significant examples of altruism was when Moses asked God to forgive the people for their sin against him. Moses petitioned God by saying, *"Oh, what a great sin these people have committed! They have made themselves gods of gold. But now, please forgive their sin—but if not, then blot me out of the book you have written"* (Exodus 32:31–32).

In the midst of the Israelites failing Moses and sinning against God, Moses EIC still wanted them spared against God's wrath because of the love he had for God and them. Unlike that of Aaron, who passed the blame on others, rather than taking accountability for his own failed leadership.

When was a time in your life when you shifted the blame in order to avoid confrontation and accountability?

....

....

....

Accountability is a huge component of EIC. It takes humility and trust in God's support and protection to step up and own your part in undesirable outcomes.

Course Correct (3 R's)

Although Moses is a High C, this case study exemplifies how he had to go in and out of

> To engage in the right behaviors, at the right time, in the right amount, we must learn to walk with God with open hearts and minds to His voice so that He can direct our steps.

DOMINANCE (D)	INFLUENCING (I)
HOW TO RESPOND TO A HIGH D • Be firm and direct • Focus on actions and goals • Confront to get his/her attention **HOW TO RELATE TO A HIGH D** • Be brief and to the point • Explain "How to acheive goals" using logic with an action plan • Allow time to consider your ideas **HOW TO REINFORCE THE HIGH D** • Repeat the plan of action, focusing on goals, objectives, and results • Give bottom line instructions • Get out of his/her way	**HOW TO RESPOND TO A HIGH I** • Be friendly and positive • Allow for informal dialogue • Allow time for stimulating and fun activities **HOW TO RELATE TO A HIGH I** • Use friendly voice tones • Allow time for them to verbalize their feelings • Help them transfer talk to an action plan **HOW TO REINFORCE THE HIGH I** • Offer positive encouragement and incentives for taking on tasks • Help to organize an action plan • Communicate positive recognition
STEADINESS (S)	**CONSCIENTIOUS (C)**
HOW TO RESPOND TO A HIGH S • Be non-threatening and patient • Allow time to process and adjust to change • Make allowances for family or team **HOW TO RELATE TO A HIGH S** • Use friendly tones when instructing • Giver personal, nonverbal acceptance and assurances • Allow time to process information **HOW TO REINFORCE THE HIGH S** • Repeat any instructions • Provide hands-on reinforcement • Be patient in allowing time to take ownership	**HOW TO RESPOND TO A HIGH C** • Be specific and accurate • Make allowance for initial responses to be cautions and/or negative • Allow freedom to ask questions **HOW TO RELATE TO A HIGH C** • Answer questions in a patient and persistent manner • Mix accurate data with assurances • Allow time to validate information **HOW TO REINFORCE THE HIGH C** • Provide a step-by-step approach • Provide reassurances of support • Give permission to validate information with third party

The Three R's for All

DISC styles to capture the leadership God intended for him. In the three Rs below, we will explain how God's EIC took him in different DISC styles.

Response: Moses's Steadiness was seen in his ability to patiently make allowances for the people he led. He saw the people for who they desired to be rather than how their behavior showed up: Grace in action.

Relate: Moses was brief and to the point when faced with a corrective decision.

Reinforce: Moses took action to Influence when he asked permission to continue on God's mission. He transferred talk into an action plan to continue the mission and save the people from God's wrath.

God had an intended role for Moses to lead His people out of slavery in Egypt to the Promised Land. Moses is relatable to all of us because he has human faults. Moses also depicts the behaviors each of us has in our life. The shedding of his old nature, where his anger over the beating of an Israelite worker caused him to kill an Egyptian, to a patient nature, when he worked as a shepherd with his father-in-law Jethro, and then to a faithful, impulsive, and passionate follower of God as he took the role of the leader of the Hebrew nation. These noticeable behavioral changes in Moses are what we experience.

To engage in the right behaviors, at the right time, in the right amount, we must learn to walk with God with open hearts and minds to His voice so that He can direct our steps.

"Whether you turn to the right or to the left, your ears will hear a voice behind you, saying, "This is the way; walk in it" (Isaiah 30:21).

As with Moses, God lays out plans and callings for us. When God calls you to do something, do you always respond with enthusiasm? Or are you sometimes, like Moses, reluctant to take on the calling God has for you? When Jesus leads you, be ready to lead by developing the behaviors needed for His calling, big or small: *"The one who calls you is faithful, and he will do it"* (1 Thessalonians 5:24).

SCRIPTURE STUDY REFERENCE 3: DEATH AND RESURRECTION OF LAZARUS—JESUS'S RESPONSE TO OUR BEHAVIORS (MARTHA AND MARY)

These next set of case studies show how God is the ultimate example of Emotional Intelligence. We have spent time in the case studies above taking a deep dive into how HE responds and adjusts to our behaviors in examples of Moses and Aaron. Jesus Christ of Nazareth modeled the highest form of emotional intelligence, connecting the hearts of humanity: love in action. The focus of the three case studies below on Martha, Mary, and Peter, will showcase Emotional Intelligence by Jesus Christ of Nazareth when He walked this earth as a man. As mentioned in the introduction, we believe Jesus Christ is the ultimate model of Emotional Intelligence; as fully man and fully God, He offers us the bridge between man and God.

Case Study 3: The Death of Lazarus—Mary/Martha Case Study/Scripture (John 11:1–44)

Now a man named Lazarus was sick. He was from Bethany, the village of Mary and her sister Martha. (This Mary, whose brother Lazarus now lay sick, was the same one who poured perfume on the Lord and wiped his feet with her hair.) So the sisters sent word to Jesus, "Lord, the one you love is sick."

When he heard this, Jesus said, "This sickness will not end in death. No, it is for God's glory so that God's Son may be glorified through it." Now Jesus loved Martha and her sister and Lazarus. So when he heard that Lazarus was sick, he stayed where he was two more days, and then he said to his disciples, "Let us go back to Judea." "But Rabbi," they said, "a short while ago the Jews there tried to stone you, and yet you are going back?"

Jesus answered, "Are there not twelve hours of daylight? Anyone who walks in the daytime will not stumble, for they see by this world's light. It is when a person walks at night that they stumble, for they have no light."

After he had said this, he went on to tell them, "Our friend Lazarus has fallen asleep; but I am going there to wake him up."

His disciples replied, "Lord, if he sleeps, he will get better." Jesus had been speaking of his death, but his disciples thought he meant natural sleep.

So then he told them plainly, "Lazarus is dead, and for your sake I am glad I was not there, so that you may believe. But let us go to him."

Then Thomas (also known as Didymus) said to the rest of the disciples, "Let us also go, that we may die with him."

Jesus Comforts the Sisters of Lazarus

On his arrival, Jesus found that Lazarus had already been in the tomb for four days. Now Bethany was less than two miles from Jerusalem, and many Jews had come to Martha and Mary to comfort them in the loss of their brother. When Martha heard that Jesus was coming, she went out to meet him, but Mary stayed at home.

"Lord," Martha said to Jesus, "if you had been here, my brother would not have died. But I know that even now God will give you whatever you ask."

Jesus said to her, "Your brother will rise again."

Martha answered, "I know he will rise again in the resurrection at the last day."

Jesus said to her, "I am the resurrection and the life. The one who believes in me will live, even though they die; and whoever lives by believing in me will never die. Do you believe this?"

"Yes, Lord," she replied, "I believe that you are the Messiah, the Son of God, who is to come into the world."

After she had said this, she went back and called her sister Mary aside. "The Teacher is here," she said, "and is asking for you." When Mary heard this, she got up quickly and went to him. Now Jesus had not yet entered the village, but was still at the place where Martha had met him. When the Jews who had been with Mary in the house, comforting her, noticed how quickly she got up and went out, they followed her, supposing she was going to the tomb to mourn there.

When Mary reached the place where Jesus was and saw him, she fell at his feet and said, "Lord, if you had been here, my brother would not have died."

When Jesus saw her weeping, and the Jews who had come along with her also weeping, he was deeply moved in spirit and troubled. "Where have you laid him?" he asked.

"Come and see, Lord," they replied.

Jesus wept.

Then the Jews said, "See how he loved him!"

But some of them said, "Could not he who opened the eyes of the blind man have kept this man from dying?"

Jesus Raises Lazarus From the Dead

Jesus, once more deeply moved, came to the tomb. It was a cave with a stone laid across the entrance. "Take away the stone," he said.

"But Lord," said Martha, the sister of the dead man, "by this time there is a bad odor, for he has been there four days."

Then Jesus said, "Did I not tell you that if you believe, you will see the glory of God?"

So they took away the stone. Then Jesus looked up and said, "Father, I thank you that you have heard me. I knew that you always hear me, but I said this for the benefit of the people standing here, that they may believe that you sent me."

When he had said this, Jesus called in a loud voice, "Lazarus, come out!" The dead man came out, his hands and feet wrapped with strips of linen, and a cloth around his face.

Jesus said to them, "Take off the grave clothes and let him go."

Case Study Highlights: The Death and Resurrection of Lazarus

The focus of the Lazarus case studies is to show the differences in Jesus's behavior as He individually spoke to both Martha and Mary on the death of their brother Lazarus. It will provide background on Martha and Mary and then explain how Jesus responds to their DISC styles based on their emotional needs.

EIC Case Study 5: Martha (death of Lazarus)

CASE STUDY HIGHLIGHTS

- Martha was the oldest and appeared to be the owner of the family home.
- Martha had the gift of hospitality.
- Martha's name is the Aramaic word for "Lord," which seems to fit her character as a meticulous, controlling homemaker.

DISC STYLE

- High D
- Task Driven

EIC Application

Encounter

"On his arrival, Jesus found that Lazarus had already been in the tomb for four days. Now Bethany was less than two miles from Jerusalem, and many Jews had come to Martha and Mary to comfort them in the loss of their brother. When Martha heard that Jesus was coming, she went out to meet him, but Mary stayed at home.

"Lord," Martha said to Jesus, "if you had been here, my brother would not have died. But I know that even now God will give you whatever you ask."

Jesus said to her, "Your brother will rise again."

Martha answered, "I know he will rise again in the resurrection at the last day."

Jesus said to her, "I am the resurrection and the life. The one who believes in me will live, even though they die; 26 and whoever lives by believing in me will never die. Do you believe this?"

"Yes, Lord," she replied, "I believe that you are the Messiah, the Son of God, who is to come into the world."

After she had said this, she went back and called her sister Mary aside.

Identified behavior(s) (Martha)

The behavior of focus for this case study was on Martha's Christ Connections (Relational Management). Martha was a high D and was driven to work toward achieving the goals and tasks at hand. Although God applied the proper course correction when Martha lacked Christ Connections (Relational Management), we can't forget that Mary and her sister were both missionaries. Jesus points to Mary's example not to rebuke Martha but as a gentle reminder that leadership demands the switch from leadership to management and vice versa. Sometimes being focused on the task and not the mission drives us to lose track of what is essential. When this happens, we must course-correct applying the EIC Model.

Course Correct (Apply the 3Rs)

Response: Jesus responds to Martha firmly and directly with an action plan.

Relate: Jesus was brief and to the point with Martha asking her belief in her brother rising again.

Reinforce: Jesus gave Martha bottom line instructions on His resurrection and life.

EIC Case Study 6: Mary (death of Lazarus)

CASE STUDY HIGHLIGHTS

- Mary was the middle sibling with a quiet, empathetic style
- Mary lived with her sister Martha
- Mary was very close with Martha and Lazarus

DISC STYLE

- High S
- Feeling Driven

EIC Application

Encounter

After she (Martha) had said this, she went back and called her sister Mary aside. "The Teacher is here," she said, "and is asking for you." When Mary heard this, she got up quickly and went to him. When Mary reached the place where Jesus was and saw him, she fell at his feet and said, "Lord, if you had been here, my brother would not have died." When Jesus saw her weeping, and the Jews who had come along with her also weeping, he was deeply moved in spirit and troubled. "Where have you laid him?" he asked. "Come and see, Lord," they replied. Jesus wept."

DOMINANCE (D)

HOW TO RESPOND TO A HIGH D
- Be firm and direct
- Focus on actions and goals
- Confront to get his/her attention

HOW TO RELATE TO A HIGH D
- Be brief and to the point
- Explain "How to acheive goals" using logic with an action plan
- Allow time to consider your ideas

HOW TO REINFORCE THE HIGH D
- Repeat the plan of action, focusing on goals, objectives, and results
- Give bottom line instructions
- Get out of his/her way

The Three R's for Dominance

Identified behavior(s) (Mary)

In contrast, the behavior of Mary in her Christ Connections (Relational Management) was appropriate. She knew how to choose the better path, which was to pay more attention to Christ than the home's activities. One could say that her Altruistic Attitude (Social-Awareness) behavior toward her sister is lacking. Mary did pay more attention to the teachings of Jesus as she sat at His feet when Jesus came to their home and not on the supper preparation for her guests. In all situations, we must look at the entire picture. Remember that it wasn't her needs she was paying attention to but that of Christ. She put Jesus's teaching first, giving attention to what is needed.

Course Correct (Apply the 3Rs)

Response: Jesus allows time for Mary to respond to His questions.

Relate: Jesus weeps with Mary showing His compassion letting her know that He understands her grief.

Reinforce: Jesus provides instructions to Mary and questions her to confirm her belief in His promise and moves to show her.

EIC Case Study 7: Jesus to Martha and Mary Summary

As we have learned, the most effective way to communicate and connect with a high D is to be firm and direct. Jesus knew this about Martha and responded to her directly about her belief and faith in Him. Jesus asked her questions that confirmed her thoughts in God's Word and was able to redirect Martha when she was going in the wrong direction toward doubt and restore her faith.

> Jesus wants you to focus your time and energy on Him and his word, understand your priorities and use good judgment.

Mary, who was a High S, was approached by Jesus indirectly and openly. Jesus went into His supporting and aligning role with her, which Mary needed at the time. He showed compassion, empathy, and patience with her being responsive to her needs as He personally connected to her grief. Remember, Jesus continually used different behaviors to meet the needs of any given situation He faced and His leadership styles were consistent with situations that were repetitive.

> ## STEADINESS (S)
>
> **HOW TO RESPOND TO A HIGH S**
> - Be non-threatening and patient
> - Allow time to process and adjust to change
> - Make allowances for family or team
>
> **HOW TO RELATE TO A HIGH S**
> - Use friendly tones when instructing
> - Giver personal, nonverbal acceptance and assurances
> - Allow time to process information
>
> **HOW TO REINFORCE THE HIGH S**
> - Repeat any instructions
> - Provide hands-on reinforcement
> - Be patient in allowing time to take ownership

The Three R's for Steadiness

Before we move onto the EIC of Jesus, take a moment to reflect on a few of your findings around your DISC or EIC assessment (links to take the assessments are found in Chapter 2). What do you want to transfer forward that will support your ability to connect your identity with Christ and practice self-control when you come face-to-face with emotionally challenging situations? For example, let's say you are sensitive to what others think of you. Knowing this, how do you want to prepare your soul in Christ so that you don't take things personally? Or maybe you have a tendency to be blunt and direct with little concern for how you come across to other people. Only 7% of effective communication are the words you use, the other factors include body language, intonation, and facial expressions. What if God said to you: "Remind your face today that I adore you and share that with others around you."

THE CHAVOUS, CUMMINS, MILLER AND VOGES EIC MODEL IN PRACTICE

SCRIPTURE STUDY REFERENCE 4: AT THE HOME OF MARTHA AND MARY

Luke 10:38–42 is another example of Jesus's love and understanding of the behaviors of Martha and Mary.

Jesus wants you to focus your time and energy on Him and his word, understand your priorities and use good judgment.

> *"But Martha was distracted by all the preparations that had to be made. She came to him and asked, "Lord, don't you care that my sister has left me to do the work by myself? Tell her to help me!" "Martha, Martha," the Lord answered, "you are worried and upset about many things, but few things are needed—or indeed only one. Mary has chosen what is better, and it will not be taken away from her."*

Jesus's behavior toward Martha was kind, compassionate, and He knew her heart and that she was worried and troubled. He calmly told her that she needn't worry about all of the preparations and that spending time with Him was all that was needed, as Mary had chosen to do. Jesus accepted Martha for who she was and let her vent, responding with love.

Mary chooses to sit with Jesus and take in the opportunity for connection with Him and His Word. She wasn't concerned with the business of hosting but fellowshipping with Him. Jesus commended Mary for giving Him her full attention, as in that moment, He called it the *one thing needed.*

Now it is time for you to practice what you've learned from the EIC Model in this piece of Scripture.

DOMINANCE (D)

HOW TO RESPOND TO A HIGH D
- Be firm and direct
- Focus on actions and goals
- Confront to get his/her attention

HOW TO RELATE TO A HIGH D
- Be brief and to the point
- Explain "How to acheive goals" using logic with an action plan
- Allow time to consider your ideas

HOW TO REINFORCE THE HIGH D
- Repeat the plan of action, focusing on goals, objectives, and results
- Give bottom line instructions
- Get out of his/her way

INFLUENCING (I)

HOW TO RESPOND TO A HIGH I
- Be friendly and positive
- Allow for informal dialogue
- Allow time for stimulating and fun activities

HOW TO RELATE TO A HIGH I
- Use friendly voice tones
- Allow time for them to verbalize their feelings
- Help them transfer talk to an action plan

HOW TO REINFORCE THE HIGH I
- Offer positive encouragement and incentives for taking on tasks
- Help to organize an action plan
- Communicate positive recognition

STEADINESS (S)

HOW TO RESPOND TO A HIGH S
- Be non-threatening and patient
- Allow time to process and adjust to change
- Make allowances for family or team

HOW TO RELATE TO A HIGH S
- Use friendly tones when instructing
- Giver personal, nonverbal acceptance and assurances
- Allow time to process information

HOW TO REINFORCE THE HIGH S
- Repeat any instructions
- Provide hands-on reinforcement
- Be patient in allowing time to take ownership

CONSCIENTIOUS (C)

HOW TO RESPOND TO A HIGH C
- Be specific and accurate
- Make allowance for initial responses to be cautions and/or negative
- Allow freedom to ask questions

HOW TO RELATE TO A HIGH C
- Answer questions in a patient and persistent manner
- Mix accurate data with assurances
- Allow time to validate information

HOW TO REINFORCE THE HIGH C
- Provide a step-by-step approach
- Provide reassurances of support
- Give permission to validate information with third party

The Three R's for All

Encounter

Describe a situation where you have felt like you have been carrying all the load and others haven't been there to support you.

Identified Behavior (s)

Write down the behavior you displayed in response to this encounter and the behavior of the other person involved.

Course Correct

How would you have course-corrected the behavior using your personal DISC style? How would you have changed this by course-correcting using the behavior of Jesus?

Having practiced EIC in both ways, reflect on the differences and how they made you feel. In what ways did your demonstration of Christlike behavior change the situation? How will you work to incorporate the EIC model to appropriately exhibit Christlike behavior and not pass judgment on others for the way they respond?

Scripture Study Reference 5: Jesus and the Miraculous Catch of Fish (John 21)

"Afterward Jesus appeared again to his disciples, by the Sea of Galilee. It happened this way: Simon Peter, Thomas (also known as Didymus), Nathanael from Cana in Galilee, the sons of Zebedee, and two other disciples were together. "I'm going out to fish," Simon Peter told them, and they said, "We'll go with you." So they went out and got into the boat, but that night they caught nothing.

Early in the morning, Jesus stood on the shore, but the disciples did not realize that it was Jesus.

He called out to them, "Friends, haven't you any fish?"

"No," they answered.

He said, "Throw your net on the right side of the boat and you will find some." When they did, they were unable to haul the net in because of the large number of fish.

Then the disciple whom Jesus loved said to Peter, "It is the Lord!" As soon as Simon Peter heard him say, "It is the Lord," he wrapped his outer garment around him (for he had taken it off) and jumped into the water. The other disciples followed in the boat, towing the net full of fish, for they were not far from shore, about a hundred yards. When they landed, they saw a fire of burning coals there with fish on it, and some bread.

Jesus said to them, "Bring some of the fish you have just caught." So Simon Peter climbed back into the boat and dragged the net ashore. It was full of large fish, 153, but even with so many the net was not torn. Jesus said to them, "Come and have breakfast." None of the disciples dared ask him, "Who are you?" They knew it was the Lord. Jesus came, took the bread and gave it to them, and did the same with the fish. This was now the third time Jesus appeared to his disciples after he was raised from the dead."

EIC Case Study 8: Jesus Reinstates Peter

"When they had finished eating, Jesus said to Simon Peter, "Simon son of John, do you love me more than these?"

"Yes, Lord," he said, "you know that I love you."

Jesus said, "Feed my lambs."

Again Jesus said, "Simon son of John, do you love me?"

He answered, "Yes, Lord, you know that I love you."

Jesus said, "Take care of my sheep."

The third time he said to him, "Simon son of John, do you love me?"

Peter was hurt because Jesus asked him the third time, "Do you love me?" He said, "Lord, you know all things; you know that I love you."

Jesus said, "Feed my sheep. Very truly I tell you, when you were younger you dressed yourself-and went where you wanted; but when you are old you will stretch out your hands, and someone else will dress you and lead you where you do not want to go." Jesus said this to indicate the kind of death by which Peter would glorify God. Then he said to him, "Follow me!"

Peter turned and saw that the disciple whom Jesus loved was following them. (This was the one who had leaned back against Jesus at the supper and had said, "Lord, who is going to betray you?") When Peter saw him, he asked, "Lord, what about him?"

Jesus answered, "If I want him to remain alive until I return, what is that to you? You must follow me." Because of this, the rumor spread among the believers that this disciple would not die. But Jesus did not say that he would not die; he only said, "If I want him to remain alive until I return, what is that to you?"

This is the disciple who testifies to these things and who wrote them down. We know that his testimony is true.

Jesus did many other things as well. If every one of them were written down, I suppose that even the whole world would not have room for the books that would be written.

The apostles returned from Jerusalem to the Sea of Galilee without their teacher Jesus."

CASE STUDY HIGHLIGHTS

- Peter was a fisherman who spent three years in the school of Jesus
- Peter went through a great transformation in his life from being impetuous to being strong and firm
- Peter's weakness was his flesh side always wanting approval and Social-Awareness and fears in not getting this

DISC STYLE

- Peter was a High I

EIC Application

Encounter

There are two significant incidents around Peter and his EIC. The first was his not recognizing Jesus as John did and the second was his being questioned as to his love for God three times.

Identified Behavior(s)

In both of the incidents above, Peter could be limited in the area of Relational Management/Christ Connections. When Jesus appeared on the shore and hollered to the disciples, Peter's Spiritual Perception was lacking, unlike that of John, who recognized Jesus immediately. Another critical thing was Jesus questioning him about the love he had for Him. Jesus took the adversities, trials, and mistakes Peter encountered to continue his love for Him. He gave him the ultimate forgiveness.

Course Correct (Apply the 3Rs)

Response: Jesus responds to Peter with an action plan to follow Him

Relate: Jesus relates to Peter with patience and love

Reinforce: Jesus gave Peter positive encouragement by restoring him publicly in front of His disciples

---

INFLUENCING (I)

HOW TO RESPOND TO A HIGH I
- Be friendly and positive
- Allow for informal dialogue
- Allow time for stimulating and fun activities

HOW TO RELATE TO A HIGH I
- Use friendly voice tones
- Allow time for them to verbalize their feelings
- Help them transfer talk to an action plan

HOW TO REINFORCE THE HIGH I
- Offer positive encouragement and incentives for taking on tasks
- Help to organize an action plan
- Communicate positive recognition

The 3 Rs for Influencing

Case Summary

There is no better case study to illustrate Jesus's perfection in EIC than the story of "Jesus and the Miraculous Catch of Fish." The story had three incidents; the fishing experience on the lake, the breakfast on the shore, and followed by the third and most important Emotional Intelligent response: It is Jesus's undoing of Peter's three denials with affirmation and publicly restoring him as the leader of Apostles in front of the disciples. In each of these situations, God teaches Emotional Intelligence to Peter and the disciples.

> God uses His Emotional intelligence to show us that He is the Lord of will, the Lord of hearts, and the Lord of our minds.

This case study showed the love and forgiveness Jesus has for us. Peter denied Christ three times during the night of Jesus's trial, but Jesus took special care to rehabilitate Peter and assure him He forgave him. He did this at the seashore. When Jesus spoke to Peter on the seashore, He asked him three times to confirm his love for Him.

Before that, Peter denied Jesus three times, which is significant and shows us how we can learn from our experiences and failures and Christ's forgiveness.

Matthew 18:21–22 says, *"Then Peter came to Jesus and asked, "Lord, how many times shall I forgive my brother or sister who sins against me? Up to seven times?" Jesus answered, "I tell you, not seven times, but seventy-seven times."*

In this story, God uses His Emotional intelligence to show us that He is the Lord of will, the Lord of hearts, and the Lord of our minds.

The case study below shows the powerful transformation within Peter from fear to faith as a result of his reconciliation encounter with the Risen Lord. Notice the faith-filled courage that leads Peter's behavior over fear.

Take some time to reflect on a time in your life when you felt like your spiritual perception was lacking? Or when you sacrifice your beliefs due to fears of what others think. What did your behaviors look like as a result of this? How did you reconnect or course-correct with God as Peter did?

....

....

....

....

....

Scripture Study Reference 6: Sanhedrin Story (Acts 4: 1–13)

> *"The priests and the captain of the temple guard and the Sadducees came up to Peter and John while they were speaking to the people. They were greatly disturbed because the apostles were teaching the people, proclaiming in Jesus the resurrection of the dead. They seized Peter and John and, because it was evening, they put them in jail until the next day. But many who heard the message believed; so the number of men who believed grew to about five thousand.*
>
> *The next day the rulers, the elders and the teachers of the law met in Jerusalem. Annas the high priest was there, and so were Caiaphas, John, Alexander and others of the high priest's family. They had Peter and John brought before them and began to question them: "By what power or what name did you do this?"*
>
> *Then Peter, filled with the Holy Spirit, said to them: "Rulers and elders of the people! If we are being called to account today for an act of kindness shown to a man who was lame and are being asked how he was healed, then know this, you and all the people of Israel: It is by the name of Jesus Christ of Nazareth, whom you crucified but whom*

God raised from the dead, that this man stands before you healed. Jesus is

"'the stone you builders rejected, which has become the cornerstone.'

Salvation is found in no one else, for there is no other name under heaven given to mankind by which we must be saved."

When they saw the courage of Peter and John and realized that they were unschooled, ordinary men, they were astonished and they took note that these men had been with Jesus."

EIC Case Study 9: Peter (Sanhedrin Story)

CASE STUDY HIGHLIGHTS

- This case study was an example of how the Holy Spirit can empower you to do God's work. The behavior that Peter was assigned went against his nature, but with the Holy Spirit, he could go against his flesh nature into the Emotional Intelligence of Christ.

DISC STYLE

- Peter was a High I

EIC Application

Encounter

Temple guards and Sadducees approached Peter and John disturbed about them proclaiming in Jesus's name the resurrection of the dead. They seized Peter and John and put them in jail. When later asked what power or what name did this, Peter was filled with the Holy Spirit and replied.

"Rulers and elders of the people! If we are being called to account today for an act of kindness shown to a man who was lame and is being asked how he was healed, then know this, you and all the people of Israel: It is by the name of Jesus Christ of Nazareth" (Acts 4:1–10).

Identified Behavior

The identified behavior for Peter was Self-Control (Self-Management) demonstrated by Peter as he stood before the Sanhedrin in Acts 4. Based on Peter's profile, taking this bold move to stand firm under the face of social pressure would be hard for him. He was a High I and they work toward relating to people through friendly and favorable situations, unlike those presented to him. But through the Holy Spirit, he modeled the behavior of Jesus and was able to take on the personality and strength of courage needed to overcome this obstacle.

> We all long to live a life for Christ, but it takes knowing Him, His EIC and modeling His behavior.

INFLUENCING (I)

HOW TO RESPOND TO A HIGH I
- Be friendly and positive
- Allow for informal dialogue
- Allow time for stimulating and fun activities

HOW TO RELATE TO A HIGH I
- Use friendly voice tones
- Allow time for them to verbalize their feelings
- Help them transfer talk to an action plan

HOW TO REINFORCE THE HIGH I
- Offer positive encouragement and incentives for taking on tasks
- Help to organize an action plan
- Communicate positive recognition

The 3 Rs for Influencing

Course Correct (Apply the 3Rs)

Response: Jesus responds to Peter by filling him with the Holy Spirit, enabling him to move past his flesh.

Relate: Jesus knew Peter and was capable of taking action.

Reinforce: Jesus gave Peter an action plan and helped him execute and communicate it.

Peter's Case Study Summary

Peter's life is a great redemption story. He was in the fishing profession known to be for the uneducated and violent. Peter demonstrates this violent behavior when he cuts off the soldier's ear in the Garden of Gethsemane at Jesus's arrest instead of reacting in love. Then, Peter's plight of spreading the Good News is found in the Book of Acts. During Jesus's ministry, Peter was a man who wanted a strong faith but faltered often.

We all long to live a life for Christ, but it takes knowing Him, His EIC and modeling His behavior.

Let's take some time to reflect:

When was a time in your life when fear shut you down emotionally and Jesus came after you to restore faith over the fear? What do you want to remember about that time to strengthen your ability to choose Christ over the emotion of fear?

When have you experienced the strength of God within you, as Peter did, that unlocked your ability to do something you would not normally think you could do with your own efforts? Which aspect of EIC was influenced by grounding your identity in Christ as Peter did? Self-control? Altruism? The ability to make connections in the midst of conflict? (Christ Connections):

Again, reflect on a moment in your life when you modeled the behavior of Christ over your natural flesh tendencies. What did you notice to be different as a result of practicing Emotional Intelligence in Christ: your ability to be aware of your emotions and with help of the Holy Spirit, manage them well?

Closing Comments on Peter's Self-Control (Self-Management)

Peter is a good case of learning from our reactions and how the Holy Spirit can guide us to the right responses. We will discuss this by looking into how Peter's negative self-management and his flesh side affected his EIC and how when Jesus's relational management strategies took over changed the outcome.

Negative Self-Management response of Peter

Accenting the positive and ignoring the negative increases flexibility because more options are open. However, eventually the overuse of these strengths results in pressure situations for I/Ds. Under pressure, they become soft and persuadable. When confronted, an emotional denial of responsibility is often their common defense response. [1]

The Apostle Peter's flesh side of Emotional Intelligence (Matthew 26:69–72)

Now Peter was sitting out in the courtyard, and a servant girl came to him. "You also were with Jesus of Galilee," she said. But he denied it before them all. "I don't know what you're talking about," he said. Then he went out to the gateway, where another servant girl saw him and said to the people there, "This fellow was with Jesus of Nazareth." He denied it again, with an oath: "I don't know the man!"

Jesus's Relational Management Strategies in responding to Peter's flesh actions (John 21:1–17)

Afterward Jesus appeared again to his disciples, by the Sea of Galilee. It happened this way: Simon Peter, Thomas (also known as Didymus), Nathanael from Cana in Galilee, the sons of Zebedee, and two other disciples were together. "I'm going out to fish," Simon Peter told them, and they said, "We'll go with you." So they went out and got into the boat, but that night they caught nothing.

Early in the morning, Jesus stood on the shore, but the disciples did not realize that it was Jesus. He called out to them, "Friends, haven't you any fish?" "No," they answered. He said, "Throw your net on the right side of the boat and you will find some." When they did, they were unable to haul the net in because of the large number of fish...When they landed, they saw a fire of burning coals there with fish on it, and some bread. . . . Jesus said to them, "Bring some of the fish you have just caught." So Simon Peter climbed back into the boat and dragged the net ashore.

It was full of large fish, 153, but even with so many the net was not torn.

Jesus said to them, "Come and have breakfast." None of the disciples dared ask him, "Who are you?" They knew it was the Lord. Jesus came, took the bread, and gave it to them, and did the same with the fish …

When they had finished eating, Jesus said to Simon Peter, "Simon son of John, do you love me more than these?" "Yes, Lord," he said, "you know that I love you." Jesus said, "Feed my lambs." Again Jesus said, "Simon son of John, do you love me?" He answered, "Yes, Lord, you know that I love you." Jesus said, "Take care of my sheep." The third time he said to him, "Simon son of John, do you love me?" Peter was hurt because Jesus asked him the third time, "Do you love me?" He said, "Lord, you know all things; you know that I love you." Jesus said, "Feed my sheep.[3]

Significance of turning Peter's answers to an action plan.

Jesus said, *"Feed my lambs."* Feed the new believers the Word of God.

Jesus said, *"Take care of my sheep."* Mentor the mature believers how to lead.

Jesus said, *"Feed my sheep."* Train the mature believers from the Word of God.

Then he said to him, *"Follow me!"* Inviting Peter and all followers of The Way, to model their leadership after Christ.

Looking back on all you have Discovered

In the Biblical DISC, you learned what you need and what others need in order to make Christ Connections. As you explored your own emotional intelligence and the emotional intelligence of Christ you learned where you are and where you want to be along with specific methods to meet those needs. Emotional Intelligence in Christ is the activation of the Holy Spirit within you to discern and manage personal emotions and behavior in a way that honors God by loving others well as Jesus did. It involves the four areas of: Personal Identity | Self-Control | Altruism | Christ Connections. We invite you to capture your learnings around your Biblical DISC and EIC in the NEXT STEPS section.

> *"Therefore Jesus said again, "Very truly I tell you, I am the gate for the sheep. All who have come before me are thieves and robbers, but the sheep have not listened to them. I am the gate; whoever enters through me will be saved. They will come in and go out, and find pasture. The thief comes only to steal and kill and destroy; I have come that they may have life, and have it to the full.*
>
> *"I am the good shepherd. The good shepherd lays down his life for the sheep. The hired hand is not the shepherd and does not own the sheep. So when he sees the wolf coming, he abandons the sheep and runs away. Then the wolf attacks the flock and scatters it. The man runs away because he is a hired hand and cares nothing for the sheep.*
>
> *"I am the good shepherd; I know my sheep and my sheep know me— just as the Father knows me and I know the Father—and I lay down my life for the sheep. I have other sheep that are not of this sheep pen. I must bring them also. They too will listen to my voice, and there shall be one flock and one shepherd"* (John 10:7–16).

NEXT STEPS

PERHAPS THIS IS the first time you have explored the impact that Jesus Christ of Nazareth had and continues to have in the lives of people who encounter Him. Jesus is after you, He adores you just as you are and loves you enough not to leave you there. If you have not had the opportunity to personally surrender your life over to Jesus, we invite you to pause and take a moment to do so now with a simple prayer:

> Dear Lord, I'm sorry for the behaviors in my life that have been clearly disconnected from the way You show up. Forgive me for every thoughtless word spoken and behavior done that has negatively impacted the life of another person and ultimately separated me from You. Today, I begin again and surrender all that I am over to You. Renew my sense of identity in You. Resurrect within me a sense of self-control over my emotions and behaviors. Fill me with the Holy Spirit and move me to forgive every individual that has negatively impacted my sense of wellbeing by careless words and or behaviors. I want to be Your ambassador in this world for the Glory of God. Come into my heart and be the Lord of my life. Lead me into Your emotionally intelligent way of loving God and loving people.

Congratulations for choosing to become a disciple of Christ. We encourage you to get involved with a Christ-centered church and Bible study group that can nourish your walk with the Lord. This is the most important choice you will make in your life.

Take some time to read through your reflections and responses that you wrote throughout this book. As is the case with new learnings, it is essential to have an action plan in place that you are willing to commit to daily in order to anchor specific behavioral shifts that support your desire to transfer and sustain EIC: Emotional Intelligence in Christ.

What are your top 7 takeaways from your experience with Emotional Intelligence in Christ?

1.
2.
3.
4.
5.
6.
7.

Take time to review what you learned about yourself-after taking the Biblical DISC assessment: https://bit.ly/3EomOBW. What specific behaviors do you want to do more of?

What is your next step and when will you start?

What specific behaviors do you want to do less of?

What is your next step and when will you start?

Take time to review what you learned about yourself-after taking the Biblical EIQ assessment: https://bit.ly/39e3f0M. What specific behaviors do you want to do more of?

....

....

....

What is your next step and when will you start?

....

....

....

What specific behaviors do you want to do less of?

....

....

....

What is your next step and when will you start?

....

....

....

Invite the Holy Spirit to help you shift the above specific behaviors in the area of the Biblical DISC and Biblical EIC assessment into the Emotional Intelligence in Christ in each of the four EIC areas. Notice the ways your Biblical DISC directly influences your EIC. For example, let's say your assessment shows a high D tendency, therefore your patience for people who take longer to process new information may trigger impatience within you as you are wired to get 'er done. What behavior do you want to focus on to draw near to Christ through the Holy Spirit to increase your ability to identify and adjust in that emotional area?

Personal Identity in Christ/Self-Awareness—Chapter 3: I commit to doing more of these behaviors in order to strengthen my personal relationship and identity in Christ: _____

_____

_____

_____

Self-Control/Self-Management—Chapter 4: I commit to doing more of these behaviors in order to strengthen my ability in Christ to activate the fruit of the Spirit in the area of self-control when it comes to my strong emotions: _____

_____

_____

_____

Altruism/Social-Awareness—Chapter 5: I commit to doing more of these behaviors in order to strengthen my ability in Christ to notice and respond to opportunities that express my concern for the wellbeing of others, as Christ did so beautifully and continues to do through His ambassadors, including me: _____

_____

_____

_____

Christ Connections/Relational-Management—Chapter 6: I commit to doing more of these behaviors in order to create intentional Christ Connections. I desire to be interruptible for God's work in people's lives. What will that look like specifically for me moving forward? _____

_____

_____

_____

If you are interested in taking the *Emotional Intelligence in Christ* course to practice and apply your learnings go to: https://EmotionalintelligenceinChrist.com

Join the Lead Like Jesus Community at:

LeadLikeJesus.com

Edge God In Podcast: EdgeGodIn.com

AUTHOR'S PERSONAL TESTIMONIES TO THE POWER OF EMOTIONAL INTELLIGENCE IN CHRIST

Estella Chavous's EIC Story

A testimony to the Holy Spirit working in me and Emotional Intelligence In Christ was how I handled the grief of losing my parents. I always thought that losing them would start a depressed, unfulfilled life and loss of control. When I did lose them, I felt all of the above, and the experience was heartbreaking.

But God has a different plan for me. He took the grief that I was feeling and increased my awareness of him through his Word giving me the peace I needed.

John 1:1 says, *In the beginning, was the Word, and the Word was with God, and the Word was God.*

His Word and the Holy Spirit in my life has allowed me to feel the good and bad with acceptance of my emotions, no matter what I am feeling. It has taught me that in the deepest part of grief, I need to give myself-time to process and heal and find comfort again. I had to learn to think less in the flesh and more in His Spirit.

1 Thessalonians 4:16—18 says, *For the Lord, himself-will come down from heaven, with a loud command, with the voice of the archangel and with the trumpet call of God, and the dead in Christ will rise first. After that, we who are still alive and are left will be caught up together with them in the clouds to meet the Lord in the air. And so we will be with the Lord forever. Therefore encourage one another with these words.*

This Word brought comfort and encouragement to me in that I know that even though my parents aren't with me now, they are in God's heart and hands, and we will be together again in eternal peace and love.

I tell you this story to say that we are never alone with the Emotional Intelligence given to us by God. He is with us always. He will turn the shock to healing, the anger to strength, and the depression to a settledness.

I believe God's Word and what it says, and I now live in acceptance, thankfulness, and hope of his calling.

Rich Cummins's EIC Story

As a child, I grew up very interested in sports, school, and the military. I was overly responsible and had a strong internal drive for success, even at an early age. After graduating from Purdue University, I decided to take a year off before graduate school to reduce my college debt. I moved back home and went to work with my father in our family business. Two months after working alongside my dad, he had a massive heart attack and died at the young age of 47.

Before he died, my dad uncovered an embezzlement. An employee had stolen over $500,000 from our company, most of which was owed to the IRS. At age twenty-two, I became a fourth generation print shop owner and inherited an undercapitalized business along with the fate of 40 families relying on my success. Facing four lawsuits to recover stolen funds from involved banks, the prosecution of our former employee, and the IRS with an intent to levy my business, I was truly being "baptized by fire."

Determined to succeed and not let the family business collapse on my watch, I put "my nose to the grindstone" and worked feverishly hard to resolve the mess that I took over. I settled the lawsuits with banks, paid off the IRS, and cooperated with the judicial process in the prosecution of the former employee.

Six years later, while on duty with the Indiana Army National Guard, I received a call from the office that dropped me to my knees. Apparently, our community was pummeled with a 100-year storm that flooded the business and caused over a million dollars of damage. I took out an SBA Disaster Assistance Loan, personally guaranteeing the debt to keep the company viable. Back to the "grindstone" I went. My resolve was unfettered as I pressed on.

By 2005, I was tired and worn out. The business challenges and chronic stress was getting the better of me. The American Dream was more of American Delusion as the treadmill of progress kept rolling without going anywhere really. It was that year that my life changed forever. A business colleague led me to the Lord, and I radically submitted my life to Jesus. For the first time in a long time, I finally felt peace. I continued to operate the business for several years but felt God nudging me in a new direction. It was at that point that our nation faced an economic recession like no other in American history.

The pressures exerted upon my business during the early days of the Great Recession forced me into a tenuous situation with the SBA. I sold the operation for equipment only to partially satisfy the financial commitment. This decision set in motion a series of events that resulted in my eventual personal bankruptcy. At any other point in my life, I would have been utterly devastated by the failure. But God! The grace that poured upon me was like a salve to utterly heal a deep wound caused by the loss of my dad and his business.

I finally knew who I was and Whose I was, and the failure didn't destroy me. My emotional intelligence in Christ gave me the Self-Awareness to understand that I was loved, even in my imperfection. My emotional intelligence in Christ helped me to manage the depression that came with the negative realities that I faced. My emotional intelligence in Christ gave me the tools to cope with the anxiety resulting from an uncertain future. My emotional intelligence in Christ also equipped me to love my young family, attend to their needs, and be emotionally present even in my greatest time of struggle. My hope in the emotionally perfect One filled me up after years of depletion and the loss I feared the most!

Lauren E. Miller's EIC Story

Prior to 2006 I assumed that my skillset was good enough to give me victory over my opponent in the Colorado State Championship for the World Tae Kwon Do Federation. I had practiced 4 hours a day, 6 days a week for a year. Within the first few minutes of the first round, I was knocked out by an illegal hook kick to my head. As the referee counted down from 10, I regained consciousness when he got to the count of 4. As soon as I realized what happened my entire body was filled with anger, frustration, and determination. I catapulted to my feet and went after my opponent like a spider monkey, losing all access to the skillset I had so diligently practiced, I was fighting from emotion out of control. I ended up winning a medal. As I was full of myself coming off of the podium after receiving my medal, my 8th degree blackbelt from Korea, who happened to be a strong Christian, quietly strolled by me and whispered: *"Lauren you lost because you let your emotions override your skillset."*

Flashing forward several years on January 6, 2006, with three young children (7, 9, 11) I found myself knocked to the mat again. I received a phone call that began with: *"are you sitting down"*…followed by a phrase you never want to hear: *"Lauren, you have cancer, and it's aggressive."* At 38 years old, one week prior to my final divorce court date I was diagnosed with advanced breast cancer. In less than a two-year period of time, by God's grace I walked through: a divorce, a double mastectomy, 16 weeks of daily radiation, a MRSA staph infection, two years of chemotherapy treatments and, due to 3rd degree burns on my chest, I had 14 surgeries, as the doctors grafted my back onto my front (so now I really don't know if I'm coming or going most days). I was told that in spite of the maximum number of treatments I was receiving, the doctors were trying to get me five more years of life.

I threw myself on the ground and wept before the Lord, overwhelmed by negative emotions. Then the reality that my three children were about to walk in the house from school hit me. The Holy Spirit stepped in and reminded me of a verse I had stored in my heart when I first accepted Christ at 17, Galatians 2: 20 *"I have been crucified with Christ and I no longer live, but Christ lives in me. The life I now live in the body, I live by faith in the Son of God, who loved me and gave himself for me."*

The light bulb went on for a moment, just enough to remind my mind of what my soul always knows: *my battle belongs to the Lord, my victory lies in my choice to surrender and reclaim my identity in Jesus: The strength of Jesus within me is my victory.* The power of the Holy Spirit filled my body and moved me to my feet at the very moment my children came through the door and the battle for life and death began with Christ as my cornerstone.

The purpose for giving you, the reader, a brief summary of my "earth school" class in suffering is to connect with you at a deeper level before you take your own personal journey into *Emotional Intelligence in Christ*. My ability to manage my emotions and the emotions of people around me during the years of intense emotional and physical pain was highly compromised to say the least, AND when I surrendered my sense of identity, as I lost my hair, breasts and marriage, over to Jesus Christ of Nazareth, I stand before you today and boldly declare: I was NEVER left empty handed in my ability to overcome what I felt had overcome me. With every storm, Jesus comes too. The same strength and ability to rise above strong emotions is available to you as well.

Gratefully, God restored my physical and emotional wellbeing. I met my husband when I was bald and breastless back in 2007 and have been happily remarried for 12 years.

Ken Voges's Story

Linda, my wife, was born with an I/C behavioral style like King David. This style is gifted with outstanding people skills blended with intense inner passion which she uses to relate with others on a personal basis. These are skills I do not have. (Opposites attract) But on the downside, when Linda experiences personal rejection and personal criticism, her "need of the moment" is to talk to someone about her feelings in random thoughts and stories.

Earlier on in my understanding of the DISC model it became clear to me that the latter behavioral response was normal. I knew this intellectually, but it didn't get to my heart when encountering one of her emotional challenges. Linda would announce she needed to talk, and I'd listen for a few minutes and then exercise my non emotional intelligence S/C/D logical skills while talking in direct tones what she needed to do. I thought I was giving her wise counsel. I dismissed and set aside her feelings. Instead, I tended to just share a logical, action plan thinking that would be helpful . . . not! At some point, it became clear to me, this strategy was not working very well but I didn't know what else to do.

Then one evening Linda again announced a need to talk. I knew it was going to be at least 30 minutes of emotional discussion and it was already 10:00 in the evening. I had had a challenging day and emotionally had no energy to offer my logical wisdom. Yeah right!

So, I decided to just listen as best I could. I put both hands under my chin and kept pressing up on it so that I wouldn't appear to be disinterested or actually fall asleep . . . I'd done both before!

I just listened to her, and every five minutes acknowledged her feelings with either "Wow" or "I'm sorry that happened to you." Gratefully, I didn't nod off and we went to bed. I was asleep as soon as my head hit the pillow.

The next morning, the first thing Linda told me was, "I can't tell how much you helped me last night." I was shocked because I didn't do anything other than listen. About that time, the "Holy Spirit" sent a lightning bolt message to my brain, "Pay attention, you finally did it right! You might want to keep doing it that way . . . listen more and talk less. Furthermore, unless Linda requests it, check your logical counsel at the door since it doesn't seem to meet the need of the moment!"

I tried to improve my listening skills. When Linda announces a need to talk, I frequently ask this question. "Do you want me to just listen, or do you want feedback?" Relationally, I classify this as my best personal model of Emotional Intelligence. Most importantly, it seems to work better. We've been at this for 57 years of marriage and we still struggle with our differences at times, but the good times have totally outweighed the bad. Other than my relationship with Christ, Linda truly has been my best friend. My love language is touch and when things get off track, Linda has a habit of just reaching out her hand and we pray together for the Lord's grace and mercy to understand what to do next. So far, He's come through every time.

FYI—I share this story whenever the Lord prompts me. It seems to connect with a lot of couples. Hope it helps you.

AUTHOR BIOS

Estella Chavous, MBA, EdD

Dr. Estella Chavous is an experienced educator, communicator, global marketer, and wellbeing consultant. She is currently a global communications lead for AVEVA based in the Netherlands, an Adjunct Professor at University of Massachusetts Global, an *Inside Timer Meditation Trainer*, Speaker, and Published author. Estella has significant professional experience in education, sales, and marketing, working in strategic leadership positions for Fortune 500 companies,

including Abbott, Amgen, and Bristol Myers-Squibb. She has built and led effective teams throughout her career, designed and implemented successful strategies, and developed and managed diverse programs enabling the transformational process. As the co-founder of *Strategic-Ladies*, Dr. Estella provides personal, family, and corporate training. In addition, she consults in all aspects of wellbeing, with a particular focus on mindful meditation and contemplative prayer. Estella is the creator of the Christ-filled assessment booklet and co-author of an Amazon best-selling book, *Let Meditation Mend You*. She is also a co-host for the Mindful Media Show, co-founder of Edge God. In addition, she is a course developer, writing a host of courses on various empowering topics used in her practice.

www.edgegodin.com

http://estellachavous.com/

Rich Cummins, MAOL, CFRE

With more than twenty-five years of senior leadership and C-suite experience, Rich is a life-long learner who is passionate about developing people and organizations while cultivating cultures built on relationships, service, and excellence. Currently, Rich serves as the President and CEO of Lead Like Jesus, a global leadership training and equipping organization with ministry centers in 24 nations. He also hosts the *Lead Like Jesus Podcast: Where Leadership Starts on the Inside*, is an Executive Coach and adjunct professor in Organizational Leadership and Executive Coaching & Consultation at Concordia University Irvine.

Rich has evidenced God's great provision in the organizations that he has served and with the people that he has invested in. He has a diverse background and leadership experience in the marketplace, military, and with Christ-centered nonprofits. Rich finds purpose in helping other leaders optimize their leadership through Self-Awareness and relational effectiveness. He believes that Jesus is the greatest leadership role model and the prime example of healthy social emotional understanding.

He has earned a Master of Arts in Organizational Leadership at Huntington University, Advanced Executive Coaching and Leadership credentials from the Townsend Institute, the Certificate in Fundraising Management from the Lilly Family School of Philanthropy at Indiana University and is a Certified Fundraising Executive with CFRE International. He is currently working towards a doctorate in Higher Education Leadership with Bethel University (MN), studying the impact of emotional intelligence on burnout. Rich also serves his church as an ordained minister.

Lead Like Jesus Website - www.leadlikejesus.com

Lead Like Jesus Podcast - www.leadlikejesus.com/podcasts

Lauren E Miller, M.Ed, MSC, ICF-PCC

As a stress relief expert, award winning author, motivational speaker, HRD trainer, Edge God In podcast host, and certified executive and life coach, Lauren facilitates fun process driven programs with guidance, support and accountability creating positive sustainable behavioral change in business and personal life.

Lauren has worked in youth and adult ministries for over 30 years. Through God's mercy, grace, and strength, she uses her experience simultaneously conquering two of life's top stressors: cancer and divorce to help others destress and successfully move through challenges.

Happily, remarried and gratefully enjoying life in Colorado with a loving husband, three grown children and two grandchildren, Lauren is often found in the kitchen dancing to her favorite worship music or rolling around on the floor with her two dogs. She enjoys fly fishing, camping, hiking and family dinners.

Lauren holds a Masters in Adult Education with a Certification in Human Resources Development | Advanced Neuro-Linguistic Programming (NLP) Basic & Master Certification | Faculty Shift Leadership Training | Master Sherpa Executive Coach (MSC) and ICF Certification PCC | 2nd degree blackbelt World Tae Kwon Do

Lauren has produced 8 CD's and five 3 minute/30 day Audio/Visual Personal Excellence/Wellness Programs. She has authored 8 books, 3 of which are Award Winners.

LAUREN'S MISSION STATEMENT
CHAMPION HUMAN POTENTIAL IN CHRIST

Equip people and teams globally with mindset skills and sustainable behavioral shifts to de-stress their lives, regain inner clarity of purpose and step into personal and professional excellence.

http://LaurenEMiller.com

Edge God In Podcast: http://EdgeGodIn.com

Ken Voges Bio

Ken Voges is the founder and President of In His Grace, Inc., a human resource consulting company. Ken was an elder at BridgePoint Bible Church for 40 years. As a Biblical behavioral scientist, he became acquainted with the DISC behavior model some 42 years ago which resulted in him authoring numerous DISC assessments, books and workbooks on the subject. Recently, in working with the Lead Like Jesus ministry , he authored an online, 46-page *Biblical Behavior Assessment*. The latter product allows an individual to match their behavior with a positive biblical model.

His passion has been to cross reference historical figures including biblical characters, Presidents, military leaders and with one of the *16 Classical Behavior* profiles. For the past 30 plus years, Mr. Voges has been a part of the DMin program at Dallas Theological Seminary focusing on team building models found in the Bible. He also lectures on five hand-of-God stories from WWII including the prayers of General George S. Patton Jr. during the Battle of the Bulge.

Ken and Linda, his wife of 57 years, have lived in Houston since 1968. The Voges's have two children, Randy and Christy and five grandchildren all of which know the Lord Jesus Christ as their personal savior.

Emotional Intelligence in Christ Course

Coming in 2022

For More Information Visit:

EmotionalIntelligenceinChrist.com

Acknowledgements

We are very grateful for the willingness of Ken Voges, Bob Jerus, Lead Like Jesus, Edge God In, and Biblical DISC™ to share their intellectual property for the purpose of the *Emotional Intelligence in Christ* experience for the reader. We are very grateful for Karen McGuire's talent and eye for detail along with Ginger Marks.

EMOTIONAL INTELLIGENCE IN CHRIST JOURNAL

Your Emotional Intelligence in Christ Journal Learning Objectives:

1. To capture the unique opportunity for learning and growth that come from your everyday life experiences as a follower of Christ. Simply put, your earth school lessons.

2. To help you transfer and apply your learnings from the book, course (EmotionalIntelligenceinChrist.com) and life using the Emotional Intelligence in Christ EIC Method:
   - Encounter Christ
   - Identified Behavior
   - Course Correct

Your journal is divided into eight sections that correspond to the eight chapters in the *Emotional Intelligence in Christ* book. If you are looking for guided prompts to help you focus journaling, please explore the suggestions below or simply write your learnings and reflections as the Holy Spirit prompts you after you read each chapter:

1. Write down your learnings and reflections.
2. Reflect and Respond on each learning as you choose which behaviors you want to do more of and less of with the aid of the Holy Spirit within you.
3. Apply the EIC Method to your daily life:
   - E: **Encounter**: Where did you encounter Christ today? Specifically in the 4 behaviors linked to EIC:

Your identity in Christ? Self-Control? Altruism? Christ Connections?
- I: **Identified Behavior:** What specific behaviors stand out to you as you reflect back on the last 24 hours of your life?
- C: **Course Correct:** Invite the Holy Spirit to show you specific behaviors He wants to adjust in order to make room for Emotional Intelligence in Christ as you course correct.

4. I commit to the following behaviors in Christ this week to increase my EIC in each of the following 4 EIC behaviors:

- **Identity in Christ**: Example: *Spend the 1ˢᵗ moments of my day in prayer reading scripture, sitting in silence before the Lord and seeking His wisdom for my day.*
- **Self-Control**: Example: *Pause, breath and pray before responding in difficult conversations.*
- **Altruism**: Example: *I choose to surrender all that I am to Christ today to be used as an instrument of His love towards others around me. Lord, give me an opportunity today to make you recognizable by being more attentive to the needs of others over my own.*
- **Christ Connections**: Example: *I reflected on the behavior of disconnecting with people who don't see situations like I do. I commit to the behavior of intentionally offering the love of Christ in my words, facial expressions and body language to each person I connect with today by remaining in prayer with the Holy Spirit. I will remind my face that Jesus adores me and share it with others to create Christ Connections.*

Your EIC Learnings and Reflections

Chapter 1: Overview of Emotional Intelligence

Emotional Intelligence in Christ Journal

Emotional Intelligence in Christ Journal

Emotional Intelligence in Christ Journal

Chapter 2: Biblical EIQ Assessment for EIC Application

Emotional Intelligence in Christ Journal

Emotional Intelligence in Christ Journal

Chapter 3: Behavior 1: Personal Identity (Self-Awareness)

Emotional Intelligence in Christ Journal

Emotional Intelligence in Christ Journal

Emotional Intelligence in Christ Journal

Chapter 4: Behavior 2: Self Control (Self-Management)

Emotional Intelligence in Christ Journal

Emotional Intelligence in Christ Journal

Emotional Intelligence in Christ Journal

Chapter 5: Behavior 3: Altruistic Attitude (Social-Awareness)

Emotional Intelligence in Christ Journal

Emotional Intelligence in Christ Journal

Chapter 6: Behavior 4: Christ Connections (Relational Management)

Emotional Intelligence in Christ Journal

Emotional Intelligence in Christ Journal

Emotional Intelligence in Christ Journal

Chapter 7: Biblical DISC Meets EIC Biblical Case Studies

Emotional Intelligence in Christ Journal

Emotional Intelligence in Christ Journal

Emotional Intelligence in Christ Journal

Chapter 8: The Chavous/Cummins/Miller/Voges EIC Method

Emotional Intelligence in Christ Journal

Emotional Intelligence in Christ Journal

Emotional Intelligence in Christ Journal